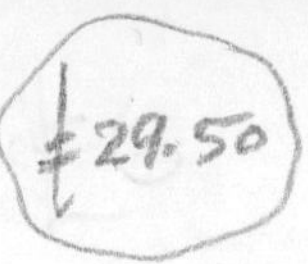

CARLYLE AND TENNYSON

Also by Michael Timko

INNOCENT VICTORIAN: The Satiric Poetry of Arthur Hugh Clough

THIRTY-EIGHT SHORT STORIES: An Introductory Anthology (*editor with Clinton F. Oliver*)

CARLYLE AND TENNYSON

MICHAEL TIMKO
Professor of English Literature
City University of New York

MACMILLAN
PRESS

First published 1988

Published by
THE MACMILLAN PRESS LTD
Houndmills, Basingstoke, Hampshire RG21 2XS
and London
Companies and representatives
throughout the world

Typeset by Wessex Typesetters
(Division of The Eastern Press Ltd)
Frome, Somerset

Printed in Hong Kong

British Library Cataloguing in Publication Data
Timko, Michael
Carlyle and Tennyson.
1. Carlyle, Thomas—Criticism and interpretation 2. Tennyson, Alfred Tennyson, *Baron*—Criticism and interpretation
I. Title
828'.808 PR4434
ISBN 0–333–43615–6

To the next generation:
Michael, Jamie, Molly,
Kim, Annie and Keith

Contents

Acknowledgements

To acknowledge and to thank all those who have helped would be impossible. I would, however, like to express my appreciation for tangible aids of various kinds from former President Saul Cohen, former Provost William Hamovitch and Dean John Reilly of Queens College, City University of New York; Harold M. Proshansky, President of the Graduate School, and Chancellor Joseph S. Murphy, CUNY. I should also like to thank Professor David Daiches, Director, Institute for Advanced Studies in the Humanities, University of Edinburgh; Professor K. J. Fielding, Department of English Literature, University of Edinburgh; Martin Ridge, Senior Research Associate, and James Thorpe, former Director of the Huntington Library, San Marino, California, where I spent a rewarding six months on an NEH–Huntington Library Fellowship. I also owe debts of various kinds to colleagues and friends at the National Library of Scotland, the University of Edinburgh Library, the New York Public Library, the CUNY Graduate School Library, the Queens College Library, and Queens College and the Graduate School of CUNY. I must give special mention to those who have read some parts of my manuscript or who have helped in more subtle ways: John Sutherland, Jerome McGann, Robert McLean, Lillian Feder, William Green, Gerhard Joseph, Aileen Christianson, John Clubbe, Horst Drescher, Lois Hughson, Robert Lyons, G. B. Tennyson, William Buckler, Susan Shatto and Allen Mandelbaum. For various kindnesses, some far reaching, I express my gratitude to Carol Pearson, Margaret Jardine, Frances Arnold, Eileen Ashcroft, Morag and the late Norrie Davidson, Margaret, Roy and Sean Davis and Lynn Kadison. My debt and gratitude to Dr Ian Campbell, Department of English Literature, University of Edinburgh, are enormous. Finally, special thanks to L.J.T., who always understands.

Michael Timko

What Wordsworth did for poetry, Carlyle has done for morality.

Harriet Martineau

Tennyson became the most representative English poet since Pope's death, the one closest to literate readers, the one most fully aware of the conflicts, the purposes, and the ideals of his time.

Jerome H. Buckley

Prologue

If one wishes to understand the Victorian period, one needs to know the work of Carlyle and Tennyson. One needs to see why they made such an impression on their age and just how lasting this impression was. One also has to ask a number of questions. Why did they choose to write about the specific subjects they did? Why did they approach these subjects the way they did? What were the influences at work on them, and how did they utilise and resist these? A proper study of the two, then, involves more than a biographical accounting or a comparison of places, events, or persons. What is required is an examination of both as 'eminent' Victorians, writers deeply involved with the movements of their day and, more important, either generators or reflectors of those movements. To take up the two is not really to concern oneself with either reputation or influence; it is, rather, to acknowledge the pervasive presence of Victorianism itself, a distinct period of literary history encompassed in the writings of these two significant Victorian figures.

The approach to each must necessarily differ. To understand Carlyle, essayist, historian, polemicist, preacher, one must primarily focus on the forces that formed his thought, character, and belief. One must come to understand the influence of family, church, education, reading and, above all, his attempts to fuse the factual and the imaginative, the real and the ideal, the natural and the supernatural. To know Carlyle one must, of course, read the works but, even more, examine the processes that caused the early 'believer' to struggle with ethics and aesthetics and wrestle with form and content in order to resolve what seemed to be irreconcilable problems of substance and style. The pervasive imagery, often compulsively employed, provides insights into his thought and art and often explains the motives behind the seemingly wild surmises and extravagant claims. Most significantly, the apparent conflict between the aesthetic and prophetic reveals the puzzled Sage becoming more and more bewildered by his inability to move the public, to show *his* misguided public the way to salvation from the perils of their age. Too often critics have sought out either the thought or the art of Carlyle instead of attempting to perceive how he himself valiantly sought to combine the two, especially under Goethe's influence, and thus bring to his readers the vision he himself through his reading of German philosophy had occasionally glimpsed: a new heaven and earth, the combination of the Beautiful and the Good. That he had occasionally glimpsed this 'true reality' and then finally lost it without ever having conveyed it to his readers embodies the tragic life of this failed prophet. It also constitutes the very essence of his Victorianism.

There must necessarily be a different approach to Tennyson, for the essence of his Victorianism is as unCarlylean as possible. One cannot deny the Carlylean influence on the younger poet, an influence evident in much of Tennyson's thought and seen at times in some of his art; however, Tennyson characteristically rejected or transformed many of the Sage's ideas, some of which seemed to him, as to many of Carlyle's contemporaries, far too radical or unorthodox or unworkable or unthinkable to be of any use. To understand Tennyson, poet and artist, one must look chiefly at his poems, his public utterances, for Tennyson was always aware of the pulse of the public. Unlike Carlyle, who often wrote what he felt, deeply and intensely, Tennyson carefully chose his words and themes and often seemed to reflect precisely what his readers were thinking and feeling. Unlike Carlyle, who often preached, Tennyson 'publicly' performed. Unlike Carlyle, who ignored such issues as Darwinism, Tennyson was always aware of them, often brooded over them and attempted to discuss them fully in his poetry. Darwinism is, indeed, a case in point. Carlyle, we know, simply refused to acknowledge the idea that, somehow, humans could be related to 'species'. He refused, or so he claimed, to read a word of Darwin. Tennyson, on the other hand, constantly worried over it, as *In Memoriam* and other poems reveal.

In the end Carlyle assumed a Ulyssean stance, conveying his own personal message to those who would listen, and his audience became smaller and smaller. At the end of his life, in spite of the national mourning at the time of his death, there were few who still believed in the words of the failed Prophet. In the case of Tennyson, however, Telemachan in nature, the influence of his poetry grew with his reputation and increased over the years. In his poems the public found, or so they believed, words that reflected domestic peace and messages that contained spiritual comfort. The Carlylean Age had given way to the Tennysonian Era.

The fascination for the modern reader lies in seeing the process of this change, viewing these two literary figures as generators or reflectors of the events and happenings of their time. Both Carlyle and Tennyson thought deeply and wrote at length on religious, social, scientific and literary issues. Their approach to and 'solution' of these various problems are instructive. Buckler has briefly characterised their methods:

> They were both learned men, though Carlyle let his learning ricochet all over the surface of his writing, while Tennyson stripped his public texts of the signs of erudition and subordinated thought to the experience of thought; Carlyle used a technique of confrontation and challenge, Tennyson a strategy of oblique insinuation.[1]

The difference in method reflects the difference in substance. Carlyle, brusque, stubborn, selfish, authoritarian, reflects all these qualities in his discussions of religious and social questions; he insists on great leaders, indeed, one great Taskmaster, and complete obedience from those who serve. Tennyson, cautious, politic, seeking compromises, openly advocating gradualism, looks for solutions that satisfy everyone. To see how and why the prophetic utterances of the one gave way to the idylic vision of the other is to gain greater understanding and new insight into a period of time that did much to form our own.

Abbreviated References

Campbell	Campbell, Ian, *Thomas Carlyle* (London: Hamish Hamilton, 1974).
CFS	Sanders, C. R., *Carlyle's Friendship and Other Studies* (Durham, N.C.: Duke University Press, 1977).
CHC	*Carlyle and His Contemporaries*, ed. John Clubbe (Durham, N.C.: Duke University Press, 1976).
CL	Carlyle, Thomas, and Jane Welsh Carlyle, *The Collected Letters of Thomas and Jane Welsh Carlyle*, Duke-Edinburgh Edition, ed. Charles Richard Sanders, Kenneth J. Fielding *et al.* (Durham, N.C.: Duke University Press, 1970ff.).
CMSB	Carlyle, Alexander (ed.), *Letters of Thomas Carlyle to John Stuart Mill, John Sterling and Robert Browning* (London: T. Fisher Unwin, 1923).
CPP	*Carlyle Past and Present: A Collection of New Essays*, ed. K. J. Fielding and Rodger L. Tarr (London: Vision Press, 1976).
Drescher	*Thomas Carlyle 1981*, ed. Horst W. Drescher (Frankfurt am Main: Peter Lang, 1983).
Froude	Froude, J. A., *Thomas Carlyle: A History of the First Forty Years of His Life, 1795–1835; A History of His Life in London, 1834–1881*, 4 vols (London: Longmans, Green, 1882; 1884).
Harrold	Harrold, C. F., *Carlyle and German Thought: 1819–1834* (New Haven: Yale University Press, 1934).
Memoir	*Alfred Lord Tennyson: Memoir*, ed. Hallam Tennyson, 2 vols (London: Macmillan, 1897).
2NB	*Two Note Books of Thomas Carlyle*, ed. C. E. Norton (New York: The Grolier Club, 1898).
NLS	National Library of Scotland, Edinburgh.

Reminiscences	Carlyle, Thomas. *Reminiscences*, ed. C. E. Norton, 2 vols (London and New York: Macmillan, 1887; Introduction by Ian Campbell (London: J. M. Dent, 1972).
Ricks	*The Poems of Tennyson*, ed. Christopher Ricks (London: Longmans, 1969); unless otherwise noted, all references to Tennyson's poems are to this volume. While the additional information in the revised (1987, 3 vols) edition supports and supplements some of my points for the specific purposes of references to lines, passages, poems, and sources, the original edition is perfectly adequate.
Wilson	Wilson, David Alec, *Carlyle*, 6 vols (London: Kegan Paul, Trench, Trubner; New York: E. P. Dutton, 1923–34).
Works	Carlyle, Thomas, *Works*, Centenary Edition, ed. H. D. Traill, 30 vols (London: Chapman and Hall, 1896–99).

Part One

Foundations

1

Carlyle: The Scottish Dimension

In the midst of all this, I for my own small share must feel as if I had got into strange latitudes, and could not for these many months take any sure Lunar. The sneaking catarrh, as you may well judge, is no help to me. In truth, I am very considerably bewildered; few landmarks in the Earth, yet, God be thanked, some stars still shining in the Heavens: I can only say with the old Hebrew, in my own diale[c]t, 'Still *trust in God, for Him to praise good cause I yet shall have': so stood it in my Father's Psalm-Book; pity for me if so much stand not also in mine! On the whole, in this wondrous condition of all things, Literary, Moral, Economical, there is need of courage, of insight; which may the bounteous Heaven, withholding what else it will, supply according to our need.*

(Carlyle to Mill, 22 February 1833; *CL*, VI, 330)

There are many studies of Carlyle, especially attempts to get at the heart of what he himself called his 'bewildered wrestlings', what Froude called his 'interpretation of human history'. That they have not wholly succeeded in helping us know fully the complex thoughts and ideas of this 'teacher of mankind' is not the fault of the authors; Carlyle escapes easy classification. 'The chief elements of my little destiny', he wrote in his *Journal* in 1848, 'have all along lain deep below view or surmise, and never will or can be known to any son of Adam' (Froude, III, 1). However, since he was, in his biographer's words, one who 'claimed "to speak with authority and not as the Scribes,"' it is important that we try to understand this 'prophet', one who 'exerted for many years an almost unbounded influence on the mind of educated England' (Froude, III, 4). It is easy enough to dismiss him as fascist, theist, idealist, but to do so is of no help to one interested in locating the foundations of his ideas and his faith.

That he is a paradoxical figure there is no doubt; with Carlyle, however, there is one area that calls for more examination: the nature of his thoughts on human beings and the world they inhabit. Froude, after publishing Carlyle's short 'essay' on religion, 'Spiritual Optics', called it 'the key to Carlyle's mind'. He concluded: 'In this faith he interpreted human history, which history witnessed in turn to the truth of his convictions. He saw that now as much as ever the fate of nations depended not on their material development, but . . . on the moral virtues, courage, veracity, purity, justice, and good sense' (Froude, II, 18).

The last quality he cites, 'good sense', brings us up short, for it seems out of place in the list of abstract virtues Froude reels off; yet, again, we see the double nature of Carlyle's thought, that same double nature that has led to his being so difficult to understand fully. That 'good sense' reminds us that in spite of Carlyle's place in literary history as a Romantic and in philosophy as a transcendentalist, he somehow seems not to belong there; there is in his thought and belief such a strong trace of practicality, a recognition of this too, too solid earth and flesh, that anyone who reads only a bit of his work begins to question both his Romanticism and his transcendentalism.

It would be useful, then, to examine closely that period during which Carlyle was experiencing, as did so many other Victorians, his 'loss and gain', a period covering his early home life, university years, and the early 1820s. An obvious first step is that which was taken by Matthew P. McDiarmid in a recent essay; one needs to look first at 'the Scottish dimension'.[1] In Carlyle's case the 'Scottish dimension' begins with his home influence, strong, as one might suspect, in matters of faith and duty. While there is no doubt that the influence of the mother was stronger than that of the father, there is also no doubt that Carlyle owes much to his father. In reading the *Reminiscences*, one is struck time and again by Carlyle's love for and admiration of his father, and the traits which he chooses to emphasise and praise are revealing. His father's dedication to work, to doing his duty as he saw it, becomes a motif of this reminiscence. 'Like a healthy man, he wanted *only* to get along with his Task: whatsoever could not forward him in this (and how could Public Opinion and much else of the like sort do it?) was of no moment to him, and not there for him', Carlyle writes. He goes on to praise his father's 'philosophy':

> This great maxim of Philosophy he had gathered by the teaching of nature alone: That man was created to work, not to speculate, or feel, or dream. Accordingly he set his whole heart thitherwards: he did work wisely and unweariedly . . . and perhaps *performed* more (with the tools he had) than any man I now know . . . he would leave nothing till it was *done*. (*Reminiscences*, p. 5)

His father's influence is seen in other areas; indeed his comments about his father's 'education' reveal as much about himself as about his father. 'A solid knowledge of Arithmetic, a fine antique Handwriting', he writes: 'these, with other limited *practical* etceteras, were *all* the things he ever heard mentioned as excellent: he had no room to strive for more'. Carlyle's view of his father's attitude towards poetry and fiction could very well be a description of his own: 'Poetry, Fiction in general, he had universally seen as treated as not only idle, but *false* and criminal'. One other aspect of his father's character that Carlyle admired (and this, too, tells us a great deal about Carlyle himself) was his willingness to concentrate on his own tasks in his own limited sphere and ignore the rest of the world. This may sound strange considering what one hears always of Carlyle's wide concerns and interest in revolution and change; however, there was always in Carlyle a deep and abiding interest in being satisfied with one's lot, even to the point of selfishness. Here is Carlyle:

> The great world-revolutions send in their disturbing billow to the remotest creek; and the overthrow of thrones more slowly overturns also the households of the lowly. Nevertheless in all cases the wise man adjusts himself: even in these times, the hand of the diligent maketh rich. My Father had seen the American War, the French Revolution, the rise and fall of Napoleon. . . . He was struck with Napoleon, and would say and look pregnant things about him: empires won, and empires lost (while *his* little household held together); and now it was all vanished like a tavern brawl!—For the rest, he never meddled with Politics: he was not there to govern, but to be governed; could still *live*, and therefore did not *revolt*. . . . To him, as one about to take his departure, the whole was but of secondary moment: he was looking towards 'a city that *had* foundations'. (*Reminiscences*, pp. 9, 30–31)

Of course part of his father's practicality was derived from the religion which he practised, the religion which the young Thomas Carlyle knew and believed in for the first fifteen years or so of his life, certainly that in which he believed until the time he went to university. 'The one immovable foundation for the Carlyle home in Ecclefechan', writes Ian Campbell, 'was religious belief; it explains the impoverishment of Carlyle's early experience, but it at least compensates for it by the early and ineffaceable teaching of the Burgher Secession community' (Campbell, p. 8). As one of a family that attended a Secession Church, Carlyle no doubt remembered such teachings as the emphasis on the reality of sin and the need to apply biblical teachings to one's own life. Since the Ecclefechan Church advocated 'individual' behaviour and the relevance of the Bible to morality in each person's life (Campbell, p. 9), it was no doubt in this spirit that Carlyle wrote to Mill from Craigenputtoch praising the Church he remembered. He told Mill:

> The History of the Scotch Presbyterian Church is noteworthy for this reason, that above all Protestant Churches it for some time was a real Church; had brought home in authentic symbols, to the bosoms of the lowest, that summary and concentration of whatever is highest in the Ideas of Man; the Idea unutterable in words; and opened thereby (in scientific strictness, it may be said) a free communication between Earth and the Heaven whence Earth had its being. (*CSMB*, p. 26)

2

New Intellectual Forces: Hume and Newton

Carlyle entered Edinburgh University in 1809 as one of the 'last products of an old system', and this system was to prove unable to help him withstand the pressures of those new intellectual forces to which he was now to be subjected. However, and this point is a crucial one, Carlyle did not, as is commonly thought, and as *Sartor* with some exaggerations records, lose faith; he was, it is true, to suffer his own 'Centre of Indifference' for a number of years, chiefly over the choice of a career. However, the exact nature of the experience at Edinburgh and in the immediate following years is one that seems closer to readjustment rather than a complete loss of faith and a subsequent miraculous recovery through readings in German literature and philosophy. The distinction is a vital one, for it alters markedly the way one views Carlyle's relationship to both science and scepticism, as well as to German literature.

Carlyle was always aware of the need for human beings first to know and then to believe—that is, faith based on evidence rather than intuition. All through his life Carlyle regarded himself as an 'enlightened sceptic', often using the term to emphasise his attitude towards the Church after his rejection of all its trappings and 'theological' beliefs. However, it also has a special and important meaning to anyone interested in the more general question of his 'interpretation of human history'. From the time of his entrance to the university, the crucial problem became for Carlyle as much epistemological as metaphysical. He never stopped believing, but it was the way of arriving at that belief that now caused him the most concern. The chief difficulty was not that of faith, which Carlyle never lacked; it was, rather, finding the ways to support and offer proof for that faith, the same proof that one could provide to explain a mathematical problem and its solution.

The pragmatic basis of Carlyle's belief cannot be ignored or dismissed. His reading and the classes he attended at the university drastically changed the course of his thinking about his early beliefs, especially as to how one arrived at them. Carlyle's chief concern became that of bringing together the inner process of knowing and the outer world of fact and things.[1] In this quest he found university study not a 'diversion' but a means to an end, that end being to find a surer foundation for his beliefs than had been provided by the old creed. That he read a great deal on his own, especially the works of great writers of the Enlightenment, is well known, and these were to have special meaning for him; Hume, Locke, mathematics, geometry were all to aid and comfort rather than deter him in his quest. Herein lies the importance of this time and these studies for Carlyle.

In his biography of John Sterling, a biography done with great sympathy, even love in the Carlylean sense, Carlyle gives some indication of the difficulties both Coleridge and Sterling had because of their inability to come to grips with 'reality'. Because of his 'ardent attendance at Highgate', Sterling was experiencing much confusion: 'Without and within, it was a wide tide of things this ardent young soul was afloat upon, at present; and his outlooks into the future, whether for his spiritual or economic fortunes, were confused enough' (*Works*, XI, p. 63). As to Coleridge himself, 'flabby and irresolute', Carlyle deplored the poet's inability to say anything concrete or meaningful:

> he spoke as if preaching,—you would have said, preaching earnestly and also hopelessly the weightiest things. I still recollect his 'object' and 'subject,' terms of continual recurrence in the Kantean province; and how he sang and snuffled them into 'omm–m–mject' and 'sum–m–mject,' with a kind of solemn shake or quaver, as he rolled along. . . . To sit as a passive bucket and be pumped into . . . can in the long-run be exhilarating to no creature . . . But if it be withal a confused unintelligible flood of utterance, threatening to submerge all known landmarks of thought, and drown the world and you! (*Works*, XI, pp. 54–6)

Carlyle, to be sure, is being unfair to Coleridge, but his purpose is clear; he was looking for 'landmarks' of thought and did not want to be drowned in rhetoric or in a 'Kantean haze-world'. What Carlyle missed in Coleridge was 'one burst of noble indignation at some injustice or depravity, rubbing elbows with us on this solid Earth'. Instead, he saw and heard only in this sad life: 'an abstract thinking and dreaming, idealistic, passed amid the ghosts of defunct bodies and of unborn ones. The moaning singsong of that theosophico-metaphysical monotony left on you, at last, a very dreary feeling' (*Works*, XI, p. 57).

What Hume offered to Carlyle, then, even before Coleridge, was a way to begin to understand this concrete world so that he could utter, as he did later, bursts of indignation at some injustice or depravity; he wanted to avoid that theosophico-metaphysical mumbo-jumbo that Coleridge offered to anyone who would listen. Hume gave him a way of understanding, even if it were not as certain a way as Carlyle would have liked. A letter from Carlyle to Robert Mitchell in 1821 gives some notion of Carlyle's attitude:

> Do not fear, my gentle brother [he tells Mitchell] that I will lead you into the mazes of Kantism; I know you have but a limited relish for such mysteries, and among my many faults, an enemy even would not reckon the inordinate desire of making proselytes. As to Kant and Schelling and Fichte and all those worthies, I profess myself but an esoteric after all; and whoever can imagine that Stewart and Hume with Reid and Brown to help them have sounded all the depths of our nature, or which is better, can contrive to overlook these mysteries entirely,—is too fortunate a gentleman for me to intermeddle with. (*CL*, I, p. 343)

That was written at a time when Carlyle was beginning to make a start in writing, and he had by this time also begun the study of German literature. Even more indicative of his Janus-like attitude towards the concrete and the mysteries, perhaps, is the thought contained in a letter written to Mitchell in 1815, just about the time Carlyle had left university and had begun to teach at Annan Academy:

> I am highly indebted to you for Hume. I like his essays better than any thing I have read these many days. He has prejudices, he does maintain errors—but he defends his positions, with so much ingenuity, that one would be almost sorry to see him dislodged. His Essays on 'Superstition & Enthusiasm,' on 'the Dignity & meanness of Human Nature' and several others, are

> in my opinion admirable both in matter & manner:—particularly the first where his conclusions might be verified by instances, with which we are all acquainted. The manner, indeed, of all is excellent:—the highest & most difficult effect of art—the appearance of its absence—appears throughout. (*CL*, I, pp 47–8)

Carlyle then goes on to add that 'many of his opinions are not to be adopted'; and he further goes on to indicate his disagreement with Hume's discussion of moral causes. 'Might it not be asserted', asks Carlyle of his friend, 'with some plausibility, that even those which he denominates moral causes, originate from physical circumstances?' 'We must admit', he adds, 'that physical causes *have* an influence on man'. He concludes: 'As a whole however [I am de]lig[hted w]ith the book, and if you can want it, I shall mo[reover] give it a second perusal' (*CL*, I, p. 48).

The chief impression one gets from reading Carlyle's many references to Hume and the other Scottish philosophers is not that he is convinced by them; on the contrary, he is often harsh on their work and ideas. However, it becomes clear that what Carlyle said in his biography of Sterling and in his *Lectures on the History of Literature*, two sources for many of his comments on Hume, is not the entire story. In the *Lectures*, for instance, he calls Hume and Samuel Johnson the 'two persons who exercised the most remarkable influences upon things during the eighteenth century'. He adds: 'two summits of a great set of influences, two opposite poles of it—the one a puller down of magnificent, far-reaching thoughts; the other, most excellent, serious, and a great conservative'.[2] After praising Johnson, chiefly for his honesty and courage, he gets to Hume and proceeds to take his usual ambivalent stance. On the one hand, Hume is sincere, 'of a noble perseverance, a silent strength', one who bore all difficulties 'like a stoic, like a heroic, silent man as he was'. However, when he gets to Hume's scepticism, Carlyle becomes stern and condemnatory:

> He starts with *Locke's Essay*, thinking . . . that logic is the only way to the truth. He began with this, and went on; in the end he exhibited to the world his conclusion, that there was nothing at all credible or demonstrable, the only thing certain to him was being that he himself existed and sat there, and that there

> were some special of things in this own brain. Any other man to him was only a spectrum. (*Lectures*, pp. 174, 175)

One would expect Carlyle to stop here, having made his point, but he does not; he goes on to credit Hume with doing a service to mankind. 'Now it was right that this should be published, for if that were *all* that lay in scepticism, the making that known was extremely beneficial to us; he did us great service' (*Lectures*, pp. 175–6).

Carlyle, however, is still not done with Hume, and feels it necessary to bring him in yet again, this time in his lecture on modern German literature. This is, I think, a most significant matching, one that Carlyle seems to have been intrigued by most of his life. Once more we have the two poles, absolute spirit and absolute material, represented by Kant and Hume. His description in 1838 of what must have been his state of mind in his earlier days is rather simply done here, but if one knows the actual events through which he passed it becomes rather moving, even touching:

> I began with Hume and Diderot, and as long as I was with them I ran at Atheism, at blackness, at materialism of all kinds. If I read Kant, I arrived at precisely opposite conclusions, that all the world was spirit namely, that there was nothing material at all anywhere; and the result was what I have stated, that I resolved for my part to have nothing more to do with metaphysics at all! (*Lectures*, p. 205)

He immediately, then, begins to discuss Goethe, without any transition from the denigration of metaphysics. For Carlyle, if not for his audience, the transition is clear. The great German philosopher was able to unite, as Carlyle was striving to do, the actual and the ideal, the spirit and the senses; and Hume was essential in the quest (Drescher, p. 135).

Readers not familiar with Carlyle might be puzzled by the difference in tone and attitude between his remarks in his lectures and those earlier in the letters, but they have no reason to be. Carlyle often remembered things not as they had actually been but as he presently wanted them to be in order to serve as an example of a point that he happened to be making. The substantive matter about his readings of and comments about Hume's writings and ideas is that they helped clarify various ideas for him. It is certain, for instance, that he saw, as he said himself, no help in metaphysical speculations; and, while he had no use for extreme scepticism either, there was something in the way that Hume, who seemed so reasonable, had 'defended his positions' and stated his ideas that appealed to Carlyle, especially at a time when he was seeking certainty of some kind.[3] Hume's interest in epistemological problems, his sincere concern for human beings, his common-sense approach to problems usually discussed in abstract terms and the substance of some of his arguments made an impact on Carlyle. While Carlyle felt free to reject many of his opinions, he still saw in Hume's works a kind of middle way between extremes. As always, Carlyle was able to recognise, as he did with the Germans later on, those ideas and qualities in Hume's writings that could serve him in his own particular need.

The influence of Hume, then, might be described in the same way that Carlyle remembered the effect of Gibbon on him when he had first read his works:

> Irving's Library was of great use to me: Gibbon, Hume, etc. etc. [the specific mention of Hume is significant]. I think I must have read it almost through;—inconceivable to me now, with what ardour, with what greedy *velocity*, literally above *ten times* the speed I can now make with any Book. Gibbon, in particular, I recollect to have read at the rate of a volume a day (twelve volumes in all) and I have still a fair recollection of it. . . . It was of all the books perhaps the most impressive on me in my then [1818] *state of investigation and state of mind* [italics mine]. I by no means completely admired Gibbon, perhaps not more than I now do; but his winged sarcasms, so quiet, and yet so conclusively transpiercing, and killing dead, were often admirably potent and illuminative to me; nor did I fail to recognise his grand power of investigating, ascertaining, of grouping and narrating. (*Reminiscences*, pp. 186–7)[4]

The impact of Hume's thought on Carlyle is evident in still another way; it may be seen in the very manner in which Carlyle expresses some of his basic ideas, especially those concerning God, nature and morality. One is struck by the closeness of certain Carlylean views and statements to those of Hume; indeed, even the language at times is strikingly similar. No doubt a large part of the attraction of Hume for Carlyle lay in the latter's Newtonian interest, one that reflected his concern with both empiricism and epistemology. 'It was', Jane Rendall reminds us, 'constantly repeated by these writers [Scottish Enlightenment figures], and most notably by David Hume, that their aim was to introduce the methods pioneered by Isaac Newton into the worlds of moral and political philosophy'.[5] By the late 1720s, she points out, within the universities 'Newtonian ideas were circulating freely; and that when Hume announced his *Treatise of Human Nature*, published in 1739, to be "an attempt to introduce the experimental method of reasoning into moral subjects", he was using a generally accepted view of the "Newtonian method"' (p. 21).

One of the most striking instances of Hume's 'presence' may be seen in Carlyle's own notions regarding 'Nature', especially as it is used as a synonym for God and the Divine order. Consider such Carlylean terms as 'Reality', 'Fact' and 'Truth' in the light of Hume's introduction to his *Natural History of Religion*: 'The whole frame of nature bespeaks an intelligent author: and no rational enquirer can, after serious reflexion, suspend his belief a moment with regard to the primary principles of genuine Theism and Religion'.[6] Hume uses the phrase 'the whole frame of nature' throughout his work, and his emphasis in the order of nature and the dependability of its laws must have impressed Carlyle at this stage of his intellectual career. Consider another statement by Hume: 'All things in the universe are evidently of a piece. Every thing is adjusted to every thing. One design prevails thro' the whole. And this uniformity leads the mind to acknowledge one author; because the conception of different authors, without any distinction of attributes or operations, serves only to give perplexity to the imagination, without bestowing any satisfaction to the understanding' (p. 30).

It is important to remember that Hume is not arguing for the existence of God from design; neither is he arguing for an anthropomorphic conception of the Deity. Rather, he wants to demonstrate that the Deity is a kind of principle of order, from which human beings can gain some idea of regularity, 'adjustment' and form. In Section IV he is as specific as he ever gets regarding the nature of the Deity.

> The only point of theology, in which we shall find a consent of mankind almost universal [he writes] is, that there is invisible, intelligent power in the word. . . . To any one, who considers justly of the matter, it will appear, that the gods of all polytheists or idolaters are no better than the elves or fairies of our ancestors, and merit as little any pious worship or veneration. These pretended religionists are really a kind of superstitious atheists, and acknowledge no being, that corresponds to our idea of a deity. No first principle of mind or thought: No supreme government and administration: No divine contrivance or intention in the fabric of the world. (pp. 37–8)

For Carlyle these attributes, while far different from the God of his mother and father, must have appeared convincing; and his later reading of Goethe and Fichte, particularly the concept of Nature as the garment of God, must have seemed compatible with Hume's 'fabric of the world'. For someone with Carlyle's ability to bring things together, to make what Elizabeth Waterson calls those 'synaptic leaps' so characteristic of him, this would not be very difficult (Drescher, p. 120).

There is still another way that Hume evidently impressed Carlyle, and that is his insistence on the need really to look at objects, concrete objects, including human beings themselves. Much attention has been paid to Carlyle's own insistence on 'wonder' and 'miracle', and one could confidently cite Hume as a source for this belief. If Carlyle found his reading in Gibbon illuminative, one can imagine his sense of revelation and delight in reading this passage in Hume:

> All human life, especially before the institution of order and good government, being subject to fortuitous accidents; it is natural, that superstition should prevail every where in barbarous ages, and put men on the most earnest enquiry concerning those invisible powers, who dispose of their happiness or misery. Ignorant of astronomy and the anatomy of plants and animals, and too little curious to observe the admirable adjustment of final causes; they remain still unacquainted with a first and supreme creator, and with that infinitely perfect spirit, who alone, by his almighty will, bestowed order on the whole frame of nature. Such a magnificent idea is too big for their narrow conceptions, which

> can neither observe the beauty of the work, nor compound the grandeur of its author. They suppose their deities, however potent and invisible, to be nothing but a species of human creatures, perhaps raised from among mankind, and retaining all human passions and appetities, along with corporeal limbs and organs. (p. 35)

Or:

> Even at this day, and in *Europe*, ask any of the vulgar, why he believes in an omnipotent creator of the world; he will never mention the beauty of final causes, of which he is wholly ignorant: He will not hold out his hand, and bid you contemplate the suppleness and variety of joints in his fingers, their bending all one way, the counterpoise which they receive from the thumb, the softness and fleshy parts of the inside of his hand, with all the other circumstances, which render that member fit for the use, to which it was destined. To these he has long been accustomed; and he beholds them with listlessness and unconcern. (p. 50)

Not only do these passages contain those ideas that would aid Carlyle in his search—the basis of knowledge, the interest in science and the concrete, the denouncing of superstition, theological or other—but there are other elements that were to become a staple of his own interpretation of human history: the recognition of the frame of nature, the sense of awe and wonder at a supreme creator, not anthropomorphic but an 'infinitely perfect spirit', and an appreciation of the beauty of the work and the grandeur of the author. Even the example that Hume cites, the hand, is found in slightly different form in Carlyle, particularly in terms of how we must not let custom prevent us from seeing the miraculous, the same theme Hume is pursuing when he talks of the 'miraculous' nature of one's hand. In the key chapter in *Sartor*, 'Natural Supernaturalism', Carlyle makes much, as does Hume, of the way that custom prevents us from recognising miracles. 'Custom', continues the Professor, 'doth make dotards of us all. . . . Innumerable are the illusions and legerdemain-tricks of Custom: but of all of these, perhaps the cleverest is her knack of persuading us that the Miraculous, by simple repetition, ceases to be Miraculous'. Then Carlyle cites the example of one's hand, in much the same way Hume has used it, to illustrate the miraculous in daily life:

> Thus, were it not miraculous, could I stretch forth my hand and clutch the Sun? Yet thou seest me daily stretch forth my hand and therewith clutch many a thing, and wing it hither and thither. Art thou a grown baby, then, to fancy that Miracle lies in miles of distance, or in pounds avoirdupois of weight; and not to see that the true inexplicable God-revealing Miracle lies in this, that I can stretch forth my hand at all; that I have free Force to clutch aught therewith? Innumerable other of this sort are the deceptions, and wonder-hiding stupefactions, which Space practises on us. (*Works*, I, pp. 206, 209)

Another 'genius' whose name appears throughout Carlyle's writings is Sir Isaac Newton; his ideas were closely associated in Carlyle's mind with such special areas as natural philosophy, physics, mathematics, astronomy and epistemology, all of which played a profound role in the development of his own doctrines (*CL*, I, p. 103, n. 4). In August 1816 he wrote to his friend Robert Mitchell:

> I return always to the study of Physics with more pleasure—after trying 'The Philosophy of Mind.' It is delightful, after wandering in the thick darkness of metaphysics—to behold again the fair face of truth. When *will* there arise a man who shall do for the science of mind—what Newton did for that of matter—establish its fundamental laws on the firm basis of induction—and discard forever those absurd theories—that so many dreamers have devised?—I believe this is a foolish question—for its answer is—never. (*CL.* I, p. 84)

Here is Carlyle again in July 1817 writing to Mitchell:

> I wish I were an Astronomer—Is it not an interesting reflection to consider, that a little creature such as man—tho' his eye can see the heaven but as it were for a moment—is able to delineate the aspects which it presented long ages before he came into being—and to predict the aspects which it *will* present when ages shall have gone by. The past the present & the future are before him. Assuredly the human species never performed a

> more honourable atchievement [*sic*] 'The boast of heraldry, the pomp of power' must disappear like those that delighted in them; but when the hand that wrote the *Principia* is reduced to a little black earth, and the spirit that dictated it is gone no one knows whither—the work itself remains in undecaying majesty to all generations. (*CL*, I, p. 103)

The implications of these Carlylean thoughts on Newton are enormous. In Froude's biography of Carlyle we learn, in Carlyle's own words, 'geometry shone before me as the noblest of all sciences, and I prosecuted it in all my best hours and moods'. His progress in that subject, he also wrote, was due 'mainly to the accident that Leslie alone of all my Professors had some genius in his business, and awoke a certain enthusiasm in me' (I, p. 26). There are good reasons for this enthusiasm. For one thing, Leslie, as did other teachers of Carlyle, including his Latin professor, Christison (who was also extremely interested in mathematics), taught his subject as all the subjects were taught in the Arts curriculum at Edinburgh, not in isolation, but with many references to and examples from other areas and disciplines.[7] Christison did not deliver any formal lectures; instead, he used to illustrate 'in a very miscellaneous way' the course of reading in his subject, 'calling in to his aid the writings of the most celebrated critics, poets and philosophers, ancient and modern'. Leslie, too, taught mathematics in the same way, using all other disciplines to illustrate his subject.

Carlyle himself describes his feelings in *Wotton Reinfred*, his early unfinished work of fiction:

> Mathematics and the kindred sciences . . . took much deeper hold of him; nay by degrees . . . almost alienated him for a long season from other studies. . . . He gloried to track the footsteps of the mighty Newton, and in the thought that he could say to himself: Thou, even thou, art privileged to look from his high eminence, and to behold with thy own eyes the order of that stupendous fabric; thou seest it in light and mystic harmony.[8]

Newton was indeed the 'mighty' Newton, not only to Carlyle but to many, including those whom Carlyle had been studying and reading. The Scottish Enlightenment figures, 'most notably' David Hume, states Rendall, had as their aim 'to introduce the methods pioneered by Isaac Newton into the worlds of moral and political philosophy. Newton appeared as the patron of empirical method, a method which was infinitely adaptable to other worlds beside that of natural philosophy' (p. 19). It was these 'other worlds' that fascinated Carlyle at this time, and he read Newton, in somewhat the same way that he read Hume and, perhaps in a more limited way, the Bible itself, for Newton was not just a mathematician. Newton had beheld the order of that 'stupendous fabric'.[9] Newton seemed to provide proof, mathematical proof, of that Author of the stupendous fabric, one aspect of the Divine in which Carlyle had always been fascinated and by which he could see for himself some visible and concrete proof of the Immensities.[10]

To assess Carlyle's response to Newton, one need only read the famous 'General Scholium' at the end of the *Principia*, in which he both demonstrates a sense of wonder at the universe and acknowledges the infinite Unnameable behind it.

> This most beautiful system of the sun, planets, and comets, could only proceed from the councel and dominion of an intelligent and powerful Being. And if the fixed stars are the centres of other life systems, these, being formed by the like wise councel, must be all subject to the dominion of One . . .: and lest the systems of the fixed stars should, by their gravity, fall on each other, he hath placed those systems at immense distances from one another.[11]

Newton then defines that Absolute, but in terms that Carlyle, even in his dissatisfaction with theology, would accept and later find supported in a much more satisfactory way in German idealism. 'The Supreme God is a Being eternal, infinite, absolutely perfect. . . . He is eternal and infinite, omnipotent and omniscient; that is, his duration reaches from eternity to eternity; his presence from infinity to infinity; he governs all things, and knows all things that are or can be done. . . . He endures forever, and is everywhere' (pp. 544–5). Newton concludes his definition with words that no doubt appealed greatly to Carlyle in his stage of thought, his religious and epistemological speculations: 'Blind metaphysical necessity', writes Newton, 'which is certainly the same always and everywhere, could produce no variety of things. All that diversity of natural things which we find suited to different times and places could arise from nothing but the ideas and will of a Being necessarily existing' (p. 546).

Again, one notes the thrust towards the concept of Deity that Carlyle would find ultimately in German transcendentalism, the 'Infinite Unnameable', whose presence could, in fact, be detected in Nature, the Garment of God, and one also responsible for the orderly framework. At this point one can assume Carlyle still was seeking the 'transcending' concept that he found in his reading of the Germans, particularly Fichte and Goethe: but Newton with his ability not only to read this wondrous universe but to place this reading on a mathematical basis, must have been truly revelatory.[12]

The fact that Newton presented his ideas mathematically was persuasive; the additional fact that he was an 'idealistic' rather than an absolute scientist also made a tremendous difference. Because of his 'idealism', his writings contained clues to what Carlyle was seeking, especially a sense of mystery and wonder. Guerlac says of Newton: 'an ideal image of nature is substituted for the crude scheme of ordered common sense which was the system of the Schools. . . . Yet there is a more important difference: precisely because their mathematical image of nature was an ideal one, these scientists recognized that the conformity of theory to reality had to be approximative and limiting. . . . That scientific truth is not absolute but probabilistic and asymptotic; that it begins in experience and ends there, too, *after passing through the mysterious alembic of mathematical deduction*, Newton expressed clearly in his *regulae philosophandi*' (pp. 18–19, my italics).

These assertions are supported clearly and dramatically by Newton's own words, and most effectively so in the last paragraph of the 'Scholium':

> And now we might add something concerning a certain most subtle spirit which pervades and lies hid in all gross bodies; by the force and action of which spirit and particles of bodies attract one another at near distances, and cohere, if contiguous; and electric bodies operate at greater distances, as well as repelling as attracting the neighbouring corpuscles; and light is emitted, reflected, refracted, inflected, and heats bodies; and all sensation is excited, and the members of animal bodies move at the command of the will, namely, by the vibrations of this

> spirit, mutually propagated along the solid filaments of the nerves, from the outward organs of sense to the brain, and from the brain into the muscles. But these are things that cannot be explained in few words, nor are we furnished with that sufficiency of experiments which is required to an accurate determination and demonstration of the laws by which this electric and elastic spirit operates. (*Principia*, p. 547)

Newton also provided Carlyle with more evidence for his view of the world as dynamical rather than mechanical. In his reference to the 'subtle spirit' or active principle that seems to be the underlying cause of motion and gravity, Newton clearly was suggesting, even if his terms were not theological or metaphysical, the concept of some Divine presence. In direct opposition to most of his contemporaries, he refused to believe that the mechanical law of impact could explain all motion, insisting that one needed to go even beyond the needs of mathematical physics to suggest the cause of gravity. 'In his most significant objection to the Cartesian explanation', Snow writes, '. . . he points to the necessary existence of some active principles of force which would conserve and compensate lost motion. . . . Newton felt that if we would assume that attraction is an attribute of matter there would be no need for a Creator, and he hoped that his *Principia* would be a proof of the existence of a God, conceived in theistic terms'.[13] Newton does, in fact, speak more openly in his *Opticks*. Towards the end of that work he begins to summarise:

> To tell us that every Species of Things is endow'd with an occult specifick Quality by which it acts and produces manifest Effects, is to tell us nothing: But to derive two or three general Principles of Motion from Phaenomena, and afterwards to tell us how the Properties and Actions of all corporeal Things follow from those manifest Principles, would be a very great step in Philosophy, though the Causes of those Principles were not yet discover'd: And therefore I scruple not to propose the Principles of Motion above-mention'd, they being of very general Extent, and leave their Causes to be found out.[14]

In spite of these reservations, however, Newton does not hesitate to talk of matters of primary interest to Carlyle, such matters as the Laws of Nature, the Cosmos, and the various parts of the 'Framework of the Heavens':

> Now by the help of these Principles, all material Things seem to have been composed of the hard and solid Particles above-mentioned, variously associated in the first Creation by the Counsel of an intelligent Agent. For it became him who created them to set them in order. And if he did so, it's unphilosophical to seek for any other origin of the World, or to pretend that it might arise out of a Chaos by the mere Laws of Nature; though being once form'd, it may continue by those Laws for many Ages. For while Comets move in very excentric Orbs in all manner of Positions, blind Fate could never make all the Planets move once and the same way in Orbs concentrick. . . . Such a wonderful Uniformity in the Planetary System must be allowed the Effect of Choice. And other Organs of Sense and Motion; and the Instinct of Brutes and Insects, can be the effect of nothing else than the Wisdom and Skill of a powerful ever-living Agent, who being in all Places, is more able by his Will to move the Bodies within his boundless uniform Sensorium, and thereby to form and reform the Parts of the Universe, than we are by our Will to move the Parts of our own Bodies. (pp. 402–3).

Newton, however, puts in a very significant proviso, one which would have great interest for Carlyle, since it would serve to make his agreement with Newton all the more complete. Newton is careful to avoid any appearance of pantheism: 'And yet we are not to consider the World as the Body of God, or the several Parts thereof, as the Parts of God. . . . For so far as we can know by natural Philosophy what is the first Cause, what Power he has over us, and what Benefits we receive from him, so far our Duty towards him, as well as that towards one another, will appear to us by the Light of Nature' (pp. 403–5). Carlyle, of course, like Newton, refused to see the world as the body of God; it was enough for him to see the world as the garment of God, thus keeping clear the division between the natural world and the Divine Spirit. Like Newton, he would have nothing to do with pantheism; he preferred the inconceivable Absolute.

For Carlyle, then, Newton represented a release from the past in several ways. He had helped sweep away the mechanistic explanation of the cosmos and had at least shown the possibility of other means of viewing it. Also, Newton 'never separated astronomy from the other sciences or mechanics from geometry: they were all one universal science, an experimental or natural philosophy, a unity of sciences. . . . The world for Newton was geometrical primarily but theological. Newton thought that his *Principia* would point to the necessary existence of God' (Snow, p. 82). To one coming from an educational system like that at Edinburgh, this unity was indeed important; to one interested in geometry and also intensely interested in finding a solid basis for belief, this was imperative. Newton had succeeded both in demonstrating the existence of the inconceivable Absolute by emphasising the cosmic order, the proof of which was mathematically unassailable, and showing that the source of that order was indeed Spirit, in terms that seemed to be theologically convincing, certainly as plausible as any other idea put forward up to then.[15]

3

The Stupendous Whole: Newton and Carlylean Belief

The stupendous whole, indeed, fascinated Carlyle all his life; his interest in (and even obsession with) it owes much to his earlier 'inherited religious faith' and his studies in Newton and other figures of the Enlightenment. As he read in Hume and Newton of the cosmic order, he connected these with those sermons he had heard and the many family worships in which he had participated. Indeed, he sounds usually nostalgic in the essay on Edward Irving when he writes of the family worship, 'what they call "Taking the Book" (or Books, i.e. taking your *Bibles*, Psalm and Chapter always part of the service)'. He also sounds usually nostalgic in speaking of old Adam Hope, a rigid Seceder, who, with a 'select group', was in 'the habit of pilgrimage for Sermon'. Carlyle emphasises the importance of attendance:

> Less zealous brethren would perhaps pretermit in bad weather; but I suppose it had to be very bad when Adam and most of his group failed to appear. The distance, a six miles twice, was nothing singular in their case; one family, whose streaming plaids, hung up to drip, I remember to have noticed one wet Sunday, pious Scotch weavers, settled near Carlisle, I was told,—were in the habit of walking fifteen miles twice for their Sermon, since it was not to be heard nearer. A curious phasis of things;—quite vanished now, with whatever of divine and good was in it.

Carlyle then adds a bit about Irving himself, a revealing observation: 'The boy Edward joined himself to Adam's pilgriming group, and regularly trotted by their side to Ecclefechan for Sermon, listening, and occasionally joining in their pious discourse thither and back' (*Reminiscences*, pp. 176–8).

There are two notes struck in these 'musings' that indicate the nature of Carlyle's own early religious practice. The first has to do with the emphasis on the Sermon; the second with the 'pious discourse' afterwards dealing with the subject of the sermon itself. 'It has been frequently remarked that Scotch piety is intellectual rather than devotional', writes Cunningham; 'and the remark is based upon the truth. The peculiarity probably arises in a great measure from the prominence which is given to preaching in the Scottish Church. There are hundreds of thousands who have no means of getting their intellects exercised, or their knowledge enlarged, but the pulpit'. Then he speaks of the 'pious discourse': 'On that day of rest, they receive from the lips of a pious and educated man truths to speak of when they sit with their families at the fireside, and to think of when they follow their plough in the field. In the villages, coteries of keen disputants discuss at the corners of the streets during the week the subjects which were discussed in the church upon the Sabbath'.[1] Cunningham has another observation that is pertinent to Carlyle's own religious upbringing. In speaking of the order of worship, he states that the service was almost uniformly begun by a Psalm (II, p. 595); and Carlyle too, in speaking of family worship, remarked that Psalm and chapter were always part of that service.

Carlyle considered Irving and himself to be 'among the last products' of the teachings and spirit of the old Seceder clergy, and part of their heritage clearly was the emphasis that the Psalms placed on 'the unity of God, His providence, authority, and goodness, and the need for men to observe His law' (Drummond, p. 183). 'The reasons for the hold of the Psalter on all branches of the Church', one commentator has written, 'are not hard to find. The Psalms offer a classical expression of the theistic basis of Christianity . . .'. They also emphasise one other aspect: 'The psalmists do not display any abstract love of nature or of the beauties of the out of doors; . . . Their real interest in the outside world is a religious one: they look upon the heavens and the earth as the handiwork of God, and they see in the so-called processes of nature the Lord's active providence'.[2]

One can grasp from this the basis of Carlyle's response to Newton, whose *Principia* seemed to give firm support for believing in God's handiwork even after much of the theological basis had been eroded. What the Psalms had emotionally depicted, Hume had epistemologically discussed, and Newton had mathematically demonstrated.[3] Newton's 'absolute space and time', identified with the 'all-comprehending mind and immanent presence of God' (Torrance, p. 18), was certainly enough for Carlyle, at least until he was to read Kant and the German writers who were to provide the final link in his search for an acceptable and defensible belief; certainly Newton's ideas were basis enough for recalling those words he had often heard in the sermons of old and in family prayers and worship. The heavens and the earth were indeed the handiwork of God, as, for instance, proclaimed in Psalm 19: 'The heavens declare the glory of God; and the firmament showeth his handiwork'; it is this Psalm, verses 1–14, which the commentator in the *Interpreter's Bible* links to Kant's 'The starry heavens above . . . and the moral law within' (IV, p. 101). 'The heavens declare his righteousness', states Psalm 97. 'Of old hast thou laid the foundation of the earth: and the heavens *are* the work of thy hands', asserts Psalm 102; while 103 proclaims that 'The Lord hath prepared his throne in the heavens; and his kingdom ruleth over all'.

Perhaps Psalm 119, called the 'greatest tour de force in the Psalter' (IV, p. 622) and Psalm 148 are the two that best illustrate the close connection that Carlyle saw and felt in reading Newton and remembering his early biblical reading and discussions. Both stress what might be called the Newtonian cosmos and the God of righteousness and justice. In the first the chief words are 'law', 'testimonies', 'statutes', and 'commandment', all favourites with Carlyle, especiallly when coupled with Nature. Heaven and earth, as established by the Lord, are also frequently mentioned: 'For ever, O Lord, thy word is settled in heaven. . . . Thou hast established the earth, and it abideth'. It is Psalm 148, however, that serves to summarise the Carlylean 'cosmos' as reflected in Newton and the Bible: 'He that also stablished them for ever and ever; he hath made a decree which shall not pass'. *Sun, moon, stars of light* are all mentioned. 'The Lord is conceived of as a transcendent being, dwelling apart from his creation', writes the commentator (IV, p. 755); in the Newtonian sense, of course, they represent bodies in an 'isotopic, necessary and unchanging frame of reference'; they are bodies 'in motion to patterns which [are] amenable to mathematico-mechanical calculation and to formalisation in immutable laws' (Torrance, p. 32).

That Carlyle did connect Hume, Newton and his early religious reading and discussions becomes evident in the use he makes of the heavens and planets, the heavy emphasis he places on God's handiwork as proof of the Almighty. References are sprinkled throughout his letters and works, and they vary from such seemingly straightforward references as this one in 'On History': 'His little crop hangs under and over the firmament of stars, and sails through whole untracked celestial spaces, between Aries and Libra; nevertheless it ripens for him in due season, and he gathers it safe into his barn' (*Works*, XXVII, p. 90); to those that reveal more of Carlyle's 'spiritual' concerns, such as that contained in the conclusion of *Characteristics*:

> Remarkable it is, truly, how everywhere the eternal fact begins again to be recognised, that there is a Godlike in human affairs; that God not only made us and beholds us, but is in us and around us; that the Age of Miracles, as it ever was, now is . . . Behind us . . . lie Six Thousand Years of human effort, human conquest: before us is the boundless Time, with its as yet uncreated and unconquered Continents and Eldorados, which we, even we, have to conquer, to create; and from the bosom of Eternity there shine for us celestial guiding stars'. (*Works*, XXVIII, pp. 42–3)

One can also hear echoes of the Psalms in Carlyle's description of Shakespeare as hero, one who is the Product of Nature; 'It is Nature's highest reward', he writes, 'to a true simple great soul, that he got thus to be *a part of herself*. Such a man's works, whatsoever he with utmost conscious exertion and forethought shall accomplish, grow up withal *un*consciously, from the unknown deeps in him;—as the oak-tree grows from the Earth's bosom, as the mountains and water shape themselves; with a symmetry grounded on Nature's own laws' (*Works*, v, p. 108). One of the most moving passages employing this image is found in a fragment dealing with the crushing effects of false education on a young soul. One must resist, writes Carlyle: 'You must learn to pass on in silence; looking to the eastern mountains whether there is yet any streak of day. Day will break, and the light of Heaven come, wherein man can see; doubt it not. Bootes and the Bear, Kyon, Prokyon, Dogstar and Lesser Dog and Orion's Belt and all the stars, with more serenity and sternly beautiful radiance glitter down as in silent prophecy and divine admonition' (*NLS*, MS 1798, ff. 64–6). Here are present, again, the cosmological handiwork and the suggestion of divine admonition, sternly radiant; Newton's 'subtle spirit which pervades and lies hid in all gross bodies' has indeed developed into a strange force, one that only Carlyle could envision.[4]

Carlyle's favourite book in the Bible was Job,

> one of the grandest things written with pen. One feels, indeed, as if it were not Hebrew; such a noble universality. . . . A noble Book; all men's Book! It is our first, oldest statement of the never-ending Problem,—man's destiny, and God's ways with him here in this earth. . . . Sublime sorrow, sublime reconciliation; . . . so soft, and great; as the summer midnight, as the world with its seas and stars! There is nothing written, I think, in the Bible or out of it, of equal literary merit. (*Works*, v, p. 49; see also Espinasse, p. 258)

As in the Psalms, Carlyle senses in Job a stern Judge (God's ways with him here on this earth) and a cosmos that reflects a possibility of 'sublime reconciliation' (world with its seas and stars), a 'stupendous whole'. His warm response to the Book of Job is clearly based largely on his sympathy for the sufferer, whose stoicism and faith in a righteous God reflect much of Carlyle's own thinking; however, there is also in the Book of Job a recognition of the Author of the Universe, 'Which commandeth the sun, and it riseth not; and sealeth up the stars; Which alone spreadeth out the heavens, and treadeth upon the waves of the sea; Which maketh Arcturus, Orion, and Pleiades, and the chambers of the south' (9:7–9).

The similarity of various passages in Carlyle's writing to many in Job's is striking. In Chapter 38 one finds an emphasis on the Lord's cosmological command: 'Canst thou bind the sweet influences of Pleiades, or loose the bands of Orion? Canst thou bring forth Mazzaroth in his season? or canst thou guide Arcturus with his sons? Knowest thou the ordinances of heaven? canst thou set the dominion thereof in the earth?' (31–3). Time and again Job uses the example of God's dominion over the heavens to demonstrate His power and glory, the thought of 22:12–14: '*Is* not God in the height of heaven? and behold the height of the stars, how high they are! And thou sayest, How doth God know? can he judge through the dark cloud? thick clouds *are* a covering to him, that he seeth not; and he walketh in the circuit of heaven'.

One can understand, too, Carlyle's appreciation of its 'literary merit', although Carlyle was no literary critic; in verses 7–14 of Chapter 26, for instance, there is demonstrated a sense of the poetic power of the Book:

> He stretcheth out the north over the empty space, *and* hangeth the earth upon nothing. He bindeth up the waters in this thick cloud; and the cloud is not rent under them. He holdeth back the face of his throne, *and* spreadeth his cloud upon it. He hath compassed the waters with bounds, until the day and night come to an end. The pillars of heaven tremble, and are astonished at his reproof. He divideth the sea with his power, and by his understanding he smiteth through the proud. By his Spirit, he hath garnished the heavens; his hand hath formed the crooked serpent. Lo, these *are* parts of his ways; but how little a portion is heard of him? but the thunder of his power who can understand?

While one must acknowledge Carlyle's debt to Kant, Goethe, Novalis and the German writers he read, then, one cannot simply dismiss his early reading and training. His view of Nature did not suddenly emerge; it gradually developed during his early years, and his final position was one that still retained many elements that can be identified with his biblical reading and his fascination with the works of Newton and Hume. His sense of discovery of German literature must be balanced with his earlier comments on Newton's *Principia*: 'the work itself remains in undecaying majesty to all generation' and on Lagrange's *Mécanique analytique*:

> The first volume is beautiful, & can be understood; great part of the second is demonstrated, he says, in the *mécanique celeste*, and I am obliged to be content with ignorantly admiring these sublime mysteries. . . . To see these truths, my good Robert—to *feel* them as one does the proportion of the sphere & cylinder! . . . Sometimes, indeed, on a fine evening, & when I have quenched my thirst with large potations of Souchong, I say to myself—away with despondency—hast thou not a soul and a kind of understanding in it? (*CL*, I, pp. 127–8)

4

The Carlylean *Weltbild*: Natural Supernaturalism

Carlyle has many things to say about German philosophy, literature, and culture, and in his letters and writings one can trace his growing interest in and complete commitment to them. He often speaks of the effect that the German writers had on him, and it soon becomes clear that he found in their writings something that was, indeed, not doctrinal; it was something that simply struck a responsive chord in his own troubled soul. In his case, however, it provided the necessary, final link in that chain of ideas to which he had been exposed. His straightforward account is in some ways more moving than that in *Sartor* because it is litotic rather than hyperbolic:

> As to their particular doctrines, there is nothing definite or precise to be said. . . . To explain them best, I can only think of the revelation, for I call it no other, that these men made to me. It was to me like the rising of a light in the darkness which lay around and threatened to swallow me up. I was then in the very midst of Wertherism, the blackness and darkness of death. (*Lectures*, pp. 201–2)

This, of course, is not helpful to one wanting to know exactly what these German writers said or did, especially since Carlyle goes on to emphasise Goethe's 'Worship of Sorrow' and his wise silences. 'But we can see that what he spoke is not the thousandth part of what lay in him' (*Lectures*, pp. 205–8). It does indicate that it was a very personal attraction, one that was an answer to his own years of unrest, especially to his doubts and frustrations.

The major elements in Carlyle's comments on these writers seem to be a working out in 'some manner an enfranchisement' of one's soul, to save oneself from 'being crushed down by the world' and to be 'in all things men'. Goethe was to be admired above all because he had turned his sufferings into useful work

(*Lectures*, p. 209). There is always in Carlyle that subjective turn, one that enables him to see everything in terms of how it can be especially helpful to *him*; from this he takes only what he needs. In German literature, as distinct from metaphysics, from which he could get nothing (*Lectures*, p. 204), he found specific ideas that, joined to what he already had gained from his earlier readings, enabled him to enfranchise his soul, to escape from the darkness which lay around and threatened to swallow him up.

There are specific 'doctrines' in German literature that did make a deep impression on Carlyle, and these have to do with man and Nature. He was able to make those synaptic leaps that ignore logic or evidence. Although he denies that German metaphysics helped him, one has to keep in mind that Kant was one influence on Carlyle, and Kant did figure in his escape from the Everlasting NO. 'You will never in the world guess', he wrote to Jane Welsh in 1826, 'what sort of pastime I have had recourse to in this windbound portion of my voyage. Nothing less than the reading of Kant's Transcendental Philosophy! So it is: I am at the hundred and fiftieth page of the *Kritik der reinen vernunft*; not only reading but partially understanding, and full of projects for instructing my benighted countrymen on the true merits of this sublime system at some more propitious season' (*CL*, IV, p. 137).

He got enough from Kant to free himself from 'grim necessity', as he describes it in *Sartor*. He now realised that his salvation lay in his intuitive self: 'But deepest of all illusory Appearances, for hiding Wonder, as for many other ends, are your two grand fundamental world-enveloping Appearances SPACE and TIME. These, as spun and woven for us from before Birth itself, to clothe our celestial ME, but dwelling here, and yet blind to it' (*Works*, I, p. 207). 'Are we not Spirits', he concludes, 'that are shaped into a body, into an Appearance; and that fade away again into air and Invisibility? This is no metaphor', he adds, 'it is a simple scientific *fact*' (*Works*, I, p. 211). Hume's 'Fabric' and Newton's 'fact' seemed to be simply versions of Kantian spiritual fact; the importance lies in Carlyle's glimpse of how these could be brought together as 'natural supernaturalism'. In a *Journal* entry of 1830, Carlyle put down:

> I have now almost done with the Germans. Having seized their opinions, I must turn to me to inquire *how* true are they? That truth is in them, no lover of Truth will doubt: but how much?

> And after all, one needs an intellectual Scheme (or ground plan of the Universe) drawn with one's own instruments.—I think I have got rid of Materialism: Matter no longer seems to me so ancient, so unsubduable, so *certain* and palpable as Mind. *I* am Mind: whether matter or not I know not—and care not.—Mighty glimpses into the spiritual Universe I have sometimes had (about the true nature of Religion, the possibility, after all, of 'supernatural' (really natural) influences &c. &c.): would they could but stay with me, and ripen into a perfect view! (*2NB*, pp. 150–1)

In conjunction with this passage there are other notations that complement the ideas Carlyle expresses in it. I cite three from around this same time:

> Every living man is a visible mystery: he walks between two Eternities and two Infinitudes. . . . Say, I am a man; and you say all. . . . Pray that your eyes be opened, that you may *see* what *is* before them! (1829, p. 136)

> Wonderful Universe! Were our eyes but opened, what a 'secret' were it that we daily see and handle, without heed! (1830, p. 142)

> What am I but a sort of Ghost? Men rise as Apparitions from the bosom of Night, and after grinning, squeaking, gibbering some space, return thither. The earth they stand on is Bottomless; the vault of their sky is Infinitude; the Life-*Time* is encompassed with Eternity. O wonder! And they buy cattle or seats in Parliament, and drink coarser or finer fermented liquors, as if all this were a City that had foundations. (1830, p. 164. Cf. *Works*, I, 10ff.; *Sartor*, Bk. I, ch. 3)

The cumulative effect of these entries is great, largely because of Carlyle's own sense of discovery. He has truly 'seized' some opinions and sincerely wants to see if they work for him as they seem to have worked for others. He feels as if writing them down makes them true. Prominent among these ideas or opinions, as he calls them, are his sense of wonder at the universe, his belief in 'natural supernaturalism', his sense of the mystery of man as a ghost, and, perhaps most importantly, his deep faith in what can be called organic unity, the importance of wholeness. 'What is a *Whole*?' he asks himself at one point in his *Journal*: 'I see some vague outline of what a *Whole* is: also how an individual Delineation may be "informed with the Infinite"; may appear hanging in the universe of Time & Space (partly): in which case is it a Poem and a Whole? Therefore, are the true Homeric Poems of these times to be written with the *ink of science*?' (*2NB*, pp. 187–8). This sense of wholeness (unity, integration) applies to everything man does and to all disciplines.

In spite of his well-known denigration of fiction and his derisive remarks on certain kinds of poetry, Carlyle always held in high esteem what he called 'true' poetry. In his essay on the state of German literature (1827) he speaks of Goethe:

> The poetry of Goethe, for instance, we reckon to be Poetry, sometimes in the very highest sense of that word; yet it is no reminiscence, but something actually present and before us; . . . looking around upon that real world itself, now rendered holier to our eyes, and once more become a solemn temple . . . (*Works*, XXVI, p. 65)

Carlyle then goes on to talk of the function of the poet and the end of poetry, and in both instances his remarks reflect his view of the importance of 'integration':

> The end of Poetry is higher: she must dwell in Reality, and become manifest to men in the forms among which they live and move. . . . The coldest sceptic, the most callous worldling, sees not the actual aspects of life more sharply than they are here delineated: the Nineteenth Century stands before us, in all its contradiction and perplexity; barren, mean and baleful, as we have all known it, yet here no longer mean or barren, but enamelled into beauty in the poet's spirit; for its secret significance is laid open, and thus, as it were, the life-giving fire that slumbers in it, is called forth, and flowers and foliage, as of old, are springing on its bleakest wildernesses, and overmantling its sternist cliffs. For these men have not only the clear eye but the loving heart. They have penetrated into the mystery of Nature: after long trial they have been initiated; and to unwearied endeavour, Art has at least yielded her secret; and thus can the Spirit of our Age, embodied in fair imaginations, look forth on us, earnest and full of meaning, from their works. (*Works*, XXVI, p. 66)

'A man with eyes', he once wrote to a correspondent, 'with a soul and heart, to tell me in candid clearness what he saw passing round him in this universe—is and remains for ever a welcome man'. On another occasion he told the same person: 'A man with a pen in his hand, with the gift of articulate pictural utterance, surely *he* is well employed in painting and articulating worthy acts and men that by the nature of them were dumb. I on the whole define all Writing to mean even that, or else almost nothing' (*LW*, pp. 285, 304).

These conclusions perhaps raise more questions than they answer. Some of the answers are found, explicitly or implicitly, in his essay on Novalis (1829), who is referred to in his *Journal* as an 'Anti-Mechanist; a deep man; the most perfect of modern spirit-seers'. 'I thank him for somewhat', Carlyle concludes (*2NB*, p. 140). Carlyle talks of Novalis's peculiar manner of viewing Nature: 'his habit, as it were, of considering Nature rather in the concrete, not analytically and as a divisible Aggregate, but as a self-subsistent universally connected Whole'. Novalis is, for Carlyle, a true poet, 'no less Idealistic [as a poet] than as a philosopher. His poems are breathings of a high devout soul, feeling always that here he has no home, but looking, as in clear vision, to a "city that hath foundations".' It is Novalis's 'peculiar' way of looking at Nature that appeals to Carlyle and makes him the most perfect of modern spirit-seers:

> He loves external Nature with a singular depth; nay, we might say, he reverences her, and holds unspeakable communings with her: for Nature is no longer dead, hostile Matter, but the veil and mysterious Garment of the Unseen; as it were, the Voice with which the Deity proclaims himself to man. These two qualities,—his pure religious temper, and heartfelt love of Nature,—bring him into true poetic relation both with the spiritual and the material World, and perhaps constitute his chief worth as a Poet. (*Works*, XXVII, pp. 28–9)

Specifically what Novalis had provided, and to some extent the other German writers, especially Goethe, was the way to account for matter. 'Nay, to the Transcendentalist, clearly enough', Carlyle writes, 'the whole question of the origin and existence of Nature must be greatly simplified: the old hostility of Matter is at an end, for Matter itself annihilated: and the black Spectre, Atheism . . . melts into nothingness forever' (*Works*, XXVII, p. 26).

Carlyle, however, always insists on the 'scientific' basis of German Idealism; indeed, he usually pairs those we would consider sceptics with these German writers or with other mystics:

> Let the reader believe us, the Critical Philosophers, whatever they may be, are no mystics. . . . Kant, Fichte, and Schelling, are men of cool judgment, and determinate energetic character; men of science and profound and universal investigation; nowhere does the world, in all its bearings, spiritual or material, theoretic or practical, lie pictured in clearer or truer colours than in such heads as these. We have heard Kant estimated as a spiritual brother of Böhme: as justly might we take Sir Isaac Newton for a spiritual brother of Baron Swedenborg, and Laplace's *Mechanism of the Heavens* for a peristyle to the *Vision of the New Jerusalem*. (*Works*, XXVI, p. 76)

His closing remarks on Fichte are particularly interesting: 'So robust an intellect, a soul so calm, so lofty, massive and immovable, has not mingled in philosophical discussion since the time of Luther. . . . For the man rises before us, amid contradiction and debate, like a granite mountain amid clouds and wind. . . . The cry of a thousand choughs assaulting that old cliff of granite: seen from the summit, these, as they winged the midway air, showed scarce so gross as beetles, and their cry was seldom even audible' (*Works*, XXVI, p. 77).

Matter was at last subduable; Carlyle seemed finally to be able to accept it as part of an orderly world. He could at last write of matter in terms of a 'universally connected Whole', the same terms he had often used to describe natural scenes, the same terms he had found in the Bible. The world, after all, partly Newtonian, partly biblical, largely transcendental, seemed to have some order. Newton's 'most subtle spirit' had become that 'mystery' of Nature, which the German poets, men with the clear eye and the loving heart, had penetrated. 'Art [had] at last yielded her secret' (*Works*, XXVI, p. 66). Carlyle's view here reflects both his 'religious' and 'philosophic' ideas, for it encompasses all he gained from his early readings and experiences as well as the important influence of his German reading. One sees in it the results of his early church-going, particularly the emphases found in the Psalms; the effects of his parents' example; his own 'reading' of the Bible; his university experience, especially his study of Hume and later, Newton: and, finally, his own characteristic stubborn desire to go his own 'prophetic' way, a way based particularly on the example of his father and his reading of the Germans. Novalis particularly had shown that Nature (Matter) was not 'dead' and 'hostile', but rather 'the Voice with which the Deity proclaims himself to man'. What had enabled Novalis to achieve this 'poetic relation' with the spiritual and the material world were his 'pure religious temper' and his 'heartfelt love of Nature'. Accordingly, then, acting on this clue, Carlyle could begin to glimpse the 'secret'; he could begin to appreciate Nature as a 'self-subsistent universally connected Whole'.

5

Prophetic Utterance: Nature, Human History, Divine Justice and the Universe

In spite of the controversy regarding his biography of Carlyle, no one would doubt Froude's depiction of Carlyle's religion as a 'Calvinist without Theology'.[1] Even less controversial are Carlyle's own words. Carlyle, for instance, nowhere expresses a belief in a 'supernatural' Deity. 'He based his faith', stresses Froude, 'not on a supposed revelation. . . . Experienced fact was to him revelation, and the only true revelation. Historical religions, Christianity included, he believed to have been successive efforts of humanity, loyally and nobly made in the light of existing knowledge' (Froude, II, pp. 2–3).

There are several examples of Carlyle's own 'creed', each illustrating a facet of his complex approach to religious belief. In his 'Inaugural Address' to the students at Edinburgh University, for instance, he refers to studies in universities at one point.

> They begin [he says] as is well known, with their grand aim directed on Theology,—their eye turned earnestly on Heaven. . . . In regard to theology, as you are aware, it has been and especially was then, the study of the deepest heads that come into the world,—what is the nature of this stupendous Universe, and what are our relations to it, and to all things knowable to man, or known only to the great Author of man and it. Theology was once the name for all this; and this is still alive for man, however dead the name may grow!

Carlyle next begins on a favourite theme of his in regard to 'theology and churches'. He continues:

> In fact, the members of the Church keeping theology in a lively condition [*Laughter*] for the benefit of the whole population, theology was the great object of the Universities. I consider it is the same intrinsically now, though very much forgotten, from many causes, and not so successful [*A laugh*] as might be wished, by any manner of means! (*Works*, XXIX, p. 454)

Carlyle then becomes serious and discusses Goethe's *Wilhelm Meister's Travels*. 'There are some ten pages of that', he states, 'which, if ambition had been my only rule, I would rather have written, been able to write, than have written all the books that have appeared since I came into the world [*Cheers*]. Deep, deep is the meaning of what is said there.' He goes on to talk of the 'three reverences' and concludes by praising the meaning of them, especially the last: 'to learn to recognise in pain, in sorrow and contradiction, even in those things, odious to flesh and blood, what divine meanings are in them; to learn that there lies in these also, and more than in any of the preceding, a priceless blessing. And he defines that as being the soul of the Christian religion,—the highest of all religions' (*Works*, XXIX, pp. 473, 474).

Another example is in *Frederick the Great*, in which Carlyle mentions Frederick's 'creed' at least two times. The first is a brief mention of Frederick's feelings and thoughts on coming back to Berlin in 1763. After the 'mythical' account of his return, Carlyle states: 'He was not without piety; but it did not take the devotional form, and his habits had nothing of the clerical' (*Works*, XIX, p. 7). The second occurs when Carlyle is describing his last moments:

> In death, I think, he has neither fear nor hope. Atheism, truly, he never could abide: to him, as to all of us, it was flatly inconceivable that intellect, moral emotion, could have been put into *him* by an Entity that had none of its own. But there, pretty much, his Theism seems to have stopped. Instinctively, too, he believed, no man more firmly, that Right alone has ultimately any strength in this world: ultimately, yes;—but for him and his poor brief interests, what good was it? Hope for himself in Divine Justice, in Divine Providence, I think he had not practically any; that the unfathomable Demiurgus should concern himself with such a set of paltry ill-given animalcules as oneself and mankind are, this also, as we have often noticed,

is in the main incredible to him. A sad Creed, this of the King's;—he had to do this duty without fee or reward. (*Works*, XIX, pp. 290–1)

There is not much in this portrait that does not apply to Carlyle as well.

In spite of these strong convictions, however, Carlyle retained the spirit of his mother's strong belief in the simple truths of the Bible. Unable to believe in ritual and revelation, he believed, as had his parents, in 'the broad facts of the Divine government of the universe'. 'It is impossible', Carlyle once said, 'to believe otherwise than that this world is the work of an Intelligent Mind. The Power which has formed us—He (or It—if that appears to any one more suitable) has known how to put into the human soul an ineradicable love of justice and truth. The best bit for me in Kant', he added, 'is that saying of his, "Two things strike me dumb with astonishment—the Starry Heavens and the Sense of Right and Wrong in the Human Soul" ' (Allingham, p. 264).

Time and time again in his letters to his mother he reassures her that he and she are not far apart in their basic beliefs. 'To you in particular, my dear Mother', he writes in 1820, 'I know that I can never be sufficiently grateful—not only for the common kindness of a mother; but for the unceasing watchfulness with which you strove to instill virtuous principles into my young mind: and tho' we are separated at the present, and may be still more widely separated, I hope the lessons which you taught will never be effaced from my memory' (*CL*, I, p. 238). His most explicit letter, however, is later that year: 'I know well and feel deeply', he tells her, 'that you entertain the most solicitous anxiety about my temporal and still more about my eternal welfare. . . . Your character and mine are far more similar than you imagine; and our opinions too, tho' clothed in different garbs, are I well know still analogous at bottom' (*CL*, I, p. 293).

To his father he owed not only his sense of duty but his ideas about what true religious feeling should be like, the concept he so well illustrated in *Past and Present* in the person of Abbot Samson. What Carlyle stresses about his father, who in 'all the area in Boundless Space he had seen was limited to a circle of some forty miles in diameter' and whose 'knowledge of the Boundless Time was derived from his Bible', is the 'culture' he had gained from the 'better men of the district': 'the Religious men, to whom as to the most excellent, his own nature gradually attached and attracted him. He was Religious with the consent of his whole faculties: . . . "Putting out the natural eye of his mind to see better with a telescope:" this was no scheme for *him*'.

His father also set an example for what Campbell characterises as Carlyle's 'religious message': 'belief as a fundamental part of his daily life, yet he *retained his rational powers of enquiry* simultaneously with the deep emotional loyalty to his faith' (*CHC*, p. 5; my italics). In more general terms, Carlyle admired a man who 'retained a strong and unquestioning religious belief of a strong authoritarian nature' and yet 'simultaneously a questioning turn of mind which takes nothing for granted'. This quality of character is what Goethe noticed. 'Carlyle', he said, 'was resting on an *original foundation*', and was 'so happily constituted' that he could 'develop out of himself the requirements of what was good and beautiful—*out of himself,* not out of contact with others' (Froude, I, p. 431).

An important subject, indeed one of the constants, overwhelmingly present in all of Carlyle's writings, was God's universe. Froude rightly gave a place of honour to Carlyle's religion, and he published 'Spiritual Optics', which, he said, contained the 'main structure' of his philosophy. 'The secret of a man's nature lies in his religion', Froude wrote, 'in what he really believes about this world, and his own place in it' (Froude, II, p. 2). In his comments on Carlyle's 'Spiritual Optics' Froude revealed not only Carlyle's ideas, but the way he conceptualised them; and at the centre was the universe, the starry heavens and the solid earth forming a solid temple. Significantly, too, as Froude described it, as the 'relative importance of man was diminished, his conception of the system of which he was a part had become immeasurably more magnificent; while every phenomenon which *had been actually and faithfully observed remained unaffected*' (my italics). Froude explained Carlyle's great ambition: 'Carlyle conceived that a revolution precisely analagous to that which Galileo had wrought in our apprehension of the material heaven was silently in progress in our attitude towards spiritual phenomena' (Froude, II, p. 5).

The implication of Carlyle's 'revolutionary' ambitions in this respect are important to those who want to know not only what Carlyle thought about spiritual phenomena but how he arrived at these ideas. We know, for instance, that when Carlyle was writing a biography or history he liked to 'see' the subject. 'It was his habit', writes Duffy, 'to paste on a screen in his workroom engraved portraits, when no better could be had, of the people he was then writing about. It kept the image of the man steadily in view. . . . There was something in a genuine portrait, he said, which one could hardly fail to recognise as authentic. It looked *like an actual man*, with a consistent character, and left a permanent image in the memory.'[2] One begins to understand better Carlyle's interest in Hume, who is intent on 'rationality' demonstrating a kind of principle of order from which can be gained some idea of regularity or order in nature, and who argues for an invisible, intelligent power in the world.

It was evidently not too far a leap, with the example of Newton, to do the same for spiritual phenomena. Froude's description of Carlyle's thoughts and Carlyle's own words illustrate his vision of the revolution that would be wrought:

> The spiritual universe, like the visible, was the same yesterday, to-day, and for ever. . . . The word God was too awful for common use, and he veiled his meaning in metaphors to avoid it. But God to him was *the fact of facts* [my italics]. He looked on this whole system of visible or spiritual phenomena as a manifestation of the will of God in constant forces, forces not mechanical but dynamic, interpenetrating and controlling all existing things, from the utmost bounds of space to the smallest granule on the earth's surface. . . . God's law was everywhere: man's welfare depended on the faithful reading of it. (Froude, II, pp. 5–6)

Tillotson talks of Carlyle's 'neglect of the important discoveries of the scientists', and yet he acknowledges just how much Carlyle does indeed owe to them. 'Carlyle's indirect debt', he concludes, almost off-handedly, 'could not be heavy because it was they who had carried on the primitive tradition of gazing hard at the spacious firmament on high, rather than consulting Holy Writ about its nature' (p. 79). Exactly! Carlyle's debt, however, was more direct than Tillotson and others acknowledge; his own words reflect heavy Newtonian influence, almost as though Newton had provided Carlyle with a 'real photograph' of the universe:

> Part of the 'grand Unintelligible', that we are now learning spiritually too—that the earth *turns*, not the sun and heavenly spheres. One day the spiritual astronomers will find that *this* is the infinitely greater miracle. The universe is not an orrery, theological or other, but a universe; and instead of paltry theologic brass spindles for axis . . . has laws of gravitation, laws of attraction and repulsion; is not a Ptolemaic but a Newtonian universe. . . .
>
> Old piety was wont to say that God's judgments tracked the footsteps of the criminal. . . . You could do no evil, you could do no good, but a god would repay it to you. It was as certain as that when you shot an arrow from the earth, gravitation would bring it back to the earth. The all-embracing law of right and wrong was as inflexible, as sure and exact, as that of gravitation. . . .
>
> Once more it is in religion with us, as in astronomy—we know now that the earth moves. But it had not annihilated the stars for us; it has infinitely exalted and expanded the stars and the universe. (Froude, II, pp. 16–18)

These thoughts are, says Froude, the key to Carlyle's mind; in this faith 'he interpreted human history'. These ideas 'governed all his judgments of men and things' (II, p. 18).

Throughout 'Spiritual Optics' one finds Carlyle visualising the universe, heaven and earth, the starry heavens, constantly referring to heavenly bodies and phenomena. 'The great Galileo, or numerous small Galileos, have appeared in our spiritual world too, and are making known to us that the sun stands still, that as for the sun and stars and eternal immensities, they do not move at all, . . . that it is we and our dog-hutch that are moving all this while giving rise to such phenomena; and that if we would ever be wise about our situation we must now attend to that fact' (Froude, II, p. 11).

With a characteristic lament over his not being able to communicate his message to others, one that becomes more and more noticeable in his writings, Carlyle then adds: 'I would fain sometimes write a book about all that, and try to make it plain to everybody. But alas! I find again there is next to nothing to be said about it in words at present. . . . A *word* to express that extensive or universal operation of referring the motion from yourself to the object you look at, or *vice versa*? Is there none?' (Froude, II, p. 11). Carlyle, in fact, was at times more comfortable with images, symbols, or emblems, as he called them, rather than with words, and his imagery is what one must look at if one is fully to understand his meaning. He devotes an entire chapter to symbols in *Sartor*, but even earlier in that work he has the Professor exclaim, 'All visible things are emblems. . . . Matter exists only spiritually, and to represent some Idea, and *body* it forth. . . . What is Man himself, and his whole terrestrial Life, but an Emblem; a Clothing or visible Garment for that divine Me of his cast hither, like a light-particle, down from Heaven?' (*Works*, I, p. 57). 'Language itself', he writes, 'is nothing but metaphors, the Garment of God'. The Professor also speculates about Symbols:

> In a Symbol there is concealment and yet revelation. . . . In the Symbol proper . . . there is ever . . . some embodiment and revelation of the Infinite. . . . By Symbols . . . is man guided and commanded, made happy, made wretched. He everywhere finds himself encompassed with Symbols. . . . the Universe is but one vast Symbol of God. (*Works*, I, p. 175)

6

The Carlylean Dilemma: The Riddle of Destiny

How can one account, then, for the 'failure' of the Sage of Chelsea to convince his readers of the validity of his vision? Why did he resort, finally, to writing latter-day pamphlets instead of essays in the vein of *Sartor Resartus*? The answer lies, it would seem, in his inability wholly to convince himself and others of his belief in the primacy of either the 'natural' or the 'supernatural'. Each seemed to have equal claim; neither could assert any kind of final proof over the other. The sky and the earth were everywhere evident, and, like so many of his followers, Carlyle simply could not fully reject one or the other. True, he professed his belief in a unified universe, and his assertive image seemed to convey this faith; in the final analysis, however, he could not come down unquestioningly on one side or the other. He refused to, or could not, answer the riddle of the Sphinx.

Between the confident affirmations of *Sartor Resartus*, 'the central book of his life', and the pessimistic outbursts of *Latter-Day Pamphlets* there is much evidence to suggest that for Carlyle there never could be 'proof' for his ideas about the universe, about man, Nature and God. As extreme as Cazamian's claim might seem, there is some truth in his statement that with *Past and Present* Carlyle 'had exhausted all his themes'.[1] Unable to believe completely in either the natural or the supernatural, Carlyle found no way to 'solve' the universe; instead, he felt it necessary to keep repeating the ideas and the imagery of his early works and days, hoping that somehow by sheer repetition he would convince himself and others that he had indeed solved the riddle of the Sphinx. While his assertive image helped to demonstrate one possible approach to the answer to the riddle of Destiny, it is clear that it was not a satisfactory solution. He could claim to understand the secret of the Universe, the true relation between Earth and Sky, but it is apparent that he was never able to account for 'Nature, Universe, Destiny, Existence, however we name this grand unnameable Fact in the midst of which we live and struggle'. He was, in his own words, 'her mangled victim' rather than 'her victorious bridegroom' (*Works*, x, p. 7).

Perhaps the final attempt to solve the riddle had been made in *Past and Present*, a work apparently written from the heart rather than the brain. While ostensibly dealing with contemporary social, economic and political problems, *Past and Present* everywhere demonstrates Carlyle's own struggle to resolve his personal problems, not the least of which was his concern with his own life and struggle. The works immediately preceding *Past and Present* indicate Carlyle's growing dissatisfaction with his own life as well as with the British nation. Indeed, *Heroes and Hero Worship*, *The French Revolution* and *Chartism* all reveal the general direction of his thoughts, one that contains disturbing tendencies towards those Carlylean ideas repulsive to most readers: order, might, authority, divine right. These were to become, in works after *Past and Present*, the chief means to subdue chaos and assert the authority of Nature in nations as well as individuals; certainly they are the chief ideas of *Cromwell*, *Frederick* and *Latter-Day Pamphlets*. In *Past and Present*, however, Carlyle is still attempting to balance the ideal and the real, the inner sphere of Fact and the outer sphere of Semblance, the natural and the supernatural. His failure to arrive at a satisfactory solution in *Past and Present* is his implicit admission that he has been unable to become Destiny's bridegroom; henceforth he will be her 'mangled victim, scattered on the precipices', an ironic image in the light of his own assertive one.

The epigraphs of *Sartor Resartus* and *Past and Present* give some indication of Carlyle's increasing disillusionment with his self and the world and his growing dependence on Justice as Force rather than Truth, on Might rather than Right. In the former he can quote three different authorities, Goethe, Novalis and Fichte, the one from Goethe perhaps striking the keynote: 'Mein Vermächtniss, wie herrlich weit und breit!/Die Zeit ist mein Vermächtniss, mein Acker is die Ziet'; but in the latter the view has darkened: 'Ernst ist das Leben'. The Heir of Time has given way to the gloomy Prophet of the Age, alternately proclaiming and preaching the need for his people to reform, for his followers to take his advice or perish. Significantly, his advice in *Past and Present* reflects his own inability to choose between the actual and ideal, fact or spirit. In contrast to the author of *Sartor*, still 'young and elastic' and certain of great changes (Cazamian, p. 127), the author of *Past and Present* falls back again and again on the dogmas and decrees of his own philosophy, one that reveals a wavering inability to come down on one side or the other. The Prophet's declarations reveal a position, not a faith; they demonstrate reactions to situations and developments, not solutions to questions of character or humility. The Carlylean message becomes one that reflects his own dilemma, and his public pronouncements, loudly (at times hysterically) proclaimed in *Latter-Day Pamphlets*, *Cromwell* and *Frederick*, demonstrate his failure to achieve a convincing compromise between the material and the spiritual. The 'altruistic curiosity' of *Sartor* turns into the prejudices and proclamations of *Past and Present* (Cazamian, p. 118).

Chartism, written three years earlier, contains hints that indicate Carlyle's rejection of 'positive' solutions to the riddle of Destiny. While Carlyle in that work and in *Past and Present* acknowledges the need for a 'fluctuating' adjustment in society and in individual lives, he nevertheless stresses as final solutions the deplorable elements of his message. Both *Chartism* and *Past and Present*, especially the latter, emphasise what he calls the 'dualism' of life, but in both he seems to assert the supremacy of Fact as vengeful Justice rather than Fact as Truth. If injustice is, as Carlyle claims, another name for disorder, then justice becomes the means for imposing order, and order becomes both might and right. In a key chapter in *Chartism*, 'Rights and Mights', Carlyle makes clear his definitions. Who, for him, is the strong man? Carlyle's reply is to the point: 'The wise man; the man with the gift of method, of faithfulness and valour, all of which are the basis of wisdom; who has the insight into what is what, into what will follow out of what, the eye to see and the hand to do; who is *fit* to administer, to direct, and guidingly command: he is the strong man'. He goes on, not surprisingly, to place the strong man in his assertive image: 'Beautiful it is, and a gleam from the same eternal pole-star visible amid the destinies of men, that all talent, all intellect is in the first place moral;—what a world were this otherwise!' (*Works*, XXIX, pp. 147–8).

There are other indications of Carlyle's reverence for Fact as retributive justice in *Chartism*, and the implications of this particular view become increasingly evident. The need for authority, strong leaders and guidance is more and more emphasised. 'What are all popular commotions and maddest bellowings, from Peterloo to the Place-de-Greve itself? Bellowings, *in*articulate cries as of a dumb creature in rage and pain; to the ear of wisdom [strong men?] they are inarticulate prayers: "Guide me, govern me! I am mad and miserable, and cannot guide myself!" ' The conclusion is spelled out by Carlyle: 'Surely of all "rights of man", this right of the ignorant man to be guided by the wiser, to be, gently or forcibly, held in the true course by him, is the indisputablest. Nature herself ordains it . . .' (*Works*, XXIX, pp. 157–8).

The Carlylean solution to the riddle of Destiny becomes clear: in the duality of life between the actual and the ideal, while both have equal status, the true meaning of the latter must wait upon the immediate working out of the former. Divine Truth will eventually prevail, but first men must come to know what Truth means here on earth, particularly regarding such matters as justice, liberty, relations with one another, with Nature and with God. With that approach it is no surprise that Carlyle insists first on 'radical' solutions, for the actual has, in fact, become so far removed from the ideal that desperate remedies are needed. The conclusion to the chapter 'Laissez-Faire' in *Chartism* asserts all this:

> Imperfection, it is known, cleaves to human things; far is the Ideal departed from, in most times; very far! And yet so long as an Ideal (and soul of Truth) does, in never so confused a manner, exist and work within the Actual, it is a tolerable business. Not so, when the Ideal has entirely departed, and the Actual owns to itself that it has no Idea, no soul of Truth any longer: at that degree of imperfection human things cannot continue living; they are obliged to alter or expire, when they attain to that.

Carlyle then resorts to the type of imagery occasionally appearing in *Past and Present* and pervasive in *Latter-Day Pamphlets*: 'Blotches and diseases exist on the skin and deeper, the heart continuing whole; but it is another matter when the heart itself becomes diseased; when there is not heart, but a monstrous gangrene pretending to exist there as heart!' (*Works*, XXIX, p. 165).

Past and Present, then, is Carlyle's final attempt to solve his own riddle: his fascination with Fact and his devotion to the Ideal. This work demonstrates both the struggle and the acknowledgement that he had resigned himself to some sort of accommodation; it represents his 'Tintern Abbey' Ode. Both had to be acknowledged, but the way to unite them finally eluded him. 'Natural Supernaturalism' was as close to certainty as he ever got, but that concept, while as compensatory for him as the 'still sad music of humanity' was for Wordsworth, remained somehow exactly that, compensatory rather than completely fulfilling. Moreover, he never could make clear to his readers exactly what he meant by the term, although he never gave up trying, notably through his assertive image.

In *Past and Present* the real and the ideal rather than past and the present are the major concerns of Carlyle; balance, not contrast, emerges as the ultimate Carlylean 'message'. Unanswerable Fact and Divine Justice are discussed, debated, analysed, dissected, but never satisfactorily fused. In typical Carlylean fashion, there is much attention paid to the need to read the secret of the Universe, but equal attention is devoted to Unanswerable Fact, the solid earth and the here and now. Not only does *Past and Present* show 'a hardening of Carlyle's dualism', but it represents his 'failure' to be the Pauline voice for his time (LaValley, p. 184). Unable either to communicate or to sustain his vision of Natural Supernaturalism, he spent the rest of his life lamenting the powerlessness of his weak voice and crippled right hand.

It does not take the reader of *Past and Present* long to sense the Carlylean dilemma, for it is early evident in the work. The first two chapters of Book I set the tone and approach; the world itself is troubled, and the key to helping it lies in understanding Midas's experience. Carlyle's own position seems to be similar to that of Midas; indeed, everything Carlyle touches turns to physical actuality rather than spiritual idealism. The vocabulary and imagery reveal everywhere hardness, concreteness, intractability. Of course the Sphinx's riddle, in spite of Oedipus's apparent success, is insoluble, and any clue or answer provided is somewhat ambivalent. Carlyle's concern with the apparently unresolvable conflict between Fact and Spirit, Earth and Sky, soon becomes translated into what appears to be a discussion contrasting past and present, order and chaos, labour and idleness, reward and punishment; however, it becomes a lament over the apparent pervasiveness of hardness of heart and meanness of spirit. Midas's defeat was made possible not through greed or ignorance, which all human beings share, but by his inability to convert his wealth into useful, productive products and goals. Everything became for Midas 'fact' or gold, and he found that it brought him only sorrow and death rather than happiness or spiritual peace. The 'outer sphere of its Semblance' proved to be far different from what was the 'inner sphere of Fact'. 'Midas asked that all he touched be turned to gold; but when even his food was so transformed, he begged Dionysus to take back his favour'.

There is, then, no real contrast; Carlyle does not condemn the gold. He insists that men come to know the difference between Fact and Semblance and that they come to know the proper relationship between the Natural and the Supernatural. The many references to concrete elements in the first two chapters of Book I persuade the reader that Carlyle, try as he might, cannot eliminate from his thoughts and beliefs the undeniable presence of the actual in this world. 'No one', he writes, 'will accuse our Lord Abbot of wanting worldly wisdom, due interest in worldly things. . . . Nay rather it might seem . . . as if he had his eye all but exclusively directed on terrestrial matters, and was much too secular for a devout man. But this too, if we examine it, was right. For it is *in* the world that a man, devout or other, has his life to lead, his work waiting to be done' (*Works*, x, p. 115). A close reading of 'Midas' and 'The Sphinx' confirms Carlyle's own great interest in 'worldly' things. England is 'thick-studded with workshops, industrial implements, with fifteen millions of workers'. He uses statistics, mentions various studies and commissions and cites specific figures. A Mother and Father poison three of their children to defraud a burial-society of 'some 31.8s due on the death of each child'. 'Twelve hundred thousand workers' in England are in workhouses. Can not 'twenty-seven million head' in the English Nation solve the riddle? There have been 'eighteen centuries' of Christian preaching.

Even more revealing are the many references to tangible things, hard, unyielding, and an overwhelming sense of suffocation and deterioration, a gradual 'rotting'. There are 'narrow walls', 'wooden benches', 'starved sieged cities' and 'dyspeptic stomachs', 'fatal paralysis' and 'chronic gangrene'. More general allusions are in the same vein: Dante's Hell, Tarpeian Rock, Adamant Tablet. It is significant, too, that the first chapter in Book III is entitled 'Phenomena', followed directly by the gospels of Mammonism and Dilettantism. Also noteworthy is Carlyle's labelling the central chapter of Book IV 'Permanence', and that it follows directly the chapter 'Captains of Industry'. To see a pattern in *Past and Present* is not so much a matter of logic as knowing Carlyle's concern to balance fact and spirit. For Carlyle permanence means not mere 'gold' or fact; it consists of understanding the difference between the inner sphere of fact (Truth, Right, Might, Centre, Inner, Nature) and the outer sphere of Semblance. When one comes to know that, then one understands the open secret, one knows true Justice. In the chapter 'Permanence' Carlyle establishes his idea of Justice in terms of labour and permanence. At the core of it is his notion of Divine Guidance, loyal workers and just despots: The Gifted and the Didactic. Fact becomes translated into order and Authority, all of which have for their basis the notion of Justice, the ability to know the difference between the inner Sphere of Fact and the outer Sphere of Semblance, the proper relationship of the Natural and the Supernatural.

The difference is described in the first two chapters of Book I, although one needs to recognise the Carlylean assertive image. The constant need to balance the two extremes drives Carlyle always to insist on the presence of 'Valhalla and Temple of the Brave' as well as the 'Adamant Tablet'. Less pervasive than the images of Fact and Earth, nevertheless there are constant reminders by Carlyle that 'unembodied Justice is of Heaven; a Spirit, and Divinity of Heaven,—invisible to all but the noble and pure of soul'. Chapter 1, while conveying the overwhelming impression of 'things', still manages to remind the reader of the presence of the Carlylean opposites of these 'things': 'The Sun shines', and 'the eye of God' still looks down. There is the Carlylean reference to 'the highest mountain apex . . . under which lies a whole mountain region and land, not yet emerged'. He concludes the chapter on Midas, one must not forget, on a distinctive Carlylean note: Midas had misjudged the celestial music-tones.

The same balance is maintained in the Sphinx chapter; indeed, the riddle of the Sphinx reflects the ambivalence of Carlyle's own thoughts, Carlyle's description captures this quality:

> There is in her celestial beauty—which means celestial order, pliancy to wisdom; but there is also a darkness, a ferocity, fatality, which are infernal. She is a goddess, but one not yet disimprisoned; one still half-imprisoned,—the inarticulate,

> lovely, still encased in the inarticulate, chaotic. . . . Of each man she asks daily, in mild voice, yet with terrible significance, 'Knowest thou the meaning of this Day? What thou canst do Today; wisely attempt to do?' Nature, Universe Destiny, Existence, howsoever we name this grand unnamable Fact in the midst of which we live and struggle, is as a heavenly bride and conquest to the wise and brave, to them who can discern her behests and do them; a destroying fiend to them who cannot. (*Works*, x, p. 7)

Opposed to the chaos and the darkness and the ferocity of this world, then, in the 'centre of the world-whirlwind', for Carlyle, 'verily now as in the oldest days, dwells and speaks a God'. He takes up this theme in the later Books, attempting always to prophesy the eventual triumph of the brave and wise, who become the Gifted and the Didactic.

What becomes evident, however, is that Carlyle transforms subtly but carefully the meaning of the terms he uses and the means by which this triumph will be accomplished. With his growing realisation that, for now at least, on this Earth and in his time, the balance of the Natural and Supernatural that he glimpses will not be maintained, indeed, it will soon become tilted in favour of the forces of chaos, Carlyle begins to equate the voice of God with his own notions of 'celestial order, pliancy to wisdom'. The tentative ideas in *Chartism* become the dogmatic pronouncements of *Past and Present*.[2] The answer to the riddle of the Sphinx, as I have already suggested, lies not so much in wisdom and beauty as in order, guidance, might, authority and more and more strong leaders. The ideal must wait while the actual works its way, through these means, to some kind of system that reflects the celestial one. The most significant change in Carlyle's thinking is his reliance on military imagery; in contrast to Tennyson's reliance on the family, Carlyle comes to see in the military hierarchy the way to salvation.

This train of thought is found as early as the Sphinx chapter. Parliament and the Courts of Law have failed and something must be done. How can one discern the 'eternal inner Facts of the Universe' from the 'transient outer Appearance thereof'? Carlyle's argument comes to rest on 'the artillery of Woolwich' and 'A heroic Wallace' and 'old Valhalla'. In short, talk and lawful proceedings must give way to strong leaders and Might that asserts Right. 'Justice' becomes a synonym for Might and Strength:

> In this God's-world, with its wild-whirling eddies and mad foam-oceans, where men and nations perish as if without law, and judgment for an unjust thing is sternly delayed, dost thou think that there is therefore no justice? It is what the fool hath said in his heart. It is what the wise, in all times, were wise because they denied, and knew forever not to be. I tell thee again, there is nothing else but justice. One strong thing I found here below: the just thing, the true thing. (*Works*, x, p. 11)

and again:

> Await the issue. In all battles, if you await the issue, each fighter has prospered according to his right. His right and his might, at the close of the account, were one and the same. He has fought with all his might, and in exact proportion to all his right he has prevailed. (*Works*, x, p. 12)

Justice becomes for Carlyle the abiding theme, and Justice will triumph; however, the end of the Sphinx chapter and Book II, with its emphasis on order and authority, make clear that Justice in the Carlylean sense in *Past and Present* is far from the commonly held concepts of Truth and the Divinity of Heaven. In the final paragraph of 'The Sphinx' Carlyle, echoing Pontius Pilate and, perhaps, John Stuart Mill, asks:

> What is Justice? that, on the whole, is the question of the Sphinx to us. The law of Fact is, that Justice must and will be done. The sooner the better; for the Time grows stringent, frightfully pressing! 'What is Justice?' ask many, to whom cruel Fact alone will be able to prove responsive. (*Works*, x, p. 13)

There is good reason, then, for Carlyle's taking up in Book II the methods used by heroic Abbot Samson to resolve the troubles of the monastery. Chapter 10, 'Government', illustrates especially well Carlyle's focus on the 'heroic' qualities of this leader, who obviously sees his charge in the same way a military leader sees his. 'Wheresoever Disorder may stand or lie, let it have a care; here is the man that has declared war with it, that never will make peace with it' (*Works*, x, p. 92). In Chapter 15, 'Practical–Devotional', Carlyle again stresses an important facet of Samson's character; his practicality, his worldliness, his willingness in the face of trouble to use force. He ruthlessly excommunicates any who cross him, lords or simple townsfolk, thereby making the troublemakers come 'suppliant, indeed nearly naked, . . . and prostrate themselves at the Church-door'. 'In fact', writes Carlyle approvingly, 'by excommunication or persuasion, by impetuosity of driving or adroitness in leading, this Abbot, it is now becoming plain everywhere, is a man that generally remains master at last. He tempers his medicine to the malady, now hot, now cool; prudent though fiery, an eminently practical man' (*Works*, x, p. 112).

It follows naturally that Samson's modern counterpart, Plugson of Undershot, would be described in terms that reflect the leadership qualities of the former. It is no surprise, too, to find in Book IV 'Horoscope' the great attention paid to the 'Captains of Industry' and the militaristic framework in which they must work. In the Plugson chapter (Chapter 10) of Book III Carlyle had already stated unambiguously that 'Man is created to fight, he is perhaps best of all definable as a born soldier; his life "a battle and a march", under the right General' (*Works*, x, p. 190). The right general, we are not at all surprised to hear, is Plugson. In 'Captains of Industry' (Chapter 4 of Book IV) Carlyle praise seems excessive, but not if we remember that it is through them that Divine Justice is to come. They are the ones who will solve the riddle of the Sphinx. They will discern once and for all the inner sphere of Fact from the outer sphere of Semblance. They are, one realises, the pure of soul. As such, Carlyle words of praise seem well deserved:

> The Leaders of Industry . . . are virtually the Captains of the world. . . . Captains of Industry are the true Fighters, henceforth recognisable as the only true ones: Fighters against Chaos, Necessity and the Devils and Jotuns; and lead on Mankind in that great, and alone true, and universal warfare; the stars in their courses fighting for them, and all Heaven and all Earth saying audibly, Well-done! (*Works*, x, pp. 271–2)

Carlyle's connecting the Captains of Industry to his assertive image provides the final clue for the reader; he truly believes that these 'Fighters' are the hope for the present. They represent the triumph of good in the actual, the only refuge until the ideal is made possible through 'true heroes', the Gifted and the Didactic. Until that time the Captains must do. Carlyle once more connects them to God's Justice and the Eternities:

> Awake, ye noble Workers, warriors in the one true war: all this must be remedied. It is you who are already half-alive, whom I will welcome into life; whom I will conjure in God's name to shake off your enchanted sleep, and live wholly! . . . Let God's justice, let pity, nobleness and manly valour, with more gold-purses or with fewer, testify themselves in this your brief Life-transit to all the Eternities, the Gods and Silences. . . . Honour to you in your kind. (*Works*, x, p. 275)

Most revealing is Carlyle's choosing to end the work with his praise of the Chivalry of Labour, despite his calling the chapter 'The Didactic'. The reason, however, is plain: Carlyle, drawn to both the actual and the ideal, finally recognised that he must put aside Natural Supernaturalism for the present and attempt to deal with the here and now. LaValley perceptively links Carlyle, Blake and Marx, asserting that the three assail 'all abstractions and systems as unreal and limiting, failures to deal with reality and fact'. He goes on to say of Marx: 'He, like Carlyle, proclaims, "We proceed from an *actual* economic fact"' (LaValley, p. 222).

Carlyle, however, could not rest there. In future works he kept insisting on those abhorrent ideas that characterise much of his later thought: order, authority, obedience, force, and he came to rely almost completely on the model of the military. In *Past and Present*, however, he can still employ his favourite image: the Worker and the Captains of Industry are blessed; they do the heroic work, subduing chaos and bringing order in this world. In terms he always used to describe the Poet as Hero, Carlyle lifts his voice to sing the praises of not the Gifted or the Didactic, but the Workers:

> Chaos is dark, deep as Hell; let light be, and there is instead a green flowery World. Oh, it is great, and there is no other greatness. To make some nook of God's Creation a little fruitfuller, better, more worthy of God; to make some human hearts a little wiser, manfuler, happier. . . . Sooty Hell of

> mutiny and savagery and despair can, by man's energy, be made a kind of Heaven; cleared of its soot, of its mutiny, of its need to mutiny; the everlasting arch of Heaven's azure overspanning *it* too, and its cunning mechanisms and tall chimney-steeples, as a birth of Heaven. (*Works*, x, p. 298)

Only Shakespeare and Goethe, as the following chapter will show, receive higher praise, but they had succeeded in doing what Carlyle had by this time envisioned only in some future time: they had succeeded in viewing Nature as a self-subsistent universally connected whole, a garment of the Unseen.[3]

7

Tennyson: Ulyssean Influences and Telemachan Modulations

Carlyle's 'failure' and Tennyson's 'success' represent their 'Victorianism'. Both were concerned with making literature relevant, both wrote about subjects that dealt with the 'signs of the times', or the spirit of the age. Carlyle failed, assuming at the end that Ulyssean stance that marked his own recognition of his inability to communicate, to deliver his message. Tennyson succeeded, assuming that Telemachan stance that conveyed his confident belief in his own powers, his ability to communicate his concerns and 'solutions' to his readers. Their relationship with one another and the eventual emergence of Tennyson as the voice of the age form an interesting chapter in literary culture.

That Carlyle had an influence on Tennyson there is no doubt; one need only read Tennyson's poetry to know that there is much in it that reflects Carlyle's ideas. While Tennyson disagreed with Carlyle's notions about poetry, and I shall say more about this below, he did agree with many of his ideas about what poetry (and literature) should deal with. As Buckler has said, they both agreed that 'they must turn the energy of their literary imaginations frankly and fully upon the crucial problems of their own day'. One must be careful, however, not to confuse a common interest in subject-matter and a general Carlylean influence with a genuine friendship. While there was, indeed, a friendship between the two, it was never an intimate or even a particularly close one. True, Carlyle did like 'Alfred', and his comments on and 'portraits' of Tennyson indicate this. The two had met at some time in the later 1830s, and from the first they seemed to hit it off; in Tennyson's words, Carlyle 'seemed to take a fancy to me'.[1] In 1840 Carlyle described 'the Poet Tennison', as he spelled the name, to his brother: 'A fine, large-featured, dim-eyed, bronze-coloured, shaggy-headed man is Alfred; dusty, smoky, free and easy: who swims, outwardly and inwardly, with great composure in an inarticulate element as of tranquil chaos and tobacco-smoke; great now and then when he does emerge: a most restful, brotherly, and solidhearted man' (*CL*, XII, p. 239). Another well-known portrait of Tennyson is contained in a letter to Emerson, this one four years after the one to his brother:

> Alfred is one of the few British or Foreign Figures . . . who are and remain beautiful to me;—a true human soul. . . . I think he must be under forty, not much under it. One of the finest looking men in the world. A great shock of rough dusty-dark hair; bright-laughing hazel eyes; massive aquiline face, most massive, yet most delicate; of sallow brown complexion, almost Indian-looking; clothes cynically loose, free-and-easy;—smokes infinite tobacco. His voice is musical metallic,—fit for loud laughter and piercing wail, and all that may lie between; speech and speculation free and plenteous: I do not meet, in these late decades, such company over a pipe.[2]

In spite of the warm feelings reflected in these particular comments, it is difficult to see how their friendship can be characterised as anything but that of two literary figures who knew each other and tried to meet with one another when convenient. In fact, there is much to support the view that Carlyle had many misgivings about Tennyson, even during the period that Sanders calls the 'happy' period of their friendship, the 1840s (*CFS*, p. 200). Even in the letters of admiration there are notes of reservation. In one letter to Emerson, for instance, Carlyle comments on Tennyson's apparent lack of ambition: 'being a master of a small annuity on his Father's decease, he preferred clubbing with his Mother and some Sisters, to live unpromoted and write Poems'. He concludes: 'We shall see what he will grow to. He is often unwell; very chaotic,—his way is thro' Chaos and the Bottomless and Pathless; not handy for making out many miles upon' (Slater, p. 363). Carlyle also writes to his brother John: 'Alfred looks haggard, dire, and languid: they *have* got him however to go and *draw* his Pension; that is reckoned a great achievement on the part of his friends! Surely no man has a right to be so lazy in this world;—and none that is so lazy will ever make much way in it, I think' (*CFS*, p. 200).[3]

He gave Emerson specific details as to what Alfred needed; writing to him in December 1847 Carlyle said:

> a truly interesting Son of Earth, and Son of Heaven,—who has almost lost his way, among the will-o'-wisps, I doubt; and may flounder ever deeper, over neck and nose at last, among the quagmires that abound! I like him well; but can do next to nothing for him. Milnes, with general co-operation, got him a Pension; and he has bread and tobacco: but that is a poor outfit for such a soul. He wants a *task*; and, alas, that of spinning rhymes, and naming it 'Art' and 'high Art' in a Time like ours, will never furnish him. (Slater, pp. 436–7)[4]

What seemed to appeal to Carlyle in Tennyson's poems, and what is strikingly evident in the poems Carlyle specifically names, was Tennyson's occasional concern with what one reviewer (to use Carlyle's term) had called 'trivial morality'. Carlyle mentions 'Dora', The 'Two Voices', 'Summer Oak', and 'The Vision of Sin', all poems dealing with rather conventional moral, religious, and ethical issues. For Carlyle, Tennyson simply was not a seer, not sincere; he was, instead, a 'Life Guardsman spoiled by poetry'.

The pity in all this is that the two had very much in common, and Tennyson, in spite of his remark that he 'never minded him in the least', had, in fact, paid a great deal of attention to Carlyle. One sees why Carlyle felt it necessary to cite the poems that he does from the 1842 volumes; they reflected his own concerns and interests. 'The Two Voices' describes the 'conflict in a soul between Faith and Scepticism', and Ricks suggests that the tone was influenced by *Job*, *Psalms* and *Ecclesiastes*. 'Dora', one of the 'English Idyls', deals with the kind of story that would appeal to Carlyle: the tale of 'a noble simple country girl', told in 'the simplest possible poetical language' would be a work done in the spirit suggested by Carlyle when he told Espinasse that the poet should stop cobbling his odes and write on worthy subjects. 'The Talking Oak', also 'idylic', in its way, not only reminds Carlyle of 'something that is best in Goethe', but it also has a passing reference to his hero Cromwell and the Commonwealth (Ricks, pp. 641, 677). 'The Vision of Sin', with its condemnation of Epicureanism and its allusions to the City of God, would have special meaning for Carlyle, especially in terms of his own assertive image.

At last I heard a voice upon the slope
Cry to the summit, 'Is there any hope?'
To which an answer pealed from that high land,
But in a tongue no man could understand;
And on the glimmering limit far withdrawn
God made Himself an awful rose of dawn.

(p. 725)

Techniques aside, there were clearly various elements to which Carlyle could respond in these specific poems: ethical and religious concerns, biblical and Goethean allusions, and reminders of his own favourite emblem, all aspects that could be brought to bear on 'problems of their own day'.

His response to 'Ulysses' is more complicated. Ulysses was a character with whom Carlyle could easily associate; he was heroic, inspiring many, and, as the lines Carlyle quotes from the poem indicate, he represented a noble soul confident in his own powers. There were for Carlyle, as for Tennyson, all the associations of 'the happy isles'; as Ricks notes, 'The Isles of the Blest were thought to lie beyond the Pillars of Hercules . . . and it is beyond the Pillars that Dante's Ulysses urges his companions to sail' (p. 565). The poem also contains Carlyle's assertive image (lines 60–1) that Ricks gives in his note as 'Odysseus "watched the Pleiads, and late-setting Bootes, and the Bear, which men also call the Wain, which ever circles where it is and watches Orion, and alone has no part in the battle of Ocean" ' (p. 565). Here was, in fact, one version of the Carlylean symbol; no wonder there were in those lines, as he said, enough to bring up in him 'what would fill whole lachrymatories' as he read.

Finally, there were in the last lines of the poem something that struck the very depths of his being. Sanders sensed that, for he comments on 'Ulysses' as expressing Carlyle's 'own dynamic spirit' (p. 194). It does more, however. In Ulysses, Carlyle must have seen his very self, including all the qualities he admired and the hopes and ambitions of his own life. Surely he must have recognised his father in Ulysses: his strength, his belief in himself, his determination, and, above all, his faith in work or action (Campbell, p. 176). Others might see these qualities in other ways; indeed, they could be viewed as arrogance, stubbornness, and inflexibility. Be that as it may, there was in Carlyle's father, in

Carlyle's heroes and in Carlyle himself those same qualities; and Carlyle must have been keenly aware of this as he read 'Ulysses'. Particularly moving must have been the lines that distinguished Telemachus ('most blameless is he, centred in the sphere/Of common duties') from Ulysses:

> that which we are, we are;
> One equal temper of heroic hearts,
> Made weak by time and fate, but strong in will
> To strive, to seek, to find, and not to yield.
>
> (pp. 564, 566)

Perhaps most telling for Carlyle was the implication of Ulysses's strong leadership, his ability to command the loyalty of his friends and followers. In the late 1830s and through the 1840s Carlyle saw himself as one who could give 'instruction' and 'shed light in this mirk midnight of human affair'; and he was willing to do much to provide leadership.

Speaking of the early 1830s, Campbell talks of the nature of the 'discipleship' that Carlyle expected: 'The discipleship was something . . . directly involved with *himself*, not with any preconceived political creed. Just as Carlyle had won his way to relief from religious doubt through a consistent loyalty to himself, as an individual, so he based his political thinking on his own convictions, rather than on adherence to political loyalties new or old' (Campbell, p. 73). Carlyle's 'individualism' and the need for followers to follow *his* ideas rather than party or creed are the characteristics that one finds in Tennyson's Ulysses, a Ulysses close to the Dantean pattern. The emphasis on the 'I' in Tennyson's poem is unmistakable: 'I cannot rest from travel: I will drink/Life to the lees: all times I have enjoyed/Greatly, have suffered greatly, both with those/That loved me, and alone': 'I am a part of all that I have met': 'I am become a name;/For always roaming with a hungry heart/Much have I seen and known'. Also unmistakable is Ulysses's sense of needing change, of having the new replace the old: 'every hour is saved/From the eternal silence, something more,/A bringer of new things'; 'To follow knowledge like a shining star,/Beyond the utmost bound of human thought'; 'Some work of noble note, may yet be one,/Not unbecoming men that strove with Gods'. Carlyle's doctrine of work and action is expressed in the poem in terms that reflect the importance that Carlyle attached to it. Wilson tells of Carlyle's comment on Froude's reaction to his wife's death: 'He resists by work, which indeed is the only human method' (Wilson, VI, p. 323). Campbell places it on a different level:

> The necessity for change is in the foreground, the sweeping away of the old, the inevitability of struggle and suffering before the new can be found to replace the old. . . . Carlyle, as an individual, is aware of the change in himself and eager to persuade others to embark on the same process. . . . With the powerful imagery which dominates *Sartor Resartus*, of fiery death and rebirth, imagery which was to pattern *The French Revolution*, Carlyle clearly makes his *credo*. (Campbell, pp. 73–4)

The poem brings up another question that bears directly on the Carlyle–Tennyson relationship. No doubt Carlyle felt, on first meeting Tennyson, that he had found an ally, one who was, in his own words, 'one true soul more, a great melodious Poet-soul, breathing the vital air along with us'. Froude regarded Tennyson and Carlyle as equals, the two of them, Tennyson in poetry and Carlyle in prose, becoming the voices for those, the best and bravest of that time, 'determined to have done with insincerity to find ground under their feet, to let the uncertain remain uncertain. . . . to learn how much and what we could honestly regard as true, and believe that and live by it' (Froude, I, p. 291). Carlyle, however, did not regard Tennyson in the same light. He might be an ally, yes, just as John Stuart Mill was to be one, but, after all, Tennyson was almost a generation removed; there was a difference of fourteen years. Also, more importantly, Tennyson, in spite of his apparent willingness to see change, seemed more 'chaotic' rather than cosmic and a bit too timid at times. Wilson supplies evidence for the latter in his discussion of Carlyle and Leslie Stephen. 'When Stephen thought the poet too timid in expressing doubts, Carlyle did not differ' (Wilson, VI, p. 323). Tennyson himself may have sensed this feeling on Carlyle's part; Hallam Tennyson writes that his father told him, 'Carlyle is the most reverent and most irreverent man I know'. Carlyle, seeing himself as Ulysses, leading his comrades to seek newer worlds, saw Tennyson as Telemachus, 'Well-loved of me, discerning to fulfil/This labour, by slow prudence to make mild/A rugged people, and through soft degrees/Subdue them to the useful and the good'.

Telemachus is indeed the son of Ulysses and carries on his work. Both are concerned with 'the isle', with that which is 'useful and good'. In spite of his own denials, then, there is much in Tennyson's writing to suggest that his poetry was in fact influenced by the older writer: its deepening morality and its greater concern with the 'crucial problems' of his own time. Certainly Tennyson must have noticed in Carlyle's letter not only the poems to which Carlyle specifically alluded, but also those which he avoided mentioning. As vague as they are, Carlyle's words must have stirred Tennyson's artistic sense and soul; moreover, his specific choices for commentary indicated to Tennyson which direction his art should go. That Tennyson chose to concentrate on the genre of the idyl and on narrative owes something to Carlyle's words of praise; that he also chose to concentrate more on poetry of ideas and themes 'in which sensuous and picturesque imagery is contained and directed by the demands of narrative form or the pressures of serious moral reflection' and less on the poetry of 'mood and fancy' also owes something to Carlyle's influence.[5] Perhaps in 1884 Tennyson, thinking back, thought he owed very little to Carlyle, but the poems themselves offer something different.

The debt to Carlyle, then, is clear; while Tennyson's claim as supreme lyricist cannot be denied, much of his later poetry reflects Carlylean moral and social concerns. In his poems from 1842 on are found many of what can be seen as matters of great interest to Carlyle the Sage, the prophet who advocated with deep conviction and intense moral earnestness the cultivation of the heroic self, demonstrated the possibility of faith without religious trappings, portrayed man's spiritual nature as the 'vital Force which dwells in him, . . . essentially one and indivisible', and insisted that 'Morality itself, what we call the moral quality of a man . . . is . . . but another *side* of the one vital Force whereby he is and works' (*Works*, v, p. 106). This was the Carlyle who influenced the younger Tennyson, especially during the 1840s when he was still writing various sections of *In Memoriam* and experiencing different crises of his own.

Tennyson was a good listener, as anyone in a 'conversation' with Carlyle would have to be, and he came away from their walks and talks impressed with the positive elements in the Carlylean 'message' and determined to incorporate them in his own poems. He also came away from these conversations, as did many others, upset and perhaps even disgusted with some of the negative aspects of the Sage's message. In his desire to overcome the evils of his age, Carlyle at times went much further than even his most loyal disciples could or would want to go. One is able to see in Tennyson's work, then, not only some rather specific Carlylean 'solutions' to the problem of his time, but also some Tennysonian transformations of various Carlylean concerns and ideas. Indeed, as I have already indicated, as Carlyle became more and more aware of his inability to get his message across to others he became more and more extreme in some of his solutions. At times he indeed seems 'desperate', and this desperation led to some unpleasant qualities that appear in his works and character. It is in this context that Tennyson is working, seeking at one and the same time to do justice to what he considers the best in the Sage's message while transforming along the lines of his own ideals the more extreme Carlylean ideas. He deplores those qualities in Carlyle that caused Arnold to call him a 'moral desperado'.

From reading the poems that contain Carlylean traces, notably *In Memoriam*, the English idyls, and the major poems that bear the 'idylic' stamp, including *Maud*, *The Princess*, and *Idylls of the King*, one overwhelming impression emerges: Tennyson did, in fact, become more and more involved with the issues and ideas of his own day. It would perhaps be unfair to say he became more Carlylean, but it still remains true that the subjects of much of his poetry from 1842 on deal with ethical, social, and religious issues that were the staple of Carlyle's conversations and essays and were of great interest to his contemporaries and to his readers. His works were read, in the same way that the 'early' Carlyle's were. Froude's comment that Tennyson and Carlyle were thought of as teachers and guides for his generation provides one piece of evidence for this claim. One is not surprised, then, to find Carlylean themes underlying Tennysonian works: a concern with heroic figures, an emphasis on transcendentalism, an abiding interest in human relationships, especially in 'idylic' terms and an overwhelming concern with social and religious matters.

One should point out, before making too strong a claim for Carlylean influence, that other pressures were being brought to bear on Tennyson. He himself, for instance, had always had wide interests, and his poetry, from the very beginning, treated a wide variety of subjects. There was also the influence of the Apostles, one not to be lightly dismissed. Indeed, James Spedding, one of the Apostles, was to write approvingly: 'His genius was manifestly shaping a peculiar course for itself, and finding its proper business; the moral soul was beginning more and more to assume its due predominance' (Palmer, pp. 40–1; also *Critical Heritage*, pp. 142–3). R. C. Trench, another Apostle, had warned Tennyson: 'Tennyson, we cannot live in art' (Martin, p. 147). There was also the powerful message of Maurice, whose Christian Socialism and belief in a loving God had some bearing on Tennyson's thought.

The question becomes one of degree: just how much of an influence was Carlyle on Tennyson? Hallam says that his father always 'valued' Carlyle's opinion, but that bland statement may mean anything. There is much to be said in favour of Valerie Pitt's notion that Carlyle had a great influence on Tennyson's poetry, for, in spite of its shortcomings, her study of Tennyson as laureate is thorough and at times convincing. Her admirable summing up of the various Carlylean themes utilised by Tennyson serves to make clear the exact nature of Carlyle's influence; it was greater in the social than the religious sphere, for Tennyson found it much easier to accept Carlyle's social doctrines than his religious ones. While he had to adapt both to his special concerns, he was much more at ease with such Carlylean doctrines as heroes and the call for measures against the cash-nexus than he was with Carlyle's ideas about the church and the deity.

There is good reason for this, although at first one is puzzled that it should be so; the younger poet's reaction is determined largely by his being a generation removed from Carlyle and therefore in some ways being more 'Victorian' in his response to his age. He is impressed especially with the social 'message' of Carlyle, especially in Carlyle's calling attention to the abuses of the time in the name of progress. There are passages in his poems that echo the Carlylean warnings against the dangers of dependence on the 'mechanic' rather than the 'organic', on the material rather than the spiritual. There are others that reflect Carlyle's insistence on the need to resist the various pressures of the age and to protect the rights of individuals. There are still others that reflect Carlyle's concern with maintaining authority in the face of a 'democratic' surge that seemed to be threatening the very stability of the nation itself. However, as with Carlyle's religious ideas, Tennyson was put off by some aspects of Carlyle's social message, and his disagreement and disapproval appear in various ways. In contrast to Carlyle's pessimistic view regarding the consequences of the commercial spirit of the age, Tennyson emphasised not the 'commercial mire' but the gradual success of the remedies. In contrast to the harshness of the Carlylean 'vision' of the future, depicted in such ways as a world in ruins and ashes in *The French Revolution* or a world of sewers and cesspools in *Latter-Day Pamphlets*, Tennyson insisted that the future world must have more love than discipline, more co-operation than drill. Most significantly, Tennyson constantly resisted the Carlylean doctrine of the need for some sort of harsh authority to keep under control what seemed to be the growing tide of anarchy; instead, he called for the greater recognition of and dependence on that one unit of society that contained all the necessary qualities for a peaceful and prosperous future life: the family.

8

The Individual and Society

Underlying the differences in approach between Carlyle and Tennyson is their basic disagreement about man himself, the one ultimately despairing, the other ultimately hopeful. Murray Baumgarten has said of Carlyle: 'He believed democracy could never control itself, for he had no faith in rationality or mediating institutions. Therefore for him we cannot be democratic and rational individuals; we must be individuals in the imperialist Calvinist mode, each man his own hero, each woman perhaps her own heroine.'[1] Since Carlyle ultimately came to believe that most men and women were 'unheroic' and needed to be shown and told what to do, his message soon became largely ignored and he himself sank into the despair of his old age. Tennyson, on the other hand, while obviously not a champion of democracy (he was active in the cause of Governor Eyre), did have faith both in the ability of men and women to be 'rational' and in mediating institutions, the most important of which were church and family.

That Tennyson responded to Carlyle's anti-materialistic writings is clear from the evidence supplied by his poems as well as the evidence of the *Memoir*. One need only read Carlyle's words in such works as 'Signs of the Times' and *Sartor* and then compare Tennyson's poetry that treats the same matters. The depth of Carlyle's feelings in *Sartor* is seen in lines often quoted from 'The Everlasting No':

> The speculative Mystery of Life grew ever more mysterious to me: neither in the practical Mystery had I made the slightest progress, but had been everywhere buffeted, foiled, and contemptuously cast out. . . . To me the Universe was all void of Life, of Purpose, of Volition, even of Hostility: it was one huge, dead, immeasurable Steam-engine, rolling on, in its dead indifference, to grind me limb from limb. O, the vast, gloomy, solitary Golgotha, and Mill of Death! (*Works*, I, 132, 133)

Nowhere in his poetry does Tennyson approach Carlyle's sense of outrage and frustration, but his words at times have a distinct Carlylean ring to them. In 'Locksley Hall', for instance, he captures the frustration:

> What is that which I should turn to lighting upon days like
> these?
> Every door is barred with gold, and open but to golden keys.
>
> Every gate is thronged with suitors, all the markets overflow.
> I have but an angry fancy: what is that which I should do?
>
> I had been content to perish, falling on the foeman's ground,
> When the ranks are rolled in vapour, and the winds are laid
> with sound.
>
> But the jingling of the guinea helps the hurt that Honour feels,
> And the nations do but murmur, snarling at each other's heels.
>
> (p. 694)

A more striking example may be gained from that little-known, justifiably so, poem 'Suggested by Reading an Article in a Newspaper', published in *The Examiner* in 1852 under the signature of *Taliessin*. 'I feel', Tennyson wrote, 'that it expresses forcibly enough some of the feelings of our time, perhaps even you may be induced to admit it' (p. 1004). After warning the Press to take heed of its wide privileges, the poet writes:

> I honour much, I say, this man's appeal.
> We drag so deep in our commercial mire,
> We move so far from greatness, that I feel
> Exception to be charactered in fire.
> Who looks for Godlike Greatness here shall see
> The British Goddess, sleek Respectability.

Ricks suggests that the indictment of 'our commercial mire' was soon followed by *Maud*, and surely that poem, especially some of its opening lines, is as Carlylean as anything Carlyle himself wrote:

And Sleep must lie down armed, for the villainous centre-bits
Grind on the wakeful ear in the hush of the moonless nights,
While another is cheating the sick of the last few gasps, as he
sits
To pestle a poisoned poison behind his crimson lights.

When a Mammonite mother kills her babe for a burial fee,
And Timour-Mammon grins on a pile of children's bones,
Is it peace or war? better, war! loud war by land and by sea,
War with a thousand battles, and shaking a hundred thrones.

(pp. 104–43)

As caught up as he is in that message, however, Tennyson, unlike Carlyle, refuses to give way to despair; he asserts an affirmative view; he seeks to mitigate those harsh Carlylean solutions that would make men automatons instead of human beings. Rather than the harsh discipline of a monastery or the autocratic rule of a captain of industry, as 'enlightened' as those in command might be, Tennyson seeks to place responsibility in the hands of those directly involved. Carlyle sees each human as either a potential or failed hero, the present as chaos, and he calls for radical changes. Tennyson stresses the unit of the family, sees it as a microcosm of the nation and the universe, and is willing to wait, seeing hope in the future. That is why Tennyson's message, even in his most despairing of poems, always ends on a hopeful note. The hero of 'Locksley Hall' can say, 'O, I see the crescent promise of my spirit hath not set./Ancient founts of inspiration well through all my fancy yet', and he can find encouragement in thoughts of possible accomplishments in the present as well as the future with the help of his fellow-humans:

And his spirit leaps within him to be gone before him then,
Underneath the light he looks at, in among the throngs of
men:

Men, my brothers, men the workers, ever reaping something
new:
That which they have done but earnest of the things that they
shall do:

For I dipt into the future, far as human eye could see,
Saw the Vision of the world, and all the wonder that would be;

. . . .

Till the war-drum throbbed no longer, and the battle-flags were furled
In the Parliament of man, the Federation of the world.

There the common sense of most shall hold a fretful realm in awe,
And the kindly earth shall slumber, lapt in universal law.

(pp. 695–6)

The narrator of *Maud*, in the same Tennysonian spirit, can 'wake to the higher aims/Of a land that has lost for a little her lust of gold'. Regardless of the controversial nature of the ending of the poem, there remains the Tennysonian emphasis on acting with one's fellow-humans for a common goal:

We have proved we have hearts in a cause, we are noble still,
And myself have awaked, as it seems, to the better mind;
It is better to fight for the good than to rail at the ill;
I have felt my native land, I am one with my kind,
I embrace the purpose of God, and the door assigned.

(pp. 1092–3)

The ending of *The Princess* is especially relevant:

'Have patience', I replied, 'ourselves are full
Of social wrong; and maybe wildest dreams
Are but the needful preludes of the truth:
For me, the genial day, the happy crowd,
The sport half-science, fill me with a faith.
This fine old world of ours is but a child
Yet in the go-cart. Patience! Give it time
To learn its limits: there is a hand that guides'.

(p. 843)

That passage contains much of what comprises Tennyson's social thought; Carlyle simply could not have written it. Tennyson has full confidence in time and the hand that guides. At the heart of his faith in and hope for the future is the family, that unit which contains all those qualities that will help right those social ills still with us. Patience is the key. With Carlyle, of course, the approach is startlingly different. Change must come quickly, and it must come not through humility and geniality but through force and guidance from without and above. Tennyson's voice—calling for patience and trust in a 'tardy grinding of the mills'—is his voice, and it is the voice of Victorian England.

We can, then, at last perceive why Carlyle can be viewed as a Ulyssean 'failure' and Tennyson a 'Telemachan' success.[2] Ulysses praises his son Telemachus, and as he turns over to him the sceptre and the isle, he remarks: 'Most blameless is he, centred in the sphere/Of common duties, decent not to fall/In offices of tenderness, and pay/Meet adoration to my household gods'. Tillotson echoes this thought as he writes of Tennyson: 'he wrote for the few and the many . . .; he had the common touch . . .' (p. 287). It is significant that Carlyle responded with great enthusiasm to the idyls in the 1842 *Poems*, for he could recognise the 'common touch' in Tennyson's poetry even though it was absent from his own writing.

9

The Religious Question

While certain aspects of Carlyle's social views seemed objectionable to Tennyson, it was the religious sphere that gave him more trouble. To the younger poet, and to others, Carlyle, especially as he got older, seemed ultimately to view all in terms of self; he became more and more Ulyssean. The result was that his writings, as DeLaura and others have pointed out, tended to be autobiographical or biographical. Carlyle's constant reduction of all the ills of society to his own personal state had a significant effect on his relationship with Tennyson.

This concern with the self is evident in the contrast between *In Memoriam* and *Sartor*; indeed, it gives an added dimension to Carlyle's praise of Ulysses. In *In Memoriam* Tennyson 'manipulates' the poem to deal with the typical rather than the individual. Carl Dawson, for instance, makes much of Tennyson's calling the poem 'a kind of *Divina Commedia*, ending with happiness'. Dawson reminds us of the poet's own words: 'It is . . . the cry of the whole human race. . . . In the poem . . . private grief swells out into thought of, and hope for, the whole world.' 'Did Tennyson', Dawson asks, 'who struggled for answers and certitudes that were assumptions to Dante, invoke *The Divine Comedy* to move beyond the merely autobiographical or elegaic, to avoid what Carlyle called "self-consciousness"?'[1] E. D. H. Johnson has also deplored the tendency 'to regard *In Memoriam* exclusively as spiritual autobiography'. Like Dawson, he wants the work read in a much wider context:

> No longer will [Tennyson] make the mistake of seeking the meaning of his experience in the cloudlands of subjective consciousness amidst the delusions of 'vacant yearning' . . . For in the wisdom sprung from associating his loss with the common lot, he can now perceive that all along 'a *human* face' had shone on him from the 'depths of death within a landscape of sorrow overarched by *human* skies'.[2]

Carlyle's 'skyey tent' is here transformed into 'human skies'; Telemachus's vision is much different from Ulysses's. *Sartor* remains, as Campbell implies, solely Carlyle's personal story, while *In Memoriam* emerges, despite its private nature, as a very public poem.

One other difference between *In Memoriam* and *Sartor* serves to demonstrate the basic difference in their views, in spite of their agreement on many issues. Despite his insistence on 'faith, and faith alone', Tennyson never lost his pragmatic approach to problems, spiritual, political, personal. His thoughts and ideas reflect his 'practical' solutions to the problems prevalent in his society. Indeed, he is a gradualist rather than one who believes, as did Carlyle, in some apocalyptic event that will instantly cure the ills of the world; his concern is with phenomena rather than with noumena, with heroes who can help in this world rather than the next. Tennyson's concern for workable solutions is far greater than Carlyle's, whose 'dilemma' prevented him from considering any compromises. It is this difference that accounts for the conclusion of *In Memoriam*, one that is not a *Sartorian* cry for 'natural supernaturalism', but is, instead, a plea for waiting (that 'one far-off divine event') and an 'exultant proclamation of progress toward the earthly paradise' (Johnson, p. 145). Again Tennyson clearly emerges as Telemachus to Carlyle's Ulysses. Carlyle is a Jeremiah, denouncing his age, a 'heaver of rocks'; Tennyson is one whose outstanding trait is his 'extraordinary sensitiveness to the moral and intellectual climate of the period and his capacity to communicate it'.[3]

Tennyson's relationship to Carlyle, then, is an ambivalent one. While demonstrating the Sage's influence on Arnold, Dickens, and others, for instance, Tillotson says almost nothing at all about Tennyson in this connection. I have already suggested some reasons for this, not the least of which is Tennyson's fierce independence of spirit and intellect. He must have been impressed by the earnestness of the older writer, but, inevitably, Tennyson must have found his dogmatism and narrowness difficult to take and impossible to follow.

Carlyle's 'Calvinism without the theology' must have been both exhilarating and disappointing. Tennyson had enough scepticism in him to be impressed by Carlyle's ideas about what constituted true religious belief, especially those concerning the 'Eternal Verities' or the 'Divine laws' of the universe, and those which

Froude calls 'the broad facts of the Divine government of the universe'. Tennyson would have responded positively to one other Carlylean concept, since it somewhat paralleled his own belief in the divine governance of the universe: Carlyle's convictions that 'This world is the work of an Intelligent Mind. The Power which has formed us—He (or It—if that appears to any one more suitable) has known how to put into the human soul an ineradicable love of justice and truth'. What in effect appealed to Tennyson in Carlyle's 'religious belief' was his independence and, at the same time, his basic 'conservatism'.[4]

What was unacceptable was Carlyle's belligerent animosity towards all theology, 'Hebrew ol' clo'es', and his Old Testament sense of vengeful Divinity, completely unforgiving and unloving, without mercy to anyone who had broken those Eternal Laws set by the Intelligent Mind. In spite of much that was positive in Carlyle's works, there was that thread of negativism that ultimately undercut his 'teaching', the thread that persuaded at least one critic to conclude that Carlyle was still struggling to a second 'Everlasting Yea'.[5] Instead, Tennyson stressed those positive aspects of religion that he felt Carlyle had either ignored or misunderstood; he was eager to offset the 'irreverent' aspects of Carlyle's religion. As a result, he modified the Carlylean 'line' in a number of ways. Rather than ignoring Darwinism, as Carlyle had, he brought it into his 'religious' system. Rather than worship a God of Wrath or a transcendental Power whose garment was Nature, Tennyson turned to a God of Love, Whom Nature served, and who emphasised love as well as right and wrong in human hearts and souls. The two major differences that emerge are Tennyson's keen awareness of the spectre of Nature as 'Darwinism' and his insistence on a loving, caring God.

From these two emerges that which finally makes Tennyson the voice of his age and Carlyle the failed Prophet. The poet, with the extraordinary sensitivity to the moral and intellectual climate of his period and with the capacity to communicate it (Pitt, p. 192), unlike the Sage who was able to communicate his 'vision' to only his devoted followers, abjured negativism and pessimism; like Telemachus he emphasised the useful and the good, eventually to arrive at an affirmative view of life, including the notion of something approaching 'God's' love. In contrast to Carlyle's bleak view of the future, Tennyson stresses the gradual working out of events towards some Divine purpose. The negativism must have been the cause of Tennyson's complaint to Elizabeth Rundle of

Carlyle's vehemence and destructiveness; he felt strongly the need to conquer this 'destructive' side of Carlyle.

One of the most striking Tennysonian modulations of the Carlylean doctrine may be seen in his 'heroic' figures, especially Wellington and Arthur. As Pitt suggests, the difference may be viewed most clearly in the way that Tennyson had made Arthur a Christian king rather than a hero in the Carlylean mould; Carlyle's heroes are heroic not by God's power but by their sense of being right, by having and insisting others follow the old heroic virtues; often they assert and bear right through might. Ulysses can be a Carlylean hero, but not a Tennysonian one. For Tennyson a Ulysses has the taint of a heathen about him; he must be balanced by a Telemachus, with his sense of the need to pay 'meet adoration' to 'household gods'.

In the same manner Wellington must be made a Telemachan rather than a Ulyssean hero, one who, in spite of his military career, paid meet adoration to household gods. Carlyle admires Napoleon; Tennyson praises those qualities in Wellington that are in direct opposition to Napoleonic ones. Wellington was clear of 'ambitious crime'. He was 'moderate', 'resolute', rich in common sense, and in 'his simplicity sublime'. Above all, Wellington was a Christian hero, one who, while doing his Carlylean duty, never neglected his Christian ones. He thirsted for the right, was humble and put service before self. Tennyson stresses the Telemachan nature of Wellington:

> Such was he: his work is done.
> But while the races of mankind endure,
> Let his great example stand
> Colossal, seen of every land,
> And keep the soldier firm, the statesman pure:
> Till in all lands and through all human story
> The path of duty be the way to glory:
> And let the land whose hearths he saved from shame
> For many and many an age proclaim
> At civic revel and pomp and game,
> And when the long-illumined cities flame,
> Their ever-loyal iron leader's fame,
> With honour, honour, honour, honour to him,
> Eternal honour to his name.
>
> (pp. 1015–16)

Arthur, too, has those heroic qualities usually associated with Christ rather than with a Carlylean hero; he also is a Telemachan rather than a Ulyssean or Carlylean hero. His heroic qualities are those praised in *In Memoriam* and 'Wellington', those important for national as well as spiritual good. The knights of the round table swear to 'reverence the King, as if he were/Their conscience, and their conscience as their King'. The Telemachan/Christian nature of Arthur is emphasised throughout the poem. In 'The Coming of Arthur' Arthur's knighthood sings: 'The King will follow Christ, and we the King' (p. 1483). In 'The Holy Grail' Arthur sounds most like Telemachus, committed to 'the useful and the good' and 'centred in the sphere/Of common duties':

> And spake I not too truly, O my knights?
> Was I too dark a prophet when I said
> To those who went upon the Holy Quest,
> That most of them would follow wandering fires,
> Lost in the quagmire?—lost to me and gone,
> And left me gazing at a barren board.
>
> (p. 1686)

Arthur, in short, is more a Tennysonian than a Carlylean hero: he is concerned with might, but only in terms of right; he is intensely spiritual and Christian; he is concerned with his kingdom, but chiefly as it exists in the context of the Kingdom of God.

10

Darwin, Nature and Man

The acceptance of change and the recognition and worship of a God who 'fulfils himself' in many ways constitute Tennyson's recognition of Darwinism and its concomitant problems, problems that Carlyle chose to ignore. In his own bewildered wrestlings with religious questions—both personal and wider—Tennyson felt it necessary to account for Darwin's theory; the relation between the natural and the supernatural was as crucial to him as it was to Carlyle, for it ultimately encompassed the relationship of man to God. Carlyle's response was largely, like Frederick's, an individualistic one, with an emphasis on stoicism and doing one's duty; Tennyson chose a more 'public' way, and placed his confidence in the 'larger hope'. He opposed the Darwinian threat with more institutional responses, emphasising the eventual working out of God's purpose, particularly through church and family.

That anxiety over Darwinism was pervasive is understandable, for in the Darwinian context old assumptions were swept away. Man was no longer attempting to explain his bestiality in the face of his 'divine' nature; instead, he had to define and assert (or attempt to) his humanity (humanness) in the face of his demonstrated place in 'nature'. In the Darwinian world, there were no longer any firm guidelines. As Walter Houghton so eloquently put it:

> To read an article like 'On Tendencies toward the Subversion of Faith', written in 1848, and to discover that the author deals only with German rationalism and biblical criticism and is not aware of Lyell or Mill's *Logic* or *The Vestiges of Creation*, let alone such future bombshells as *The Origin of Species* and Huxley's 'Physical Basis of Life,' is to realize how terribly exposed the Victorians were to a constant succession of shattering developments.[1]

Gone were any hopes for man of any divine hierarchy or even the chain of being; even the 'unorthodox' hope of pantheism that had sustained so many of the Romantics was no longer available. The publication of Darwin's *The Origin of Species* in 1859, in short, was the climax, not the beginning, of Darwinism.

In the face of all this, Carlyle's refusal to get involved in any way is puzzling. Perhaps there are good reasons for his reactions; 'Nature', to him, was simply the garment of God, and as such far removed from any attempts by scientists to change things. He had also found a way to annihilate space and time. Perhaps his lack of concern is understandable only in terms of his arrogance or fear. For Tennyson it—man's place in nature—was the question of questions. Unlike Carlyle, Tennyson had to incorporate somehow, in some way, that concept which seemed to make man simply another animal, a 'monster', in the realm of natural development, a 'natural object' rather than a special creation of the Deity.

There is, in Tennyson's poetry a much more pronounced awareness of the implications of science and especially of Darwinism.[2] The fear of the 'materialistic tendencies' of science is especially evident. Carlyle's distinction between 'wisdom' and 'knowledge' was of some help to the poet in this respect, and Tennyson fell back on it at various times: 'We have but faith: we cannot know;/For knowledge is of things we see;/And yet we trust it comes from thee,/A beam in the darkness: let it grow./Let knowledge grow from more to more,/But more of reverence in us dwell' (p. 283).[3] Knowledge combined with 'reverence' equalled wisdom, which was very much like Carlylean 'Reason' as opposed to mere 'Understanding'.[4] The same distrust of empiricism is found in 'The Higher Pantheism', although one wonders, as Swinburne suggested in his parody of the poem, whether Tennyson himself knew exactly what he was suggesting should be the basis of one's faith.

One area in which Tennyson did not get any aid from Carlyle was in meeting the threat posed by the new sciences, especially astronomy and palaeontology. Unable simply to annihilate time and space, as had Carlyle, Tennyson expressed in his various poems the fear and doubts that came from the new and chilling perspectives of human life brought about by these new sciences. His readings in Lyell and Chambers and his openness to all things current, in contrast to Carlyle's parochialism, convinced Tennyson that there were real dangers to the spirit and one needed somehow to meet these. 'All at once', Carlyle had written in *Sartor*, 'there rose a Thought in me, and I asked myself: "What *art* thou afraid of?"' He had expressed his defiance of death and the universe: 'I am not thine, but Free, and forever hate thee!' Tennyson responds in an entirely different way; his fears of a universe 'void of life and purpose' and the death of Hallam have forced him to think of human life in larger contexts than his own parochial interests:

> I trust I have not wasted breath:
> I think we are not wholly brain,
> Magnetic mockeries; not in vain,
> Like Paul with beasts, I fought with Death.
>
> Not only cunning casts in clay:
> Let Science prove we are, and then
> What matters Science unto men,
> At least to me? I would not stay.
>
> (pp. 970–1)

In *In Memoriam* he laments specifically the horrors of a purposeless Universe, one with only 'waste places' and stars that 'blindly run'; 'Nature' has become, in Darwinian terms, a phantom echoing his own cries. In 'Vastness', a work much later than *In Memoriam*, the poet asks:

> What is it all, if we all of us end but in being our own corpse-coffins at last,
> Swallowed in Vastness, lost in Silence, drowned in the deeps of a meaningless Past?
>
> (p. 1348)

No wonder Nicolson could write that Tennyson tried all his life to rid himself of 'this obsession' of time and space; what Nicolson neglected to add, however, was that this obsession is strong evidence of Tennyson's complete identification with his own time.[5] Only one who had the arrogance, selfishness, and parochialism of a Carlyle could blissfully ignore the whole movement we now call Darwinism, of which these new discoveries were a part. Tennyson was very much concerned with both 'the purpose and quality' of life and in the means by which humans had reached their present state and the purpose for which their maker had placed them here. His keen interest in Darwinism and related matters was deep and abiding.

'My father brought "Evolution" into poetry', Hallam Tennyson wrote. 'Ever since his Cambridge days he believed in it'. On 17 August 1868, Darwin visited Tennyson at Farringford. He seemed to be 'kindly, unworldly, and agreeable', Emily Tennyson noted. 'A. said to him, "Your theory of Evolution does not make against Christianity": and Darwin answered, "No, certainly not" ' (*Memoir*, II, p. 57). From these comments one may perceive a number of things, not the least of which is, if Hallam is to be believed, that the poet believed in 'it' and that he thought that it did not make against Christianity. Presumably he believed in it because it gave assurance of man's progress. Again, one has to depend a bit on Hallam Tennyson's remarks; speaking of 'By an Evolutionist', written in 1888 when Tennyson was dangerously ill, Hallam comments: 'he conceived that the further science progressed, the more the Unity of Nature, and the purpose hidden behind the cosmic process of matter in motion and changing forms of life, would be apparent'. Hallam further tells us that

> he was inclined to think that the theory of Evolution caused the world to regard more clearly the 'life of Nature as a lower stage in the manifestation of a principle which is more fully manifested in the spiritual life of man, with the idea that in this process of Evolution the lower is to be regarded as a means to the higher'. (*Memoir*, I, p. 323)

Hallam then goes on to quote from section 118 of *In Memoriam*.

Of course, the same emphasis on the 'hidden purpose' behind the cosmic process is revealed in other poems. In 'The Two Voices' Tennyson traces this progress, and in rejected stanzas from 'The Palace of Art' he touches specifically on the idea of evolutionary progress:

> 'From change to change four times within the womb
> the brain is moulded', she began,
> 'So through all phases of all thought I come
> Into the perfect man.

'All nature widens upward: evermore
  The simpler essence lower lies.
More complex is more perfect, owing more
  Discourse, more widely wise.

'I take possession of men's minds and deeds.
  I live in all things great and small.
I dwell apart, holding no forms or creeds,
  But contemplating all.'

(p. 409)

While Tennyson firmly believes in the cosmic process, it is also clear, from the many references to the lower phases, that he is always aware of the conflict going on during that process. 'Nature', that favourite word of Carlyle's, also is often on the poet's lips. Before this process can complete itself there has to be the clear recognition of occasional setbacks; man, after all, is still man. The Darwinian question needs to be answered: How is man to escape his bestial nature and become heroic, Godlike? Tennyson frequently points out how slow this 'progress' can be; in *Idylls of the King*, for instance, he describes the first two stages of mankind: 'And in the lowest beasts are slaying man,/And in the second men are slaying beasts'. In 'Locksley Hall Sixty Years After' he presents another variation:

Gone the cry of 'Forward, Forward,' lost within a growing
  gloom;
Lost, or only heard in silence from the silence of a tomb.

Half the marvels of my morning, triumphs over time and
  space,
Staled by frequence, shrunk by usage, into commonest
  commonplace!

'Forward' rang the voices then, and of the many mine was
  one.
Let us hush this cry of 'Forward' till ten thousand years have
  gone.

(p. 1362)

In *Maud* cruel nature becomes something to be feared; the narrator finds himself in his 'own dark garden ground':

Listening now to the tide in its broad-flung shipwrecking roar,
Now to the scream of a maddened beach dragged down by the
wave,
Walked in a wintry wind by a ghastly glimmer, and found
The shining daffodil dead, and Orion low in his grave.

(p. 1048)

A short time later he observes this 'nature':

For nature is one with rapine, a harm no preacher can heal;
The Mayfly is torn by the swallow, the sparrow speared by the
shrike,
And the whole little wood where I sit is a world of plunder and
prey.

Where do human beings fit in this world:

We are puppets, Man in his pride, and Beauty fair in her
flower;
Do we move ourselves, or are moved by an unseen hand at a
game
That pushes us off from the board, and others ever succeed?
Ah yet, we cannot be kind to each other here for an hour;
We whisper, and hint, and chuckle, and grin at a brother's
shame;
However we brave it out, we men are a little breed.

(pp. 1049–50)

In *The Promise of May*, the only play of Tennyson's set in contemporary times, we find nature's cruelty emphasised right from the beginning of the drama: Dora enters singing her strange song:

But a red fire woke in the heart of the town,
And a fox from the glen ran way with the hen,
And a cat to the cream, and a rat to the cheese;
And the stock-dove coo'd, till a kite dropt down,
And a salt wind burnt the blossoming trees;
O grief for the promise of May, of May,
O grief for the promise of May.

'I don't know why I sing that song', Dora remarks; 'I don't love it'.[6] A short time later Edgar, the villain of the piece, described variously as a 'freethinker' and a 'tendentious rationalist', comes in and justifies his amorality by the example of nature:

> The Gods! but they, the shadows of ourselves,
> Have past forever. It is Nature kills,
> And not for *her* sport either. She knows nothing.
> Man only knows, the worse for him! for why
> Cannot *he* take his pastime like the flies?
> And if my pleasure breed another's pain,
> Well—is not that the course of Nature too,
> From the dim dawn of Being—her main law
> Whereby she grows in beauty—that her flies
> Must massacre each other?
>
> (*WAT*, p. 781)

These lines are very much in the spirit of the deservedly famous 55th and 56th stanzas of *In Memoriam*:

> Are God and Nature then at strife,
>   That Nature lends such evil dreams?
>   So careful of the type she seems,
> So careless of the single life;
>
> . . . . . .
>
> 'So careful of the type?' but no.
>   From scarpèd cliff and quarried stone
>   She cries, 'A thousand types are gone:
> I care for nothing, all shall go.
>
> . . . . . .
>
> No more? A monster then, a dream,
>   A discord. Dragons of the prime,
>   That tare each other in their slime,
> Were mellow music matched with him.
>
> O life as futile, then, as frail!
>
> (pp. 910–12)

11

God and Man

The above lines express Tennyson's 'Everlasting No', his lowest spiritual state. To trace his emergence, however, is to see the way that he transformed Carlyle's ideas. Hallam Tennyson has written that his father would not formulate his creed for people because they would not understand him if he did. 'He considered', concluded Hallam, 'that his poems expressed the principles at the foundation of his faith' (*Memoir*, I, pp. 308–9). Tennyson's basic religious beliefs are, in fact, clearly discerned in his poems. There is, above all, the belief in a God who has a purpose for this world, this purpose being brought about through 'spiritual' evolution. Also evident are his faith in immortality and his abiding trust in a God of Love. The first of these, of course, a purposeful God was his 'solution' to the dilemma posed by the conflict of God and Nature. Ultimately, in spite of all the apparent setbacks to progress, God's purpose would be achieved and that conflict would be resolved. The conclusion to *In Memoriam* is merely one version of that resolution, although it is, by far, the most eloquent statement of it.

As early as 'The Two Voices' the thought of a purposeful God had been the chief solace of the narrator; after he has seen the family on its way to church, a second voice, in a 'little whisper silver-clear', murmurs: 'Be of better cheer'; it assures him: 'I see the end, and know the good' (p. 540). In both 'Locksley Hall' poems the same message is emphasised; indeed, DeVane observed that the first 'Locksley Hall' was 'immensely popular . . . chiefly because it expressed better than anything else the spirit of progress and hope prevalent in England in the Forties'.[1] Not only does that poem contain the stirring lines, 'Men, my brothers, men the workers, ever reaping something new:/That which they have done but earnest of the things that they shall do:/For I dipt into the future, far as human eye could see,/Saw the vision of the world, and all the wonder that would be'; but also: 'Yet I doubt not through the ages one increasing purpose runs,/and the thoughts of men are widened with the process of the suns' (pp. 695, 696). The second 'Locksley Hall', while less confident, continues the thought; however, Tennyson warns against expecting a straight line of development: 'Evolution ever climbing after some ideal good,/And Reversion ever dragging Evolution in the mud'. The final 'message' is a positive one, in spite of the occasional reversions: 'Forward then, but still remember how the course of Time will swerve. / Crook and turn upon itself in many a backward streaming curve' (pp. 1367, 1368). 'The Making of Man', 'written at the end of his life', as Hallam tells us, also reminds us of the slowness of that progress, although there is still the faith in the purposeful God:

> Man as yet is being made, and ere the crowing Age of ages,
> Shall not aeon after aeon pass and touch him into shape?
> All about him shadow still, but, while the races flower and fade,
> Prophet-eyes may catch a glory slowly gaining on the shade,
> Till the people all are one, and their voice blend in choric
> Hallelujah to the Maker 'It is finished. Man is made.'
>
> (p. 1454)

This same 'prayer' is at the heart of *In Memoriam* and the ending of that poem puts into personal terms the thought expressed above. Hallam is that 'finished' man:

> Whereof the man, that with me trod
> This planet, was a noble type
> Appearing ere the times were ripe,
> That friend of mine who lives in God,
>
> That God, which ever lives and loves,
> One God, one law, one element,
> And one far-off divine event,
> To which the whole creation moves.
>
> (p. 988)

This confidence in the fulfilment of God's purpose through progress is clearly not Ulyssean, which always carries the Dantean taint of arrogance and pride through its emphasis on what seems to be the desire to go on simply for the sake of going on, regardless of the goal, self-fulfilment rather than the fulfilment of God's plan. (See Buckley, *Tennyson*, pp. 60–1.) Tennyson's trust is in progress that is bringing about the plan of not only a purposeful God, but a caring one as well. In one of his lectures on Arnold, R. H. Super remarked that whatever 'of transcendentalism there is in Arnold's view of the State is . . . an inheritance from Carlyle'.[2] One could very well say the same of Tennyson's 'proof' for God, which rests on faith rather than knowledge, faith that is the principal basis of wisdom. 'I hate utter unfaith', Hallam reports his father saying at one time; 'one can easily lose all belief, through giving up the continual thought and care for spiritual things' (*Memoir*, I, p. 309). Tennyson, however, transforms Carlylean philosophic transcendentalism to something much more Christian. Thus Tennyson's God is not the Carlylean Judge but something much more personal:

> Strong Son of God, immortal Love,
>   Whom we, that have not seen thy face.
>   By faith, and faith alone, embrace,
> Believing where we cannot prove.
>
> (p. 861)

Even more Tennysonian than Carlylean is the way that the poet's transcendentalism functions to make Nature not so much the garment of God as His means to help Man. Indeed, space and time as well as Nature are incorporated into the sphere of Tennyson's 'transcendental' Christianity. The poet is no longer frightened by the spectres of space, time and Science:

> There rolls the deep where grew the tree.
>   O earth, what changes has thou seen!
>   There where the long street roars, hath been
> The stillness of the central sea.
>
> The hills are shadows, and they flow
>   From form to form, and nothing stands;
>   They melt like mist, the solid lands,
> Like clouds they shape themselves and go.

But in my spirit will I dwell,
  And dream my dream, and hold it true;
  For though my lips may breathe adieu,
I cannot think the thing farewell.

(p. 973)

It is no accident that Tennyson follows these verses that emphasise his transcendental view and belief in immortality with those climactic ones that 'explain' as much as any in the poem his concept of the Deity. One of the manuscript notes for 'Vastness' states: 'What matters anything in this world without full faith in the Immortality of the Soul and of Love?' (*Memoir*, II, p. 343). Surely stanza 124 serves to summarise Tennyson's ideas on God, Nature and Immortality, especially the last verse:

And what I am beheld again
  What is, and no man understands;
  And out of darkness came the hands
That reach through nature, moulding men.

(pp. 973–4)

It is tempting to read into Stanza 124 some of Tennyson's feeling about Carlyle's 'irreverence'. One might find, for instance, an implied criticism of Carlyle's 'philosophic' attitude towards 'Reason' as final arbiter in all matters as something detrimental to faith in the Tennysonian sense. In the same way, the reference to the 'wrath' in man might apply to that Carlyle who could be so disagreeable at times, 'so vehement and destructive'. Certainly one of the major differences between the two is Carlyle's 'radical' attitude towards the Church, one that Tennyson refused to share. Indeed, as with his 'public' stance towards social matters, Tennyson thought Carlyle's 'vehemence' and 'destructiveness' towards established religion detrimental to any chance of reconciliation of differences among sects and even nations. Again, while one has to be cautious in reading the *Memoir*, there seems to be some basis for believing Hallam's comments in regard to Tennyson's view in this matter. 'Father Haythornewait, W. G. Ward's chaplain', Hallam writes, 'reminds me of one of Ward's stories about my father and Cardinal Manning. . . . "Why did you show such deference to Manning?" reprovingly asked an agnostic friend of Tennyson. . . . "Because Manning", Tennyson had replied, "is the distinguished head of a great Church."' He further notes: 'Tennyson clearly saw the need of Churches. . . . He wished that the Church of England could embrace, as he felt that Christ would have it do, all the great Nonconformist sects that loved the name of Christ. He recognised to the full that an organised religion was the needful guardian of morality' (*Memoir*, II, p. 169). On 4 May 1846, telling of a visit at Tennyson's London lodgings, FitzGerald wrote to his friend Barton,

> They two discussed the merits of this world and the next til I wished myself out of *this*, at any rate. Carlyle gets more wild, savage, and unreasonable every day; and I do believe, will turn mad. 'What is the use of ever so many rows of stupid, fetid, animals in cauliflower wigs—and clean lawn sleeves—calling themselves Bishops—Bishops, I say, of the Devil—not of God—obscene creatures, parading between men's eyes and the eternal light of Heaven.' etc., etc. This, with much abstruser nonconformity for two whole hours![3]

Wilson writes of a time when Tennyson had been telling Carlyle and FitzGerald of his 'Certainty of life for men after death':

> When he finished, FitzGerald was silent. For half a century 'good form' in England had required that gentlemen should either say they believed in immortality or else be silent. So Tennyson felt pretty safe, and did not want an answer; but instead of the hoped-for 'grunt' of acquiescence, Carlyle let out between the puffs some words that must have made a deep impression, for Tennyson's report to Miss Thackeray is the same in effect as what he told his son in extreme old age.
>
> 'Eh! Old Jewish rags! Ye must clear your mind of all that! Why should we expect a hereafter? Your traveller comes to an inn and he takes his bed. It's only for one night, and another takes it after him'.
>
> 'Your traveller comes to his inn', said Tennyson, 'and lies down in his bed almost with the certainty that he will go on his journey rejoicing the next morning'. (Wilson, III, p. 326)

FitzGerald delightedly told Tennyson that he had won that round, but more to the point is the clear difference between the two in this matter of Church and State. No wonder Tennyson thought Carlyle destructive.

Tennyson's poems do, indeed, express the principles of his faith, one of which is the need for some form of old Jewish clothes, 'organised' religion. Tennyson's private self and his public poetry are the same. Particularly striking is Tennyson's identification with his readers, both in understanding and expressing their concerns. Unlike the Sage of Chelsea, whose 'solutions' remain individual and private, Tennyson provides in his poems not only words of comfort, but elements of faith. One thinks of Carlyle's frustrations in not being able to get the people to listen to him; Tennyson had no such trouble. Somervell correctly observes that 'Tennyson . . . was an exponent rather than a critic of the orthodoxy of his day', and Scaife, too, makes this same point: 'Very largely the reactions against Tennyson can be measured by the extent to which he expressed the ideas of the age in which he lived'.[4] In contrast to Carlyle's call for apocalyptic change and what amount to a new religion, although he never specifically cites any 'principles' except that of the need for faith in Divine Laws, Tennyson provides some rather concrete ones: a God of Love, belief in immortality and confidence in a purposeful existence. While Carlyle's religious writings call for a radical change in the self, the prominent feature of Tennyson's seems to be the proper recognition of the relationship between the self and society. Carlyle prefaces *Sartor* with a quotation from Novalis: 'The world is a universal trope of the spirit, a symbolic picture of it'. Tennyson ends his poem with a marriage, from which union a 'soul' shall come forth and result in man. Reading *In Memoriam* to James Knowles, Tennyson remarked: 'It is rather the cry of the whole human race than mine. In the poem altogether private grief swells out into thought of, and hope for, the whole world' (p. 859).

Part Two

Prophet and Poet

12
Carlylean Caprice

Tennyson resisted or transformed many of Carlyle's ideas about society and religion, and one should not be surprised that he took the same approach to Carlyle's ideas about literature and art; indeed, anyone who wishes to know more about the causes for the direction that Victorian literature took needs to know about this relationship. The way that these two founders 'used' literature to convert 'man's perception of the world about him' helps one to understand better the distinctive quality of Victorian literature. Their relationship also demonstrates the causes for Carlyle's ultimate 'failure' and the basis of Tennyson's 'success', his great appeal to the readers of his day.

Carlyle's comments on Tennyson's poetry illustrate his poetic criteria as well as his chief differences with Tennyson and, one might generalise, with accepted Victorian views on poetry. In a notebook entry for 5–6 May 1848 Emerson recorded what he remembered of a conversation with Tennyson. 'Tennyson & all Carlyle's friends,' he wrote, 'feel the caprice and incongruity of his opinions' (Lang, pp. 284–5). 'Caprice and incongruity' describe well Carlyle's opinions in the late 1840s, for by that time he was beginning to realise that fewer and fewer were listening to him. Martin writes that by the end of the 1870s Tennyson made 'a determined effort to overcome his neglect of Carlyle', and he ascribes this neglect to the fact that both men were 'difficult'; citing Spedding, he adds: 'Carlyle always needed the kind of indulgence that most of us need in a fit of violent toothache'.[1] The truth is, however, that there existed between the two enough differences of opinion on so many matters that Tennyson's reluctance to visit Carlyle and the Carlyles' reluctance to visit Farringford are completely understandable without putting the blame on personalities or on Carlyle's need for indulgence. One need only recall Tennyson's eagerness to read his own poetry, especially *Maud*, to anyone who would listen to know why the Carlyles refused the many invitations to Farringford; indeed, one need only read some of Carlyle's comments on Tennyson's poetry to see why the poet would 'neglect' the Sage.

Carlyle never distinguished the man from the poet; one of his aesthetic principles, through Goethe, was 'Be *men* before attempting to be *writers*!' Carlyle quotes this in a letter to Jane, the main point of which is that literature does not constitute the 'sole nourishment of any true human spirit'. He emphatically concludes: 'Literature is the *wine* of life; it will not, cannot, be its *food*' (*CL* III, p. 244). For Carlyle, Tennyson seemed obsessed with 'literature', the wine of life; he seemed to neglect its food. How else can one explain his attempts to advise the poet? The tenor of his remarks on Tennyson's poetry becomes clear; Tennyson must become more of a man, take more interest in subjects that deal with life and human nature.

Espinasse tells of a visit to Carlyle. The latter, he reports, was

> full of the story of the dealings of an early Christian mission with some Scandinavian and heathen potentate. 'Alfred,' he declared, 'would be much better employed in making such an episode interesting and beautiful than in cobbling his odes,' the occupation of which, when visiting him some time before, Carlyle had found him engaged, and with the futility of which he had then and there reproached him. I asked Carlyle [continues Espinasse] if the Laureate did not 'stand up' for his literary procedure. 'No! he lay down for it,' Carlyle replied, doubtless with a reference to 'Alfred's' careless, indolent ways.[2]

Carlyle made many other comments on Tennyson's poetry. Margaret Fuller tells of a dinner-party at which Carlyle said that Tennyson wrote verse 'because the schoolmasters had taught him that it was great to do so, and had thus, unfortunately, been turned from the true path for a man' (Wilson, III, p. 348). In the *Memoir* we read of the year 1851:

> In the summer they met the Carlyles again. About this time he described my father to Sir J. Simeon as 'sitting on a dung-heap among innumerable dead dogs.' Carlyle meant that he was apt to brood over old-world subjects for his poems. Once many years after, when we called upon him, my father teazed him about this utterance, and Carlyle replied, 'Eh! that was not a very luminous description of you.' (*Memoir*, I, p. 340)

To Carlyle Tennyson was, as he often reminded him, 'a Life-Guardsman spoiled by making poetry' (*THF*, p. 133), and his pronouncement on *The Princess*, when it was published, was that it 'had everything but common-sense' (Espinasse, pp. 213–14). His remarks to Lady Ashburton were even harsher: 'very gorgeous, fervid, luxuriant, but indolent, somnolent, almost imbecile' (*CFS*, pp. 205–6).

Even *Idylls of the King* did not escape Carlyle's disapproval: 'We read, at first, Tennyson's *Idylls*, with profound recognition of the finely elaborated execution, and also on the inward perfection of *vacancy*,—and, to say truth, with considerable impatience at being treated so very like infants, tho the lollipops were so superlative' (Slater, pp. 552–3). He also characterised the later poetry of Tennyson as 'tender to the "happy views" of secluded ladies'; and he told Stephen that the *Idylls* demonstrated that 'Tennyson had declined into a comparatively sentimental and effeminate line of writing, mere aestheticisms, instead of inspiring a courageous spirit to confront the spiritual crisis'. To cap this particular line of criticism, Carlyle condemned the *Idylls* with one of his harshest curses: 'The *Idylls of the King* could not be the epic of the future, but at best a melodious version of conventional and superficial solutions of the last problem. King Arthur has too much of the "Gigman" (snob) to be a great leader of modern men' (Wilson, VI, pp. 323–4).[3]

What, then, did Carlyle find to praise in Tennyson's poetry? Martin writes that Sterling 'reported' to Tennyson that Carlyle 'had said more in his "praise than in any one's except Cromwell & an American Backwoodsman who has killed 30 or 40 people with a bowie-knife & since run away to Texas"' (Martin, p. 267). Sanders states that Carlyle 'never completely lost his faith in Tennyson as a poet' (*CFS*, pp. 218–19). The evidence suggests, however, that Carlyle's relationship to Tennyson resembles to some degree his relationship to Mill. There was not the separation as with the latter, of course, but there is nothing to suggest that Carlyle, after a first burst of enthusiasm, came to regard Tennyson only as a poet and artist who once had had some potential. One need merely compare Carlyle's fulsome praise of Goethe, Shakespeare, even Burns, to see the difference; there is little to warrant any belief in Carlyle's seeing in Tennyson a poet whose writing would inspire 'a courageous spirit to confront the spiritual crisis'.

Indeed, Carlyle's specific statements on Tennyson's poetry differ in no way from his comments on other poets and literature in general: there are a few vague generalisations and some comparisons with his favourite books and writers. The chief document often brought in as evidence of Carlyle's praise of Tennyson's poetry is the letter written by Carlyle to Tennyson after he had 'read' the 1842 poems, the original of which, incidentally, cannot be located. Sanders states that the letter, 'apart from its function of encouraging the poet', is 'an excellent piece of literary criticism'. While one can agree with the first point, it is difficult to see the basis of the second; there is little in the way of 'literary criticism'. There is much in the Carlylean manner of criticism:

> Truly it is long since in any English Book, Poetry or Prose, I have felt the pulse of a real man's heart as I do in this same. A right valiant, true fighting, victorious heart; strong as a lion's, yet gentle, loving and full of music: what I call a genuine singer's heart! there are tones as of the nightingale; low murmurs as of wood-doves at summer noon; everywhere a noble sound as of the free winds and leafy woods. The sunniest glow of Life dwells in that soul, chequered duly with dark streaks from night and Hades: everywhere one feels as if all were fill'd with yellow glowing sunlight, some glorious golden Vapour; from which form after form bodies itself; naturally, *golden* forms. In one word, there seems to be a note of 'The Eternal Melodies' in this man; for which let all other men be thankful and joyful! (*Memoir*, I, p. 213; *CL*, XV, p. 216)

One recognises many of Carlyle's favourite expressions: 'real man's heart'; 'right, valiant, true fighting, victorious heart'; 'genuine singer's heart'; 'Eternal Melodies'. Sanders cites as important Carlyle's praise of the 'interweaving of glorious gold with black' in the poetry and 'the pulse of a real man's heart'. The latter praise, he says, indicated Carlyle's recognition in Tennyson's poetry of 'its humanity and the invincibility of the human spirit'. Perhaps, but this same enthusiasm was never to be seen in Carlyle's reading of Tennyson's other works, and one wonders why. The 1842 poems are not unique in the Tennyson canon; indeed, they reflect most of his regular techniques and interests. The thought that crosses one's mind is that Carlyle may have seen in them the same potential he had seen in Mill's works, and with the same lack of real foundations for that belief.

The rest of the letter to Tennyson, which Tennyson had his sister Emily copy and send to his wife, is vintage Carlyle, in that just when one expects detailed criticism of specific poems Carlyle resorts to his favourite devices:

> Your 'Dora' reminds me of the *Book of Ruth*; in the 'Two Voices,' which I am told some Reviewer calls 'trivial morality,' I think of passages in *Job*. For truth is quite *true* in Job's time and Ruth's as now. I know you cannot read German: the more interesting it is to trace in your 'Summer Oak' a beautiful kindred to something that is best in Goethe; I mean his 'Müllerinn' (Miller's daughter) chiefly, with whom the very Mill-dam gets in love; tho' she proves a flirt after all and the thing ends in satirical lines! very strangely too in the 'Vision of Sin' I am reminded of my friend Jean Paul. This is not babble, it is speech; true deposition of a volunteer witness. And so I say let us all rejoice somewhat. (*Memoir*, I, pp. 213–14; *CL*, xv, p. 217)

These various statements constitute the bulk of the favourable comments by Carlyle on Tennyson's poetry. In March of 1843 Jane writes to her cousin and tells her to get Tennyson's poems. She elaborates: 'read the "Ulysses," "Dora," and the "Vision of Sin," and you will find that we do not overrate him. Besides', she adds, 'he is a very handsome man, and a noble-hearted one' (*CFS*, p. 200). One recognises immediately the same poems praised and the same terms used; there is nothing new in this letter except that Tennyson is a handsome man. Perhaps Martin is right in saying that Carlyle's 'philistine objections' were swept away when he read the volumes, but one wishes Carlyle had been more specific. What is evident in his praise are the same kinds of general observations he was wont to make when he either had not read the works or was basing his judgement strictly on the man rather than the writings.

A comment by Walt Whitman will illustrate one trait that caused potential 'disciples' to reject or modify Carlyle's message to his age, one that has to do with his view of art and artists, his aesthetic theory: 'He clears away jungle and poison-vines and underbrush—at any rate hacks valiantly at them, smiting hip and thigh. Kant did the like in his sphere, and it was all he profess'd to do; his labors have left the ground fully prepared ever since—and greater service was probably never perform'd by moral man'. Then Whitman adds significantly:

> But the pang and hiatus of Carlyle seem to me to consist in the evidence everywhere that amid a whirl of fog and fury and cross-purposes, he firmly believ'd he had a clue to the medication of the world's ill, and that his bounden mission was to exploit it. . . . He seems . . . to have been haunted in the play of his mental action by a spectre, never entirely laid from first to last, (Greek scholars, I believe, find the same mocking and fantastic apparition attending Aristophanes his comedies,)—the spectre of world-destruction.[4]

Carlyle's obsession with the 'universe' then, is the basis not only of his religious and philosophical thought, but also of much of his aesthetic theory, more particularly his ideas concerning 'natural supernaturalism' or 'the problem of comprehensiveness and correspondence'.[5]

While a great deal has been written on Carlyle's scattered ideas on poetry and poets, no one has treated or touched on those Carlylean views that are derived from his notion of 'comprehensiveness' and wholeness and his fascination with a Newtonian 'universe' that reflects 'emblematically' the world of the Psalmist.[6] There has also been little discussion of the close connection between his great early interest in mathematics and science and his aesthetic insistence on wholeness and concreteness, on 'Fact'. When one discusses Carlyle's aesthetics today, one immediately thinks of his dismissal of poetry and fiction as 'lies' or idle amusements and his advising writers to turn to 'serious' writing, such as history and biography. At one point in his life, however, Carlyle had praised literature, fiction and poetry especially, as the highest task to which man could devote himself. Froude talks of his Craigenputtoch Essays, in which Carlyle had 'spoken of literature as the highest of human occupations, as the modern priesthood, &c.', but, states Froude, 'he thought of it [in that way] only when it was the employment of men whom nature had furnished gloriously for that special task, like Goethe and Schiller' (Froude, IV, p. 264). For the 'writing function in the existing generation of Englishmen he had nothing but contempt', concludes Froude.[7]

13

Carlyle's Aesthetic Theory: The Aesthetic Whole

While loss of religious faith played a part in Carlyle's disparagement of creative literature, certainly one cannot ignore his theories concerning the world itself, God's universe. There are, in this respect, at least two overriding beliefs that influenced Carlyle's aesthetic theory: his acute awareness of the wholeness of things, organic unity; and his view of the necessity of seeing the concrete in the abstract, the real in the ideal, his natural supernaturalism. In the latter concept, what was needed in art was for the artist to capture the spirit of the times, to do, in effect, what Browning's Fra Lippo Lippi indicated it was important for the artist to do: enable one to *see* things as if for the first time.

The key texts for this Carlylean gospel of art are found in a number of his essays on the Germans, especially those on the state of German literature and on Novalis. In the former, speaking of Goethe, he writes:

> The poetry of Goethe, for instance, we reckon to be Poetry, sometimes in the very highest sense of that word; yet it has no reminiscence, but something actually present and before us; no looking back into an antique Fairyland, divided by impassable abysses from the real world as it lies about us and within us; but a looking round upon that real world itself, now rendered holier to our eyes, and once more become a solemn temple, where the spirit of Beauty still dwells, and is still, under new emblems, to be worshipped as of old. (*Works*, XXVI, p. 65)

One notes the Carlylean code words, 'solemn temple', 'emblems', 'real world'. The Carlylean conclusion comes a few sentences later: 'The end of Poetry is higher: she must dwell in Reality, and become manifest to men in the forms among which they live and move'. He then expands on this idea:

> The coldest sceptic, the most callous worldling, sees not the actual aspects of life more sharply than they are here delineated: the Nineteenth Century stands before us, in all its contradiction and perplexity; barren, mean and baleful, as we have all known it, yet here no longer mean or barren, but enamelled into beauty in the poet's spirit; for its secret significance is laid open, and thus, as it were, the life-giving fire that slumbers in it is called forth, and flowers and foliage, as of old, are springing on its bleakest wildernesses, and overmantling its sternest cliffs. For these men have not only the clear eye, but the loving heart. They penetrated into the mystery of Nature; after long trial they have been initiated; and to unwearied endeavour, Art has at last yielded her secret; and thus can the Spirit of our Age, embodied in fair imaginations, look forth on us, earnest and full of meaning, from their works. As the first and indispensable condition of good poets, they are wise and good men: much they have seen and suffered, and they have conquered all this, and made it all their own. . . . In a word, they are believers; but their faith is no sallow plant of darkness; it is green and flowery, for it grows in the sunlight. And this faith is the doctrine they have to teach us, the sense which, under every noble and graceful form, it is their endeavour to set forth. (*Works*, XXVI, pp. 66–7)

The implications of this passage are immense; in it are found the various reasons for the deep depression of Carlyle's later years, a depression partly due to the death of Jane but caused chiefly by the recognition of his inability to become a 'Poet' in the Goethean, German sense. Here were artists capable of penetrating the mystery of Nature, writers with clear eyes and loving hearts who were able, through their art, to 'enamel' into beauty, through their spirit, the complex and contradictory events of time in which they themselves lived. The spirit of the age became earnest and full of meaning from their works, works that had first been 'embodied' (presented emblematically one could say) in their imaginations. No wonder he would write when his own failure as 'artist' was clear to him: 'I do not believe in "Art"—nay, I do believe it to be one of the deadliest *cants*; swallowing, it too, its hecatombs of souls.' Indeed, the next sentence is indicative of his own state of mind, his disgust with the world that had refused his message:

> So that the world, daily growing more unspeakable in meaning to me, . . . and I am quite indisposed to *try* speaking to it, the result has been silence and fallow, which, unless I will go *mad*, must end, as I begin to see, before long. 'Too much to say,' I suppose, is not so bad a complaint as 'too little;' but it too is very troublesome. In brief, nothing is—but by *labour*, which we call sorrow, misery, &c. Thou must gird up thy loins again and work another stroke or two before thou die.

'Dialogues with his own heart', Froude called his entries, 'and in that one may be seen not only the shift in his aesthetic views, a shift which occurred much earlier than 1848, but also his own despair over his failure as artist' (Froude, III, pp. 420, 421).

This is to anticipate a bit, however, for in his essays on the state of German literature and on Novalis he still saw himself as a potential Goethe. In the essay on Novalis, a poet as well as a philosopher, he points out Novalis' ability to relate both the material and spiritual world. Carlyle quotes with approval the following passage: 'The division of Philosopher and Poet is only apparent, and to the disadvantage of both. It is a sign of disease, and of a sickly constitution' (*Works*, XXVII, pp. 28–9, 41). Perhaps the best and clearest statement is found in his short essay on Goethe's portrait (1832), in which he states his conception of the roles of art and the artist. 'Reader: within that head the whole world lies mirrored', he writes,

> in such clear ethereal harmony as it has done in none since Shakespeare left us: even *this* rag-fair of a world, wherein thou painfully strugglest, . . .—all lies transfigured here, and revealed authentically to be still holy, still divine. What alchemy was that: to find a mad universe full of scepticism, discord, desperation; and *transmute* it into a wise universe of belief, and melody, and reverence! Was not *there* an *opus magnum*, if one ever was? This, then, is he who, heroically doing and enduring, has accomplished it. (*Works*, XXVII, p. 372)

'Work, then, even as he has done, and does', Carlyle concludes his essay, advice which he was unable in his own career to follow (*Works*, XXVII, p. 373).

The basis of Goethe's art and his ability to transmute discord into a 'wise universe of belief, and melody, and reverence' evidently lay in the German poet's ability to envision the universe itself as a whole. The universe itself was the best representations, a 'solemn temple'. 'Go where we may', he once wrote, 'the deep *heaven* will be round us' (Froude, II, p. 96). He has another notation regarding the sense of the whole:

> What is a *Whole*? or how specifically, *does* a Poem differ from Prose? Ask not a definition of it in words, which can hardly express common logic correctly; study to create in thyself a *feeling* of it; like so much else, it cannot be made clear, hardly even to thy thought (?) . . .
>
> I see some vague outline of what a *Whole* is: also how an individual Delineation may be 'informed with the Infinite'; may appear hanging in the universe of Time & Space (partly): in which case is it a Poem and a Whole? Therefore, are the true Heroic Poems of these times to be written with the *ink of Science*? Were a correct philosophic Biography of a Man (meaning by philosophic *all* that the name can include) the only method of celebrating him? The true History (had we any such, or even generally any dream of such) the true Epic Poem?—I partly begin to surmise so. (*2NB*, pp. 187–8; Froude, II, pp. 97–8)

It soon becomes clear that Carlyle connects this idea of the whole, specifically the aesthetic whole, with the concept of the 'true' artists's being able to read the secret of his age, isolate those various currents and movements that are significant, organise them, 'enamel' them, and then become the spokesman for his era: 'Thus the History of a nation's Poetry is the essence of his History, political, economic, scientific, religious'.[1] It is only another step further to define poetry as truth. There is that curious passage in the 'Proem' of *Frederick*, in which Carlyle, after characterising fiction as akin to lying, goes on:

> But I think all real *Poets*, to his hour, are Psalmists and Iliadists after their sort; and have in them a divine impatience of lies, a divine incapacity of living among lies. Likewise, which is a corollary, that the highest Shakespeare producible is properly the fittest Historian producible. . . . I believe that the world will not always waste its inspired men in mere fiddling to it. That the man of rhythmic nature will feel more and more his vocation

> towards the Interpretation of Fact; since only in the vital centre of that, could we once get thither, lies in real melody; and that he will become, he, once again the Historian of events.

History (or poetry) will then become, in Carlyle's words, once again, 'the inspired gift of God employing itself to illuminate the dark ways of God. A thing thrice-pressingly needful to be done!' (*Works*, XII, pp. 18–19).

TRUTH, BEAUTY AND FACT

Carlyle thus characteristically succeeds in stating his belief in such a way that one can read it a number of ways, a phenomenon that explains much of what has been written about Carlyle's notion of what 'real Poets' are and his view that a 'true' Poet has the ability to interpret facts and to communicate these facts 'musically'. All else seem unimportant. The confusion arises when Carlyle equates fiction with lies (apparently because fiction deals not with facts but with imaginative ideas) and equates poetry with 'fiddling to the world'. It becomes logical for him, then, to see history and biography as the only genres capable of taking up what he calls 'facts'.

In his writings, however, Carlyle keeps hedging, and his ambivalence becomes especially evident on the vital matter of the meaning of a 'true poet' and 'man of rhythmic nature'. For Carlyle, this definition finally becomes an insurmountable obstacle, especially when applied to himself and his own writings, and he turns more and more simply to insisting on facts in prose form, specifically history and biography. Finally, he is able to write to a correspondent that he no longer can bear to read 'so-called poetry', but he wants 'a man with eyes, with a soul and heart, to tell me in candid clearness what he saw passing round him in this universe'. 'Fact' becomes more important than melody. He can also write to the same correspondent: 'A man with a pen in his hand, with the gift of articulate pictural utterance, surely *he* is well employed in painting and articulating worthy acts and men that by the nature of them were dumb. I on the whole define all Writing to mean even that, or else almost nothing'. He also can tell this same correspondent: 'all writing means Biography;

utterance in human words of Heroisms that are not fully utterable except in the speech of gods!' (*LW*, pp. 210, 228, 229). He can praise the correspondent's last work: 'such a deep, what I call an unconscious soul of method lying under it:—the work of an Artist' (*LW*, p. 210). One begins to see that Carlyle's *Reminiscences* are more than dutifully written works in memory of loved ones; he saw them as 'utterances in human words of Heroisms'.

In these last statements there is one common thread throughout: 'pictural utterance', 'speech of gods', 'unconscious soul of method', 'Artist'. Herein lies the Carlylean vision and the Carlylean failure. He knows and can describe that which makes Goethe and the German writers artists: 'beauty', which entails harmony and a sense of wholeness. In his comments on Carlyle's views of literature, Roe seems to overlook the significance of this particular aspect, especially the meaning it had for Carlyle. 'Carlyle sometimes identifies this truth in art with beauty', he writes, 'but not by entering the mazes of aesthetic theory as do Schiller and Goethe' (Roe, p. 29). Carlyle did, however, try to enter this maze, but he was unable to solve it. Later on, having tried and failed to understand and to master it, he turned to 'facts' and morality, disparaging 'beauty' as an aesthetic concept. The term 'beauty' is connected with the 'wholeness' of the artist, and Carlyle found himself unable to realise it.

Typical of his 'attempts' to enter the maze before his abandonment of the concept are the following examples from his *Journal*, the cumulative effect of which is impressive. He begins by revealing a certain puzzlement over the notion:

> Schiller seems to have been a very worthy character, possessed of great talents, and fortunate in always finding means to employ them in the attainment of worthy ends. [Carlyle would indeed envy one who had found the means to employ his talents, since he had been unable to find his proper place in the universe.] The pursuit of the Beautiful, the representing of it in suitable forms, and the diffusion of the feelings arising from it, operated as a kind of religion in his soul. He talks in some way of his essays about the *Aesthetic's* being a *necessary* means of improvement among political societies. . . . One is tired to death with his and Goethe's *palabra* about the nature of the fine arts. Did Shakespeare know aught of the *aesthetic*? Did Homer? (*2NB*, pp. 40–1)

A short time later he seems to have thought about this matter: 'Poet should preach or poetize for his *age*, should elevate and beautify the ideas which are current in it: be *Zeitbürger* as well as *Staatsbürger*.—[Schiller] Review of Bürger' (*2NB*, p. 48). He comes back to the idea a short time later: 'Goethe (Dichtung und Wahreit II.14) asserts that the sublime is natural to all young persons and peoples; but that day-light (of reason) destroys it, *unless* it can unite itself with the Beautiful, in which case it remains indestructible.—A fine obs' (*2NB*, p. 128). The next jotting in the *Journal* on this subject reveals Carlyle's genuine concern with this particular problem: 'What is Poetry? Do I really love Poetry? I sometimes fancy almost, not. The jingle of maudlin persons, with their mere (even genuine) "sensibility" is unspeakably fatiguing to me. My greatly most delightful reading is, where some Goethe musically *teaches* me. Nay, *any* fact, relating especially to man, is still valuable and pleasing' (*2NB*, p. 151).

This was written in 1830, at a time when his own career was in balance. He had written a number of articles for various journals and was working on *Sartor*. He had published 'Signs of the Times', and it was clear to him already that he was having trouble attaining that 'wholeness' the German writers were able to achieve; certainly he was finding it difficult to 'poetise' for his age, to 'elevate and beautify' the ideas in it. His dilemma is evident in his comments: 'Wrote a Paper on *Voltaire* for the Foreign Review (sometime in March & April 1829). It appears to have given some (very slight) satisfaction: pieces of it breathe afar off the right spirit of composition. When shall I attain to write wholly in that spirit?' (*2NB*, p. 140). A bit later he notes: 'Paper on *Novalis* for F. R. just published. . . . Generally poor. . . . Also just finished an Article on the *Signs of the Times*, for the Ed. Review; as Jeffrey's last speech. Bad in general' (*2NB*, p. 140).

This 'writing' problem, it becomes clear, is not in the actual composition. Carlyle himself asks: '*Ought* any writing to be transacted with such intense difficulty? Does not the True always flow *lightly* from the lips and pen? I am not clear in this matter; which is a deeply practical one with me. . . . This, however, I must say for myself: It is seldom or never the Phraseology, but always the Insight, that fails me, and retards me' (*2NB*, pp. 264–5). The chief problem lay in coming to understand and believe in the German notion of Beauty and the Aesthetic. Carlyle continues to puzzle over this: 'What *is* Art and Poetry? Is the Beautiful really higher than the Good? A higher *form* thereof? Thus were a Poet not only a Priest but a High-Priest' (*2NB*, p. 180).

The problem becomes closely connected with the writing itself and the relationship of the 'moral' to the 'artistic'. 'Sent to Jack to liberate my *Teufelsdreck* from Editorial durance in London, and am seriously thinking to make a Book of it. The thing is not right, not *Art*; yet perhaps a nearer approach to Art than I have yet made. We ought to try' (*NB*, p. 183). 'Is Homer or Shakespeare', the most pertinent entry asks, 'the greater genius? Were hard to say. Shakespeare's world is the more complex, the more spiritual, and perhaps his mastery over it was equally complete' (*2NB*, p. 187). By 'mastery' one assumes Carlyle means both wholeness and harmony, two of the favourite ways he found to express the aesthetic success of a work.

The next entries on this subject appear in 1831. His essay 'On History' had appeared in *Fraser's Magazine* in 1830, and in it Carlyle had not only 'enunciat[ed] his views on the meaning of history and the writing of history', but he had presented his 'theory of the commanding role of biography in history', thus anticipating the 'doctrine of the hero'.[2] In that essay Carlyle had also distinguished the Artist in History from the Artisan in History; the former was the one who could 'inform and enoble the humblest department with an Idea of the Whole, and habitually know that only in the Whole is the Partial to be truly discerned' (*Works*, XXVII, p. 90). In that same work he had also touched on the specific problem that was bothering him:

> He who should write a proper History of Poetry, would depict for us the successive Revelations which man had obtained of the Spirit of Nature; under what aspects he had caught and endeavoured to body forth some glimpse of that unspeakable Beauty, which in its highest clearness is Religion, is the inspiration of a Prophet, yet in one or the other degree must inspire every true Singer, were his theme never so humble. (*Works*, XXVII, p. 94)

One begins to realise the tremendous gravity of Carlyle's concern, and his entries take on an added seriousness when one realises the personal stake he has in all this:

> On the whole I wish I could define to myself the true relation of moral genius to poetic genius; of Religion to Poetry. Are they

> one and the same, different forms of the same; and if so which is to stand higher, the Beautiful or the Good? Schiller and Goethe seem to say the former, as if it included the latter and might supersede it: how truly I can never well see.—Meanwhile that the *faculties* always go together seems clear. . . . I have observed in these also the taste for Religion and for Poetry go together.
>
> Canst *thou* in any measure spread abroad Reverence over the hearts of men? That were a far higher task than *any* other. Is it to be one by Art; or are men's minds as yet shut to Art and open only at best to oratory; not fit for a *Mesiter*, but only for a better and better *Teufelsdreck*. . . . (*2NB*, pp. 188–9, 203–4)

The personal note is strong, and the contrast between the positive statements in 'On History' and the tentativeness found in the *Journal* is striking. Perhaps the passage that best depicts Carlyle's inner struggle is the following:

> When Goethe and Schiller say or insinuate that Art is higher than Religion, do they mean perhaps this: That whereas Religion represents (what is the essence of Truth for men) the Good as *infinitely* (the word is emphatic) different from the Evil, but sets them in a state of *hostility* (as in Heaven and Hell),—Art likewise admits and inculcates this quite infinite difference; but *without* hostility, with peacefulness; like the difference of two Poles which *cannot* coalesce, yet do not quarrel, nay should not quarrel for both are essential to the whole? In this way is Goethe's morality to be considered as a *higher* (apart from its comprehensiveness, nay universality) than has hitherto been promulgated?—*Sehr einseitig!* Yet perhaps there is a glimpse of the truth here. (*2NB*, pp. 204)

Once again one is struck by the contrast between this statement, with its Carlylean sense of reaching for 'the whole', and an essay like *Characteristics* (1831), in which Carlyle sets up oppositions in every topic he takes up and emphasises the need for morality and conduct: 'If in any sphere of man's life, then in the Moral sphere, as the inmost and most vital of all, it is good that there be wholeness; that there be unconsciousness, which is the evidence of this' (*Works*, XXVIII, p. 8). While he is writing these words,

Carlyle is wrestling with a concern of another dimension: 'Is *Art* in the old Greek sense possible for man at this late era? Or were not . . . the Founder of a Religion our true Homer at present?—The *whole Soul* must be illuminated, made harmonious: Shakespeare seems to have had no religion, but his Poetry.—' (*2NB*, p. 215). 'Everywhere and Everywhen lie the materials of Art. . . . Man and his ways reach always from Heaven to Hell. But *where*, O where is the Artist that can again body this forth!—Not yet born?' (*2NB*, pp. 227–8). Then there are those passages that show how much this means to Carlyle personally: 'The whole thing I want to write seems lying in my mind; but I *cannot get my eye on it*' (*2NB*, p. 263). And there is the cry from the heart: 'How sad and stern is all Life to me! . . . Why cannot I be a kind of Artist!' (*2NB*, p. 226).

Why cannot I be a kind of Artist? This question of 1831 indicates more than simply an adolescent yearning. After all, Carlyle is thirty-six years old at this time, and his career in literature is clearly set. Before him lie most of the works that were to fill thirty volumes. The question, however, is indicative, as I have already suggested, of Carlyle's dilemma: his vision of the true Artist and the failure he saw himself to be. It is no accident, then, that from this time on Carlyle's work becomes identifiable in several ways, but never as 'creative' or 'artistic', labels which he would have regarded with some favour then. He was unable, clearly, to write a work in the 'German' vein, a Goethean or Schillerian artistic whole. Instead, his work after *Characteristics* can be seen from different perspectives, all of which exclude complete 'mastery' (the coalescence of opposites) of subject matter and *musical* teaching.[3]

14

Carlyle's Moral Aesthetic

One can perhaps best illustrate Carlyle's essentially 'moral' aesthetic by examining his relationship with the Romantics, that generation of poets with whom he sometimes has been connected. It is important to keep in mind, however, that Carlyle was born in 1795, three years before *Lyrical Ballads*, and he was in his early teens when Byron took his seat in the House of Lords and published *English Bards*. There was never any question of Carlyle's basic hostility to the Romantics, for his approach to art and poetics, no matter what he might pay lip service to, was one that could in no way embrace the poetics of the Romantics, even granting their own varied views on art and poetry. In examining Carlyle's responses to the major poets of the early nineteenth century, Wordsworth, Coleridge, Byron, Shelley, and Keats, one can see instantly that there was never any basis for agreement; each had his own faults or distortions in terms of the Carlylean aesthetic, faults generally based on moral rather than aesthetic grounds. Of the lesser poets and writers, he also has responses based on matters other than aesthetics. Lamb was simply insane; Hunt, a personal friend, was regarded most highly. His poetry had 'a genuine tone of *Music*', although that is as far as Carlyle ever got to defining one of the terms he was so fond of using.[1] Carlyle's emphasis was always, after he had got over his brief fling with the German notion of Beauty, on the man rather than his work, the content rather than the form. 'What we want to get at', he intoned in 'The Hero as Poet', 'is the *thought* the man had, if he had any: why should he twist it into jingle, if he *could* speak it out plainly?' It was this moralistic bias and his veneration, for that is really the only word one can use, of Goethe that worked against any chance that he would respond to the Romantics; they were as dwarfs compared to the only 'true' Artist Carlyle had ever known.

Although some have made notable attempts to demonstrate what Carlyle meant by the various terms he used, there remains the real problem of attempting to arrive at any useful definitions.

Carlyle, for instance, often talks, as we have seen, of Beauty. Ultimately he gave up attempting to achieve this vision of Beauty in his own work, the Beauty that would incorporate the Good, and settled reluctantly for the latter only. He kept on using the term, however, even though he himself had repudiated it. In 'The Hero as Poet', the most specific essay in some ways on his own idea of what constitutes a 'poet', he falls back on the term once more. 'A saying of Goethe's', he writes, 'which has staggered several, may have meaning: "The Beautiful", he intimates, "is higher than the Good; the Beautiful includes in it the Good."' This saying, we know, had 'staggered' Carlyle himself, who could never really bring himself to accept it fully; he needs to qualify it in his own 'Carlylean' way. 'The *true* Beautiful; which however, I have said somewhere, "differs from the *false* as heaven does from Vauxhall!"' (*Works*, v, pp. 81, 82). Once he qualifies beauty in this way then Carlyle can accept the term.

He goes on, then, to talk of 'Poets who are accounted perfect', but again we find that he is less than helpful in giving us concrete terms that can aid one in arriving at a Carlylean poetic. In the passage that comes closest to defining what he means by a Poet, we read:

> At bottom, clearly enough, there is no perfect Poet! A vein of Poetry exists in the hearts of all men; no man is made altogether of Poetry. We are all poets when we *read* a poem well. . . . We need not spend time in defining. Where there is no specific difference, as between round and square, all definition must be more or less arbitrary. A man has *so* much more of the poetic element developed in him as to have become noticeable, will be called Poet by his neighbours. World-Poets too, . . . are settled by critics in the same way. One who rises *so* far above the general level of Poets will, to such and such critics, seem a Universal Poet; as he ought to do. And yet it is, and must be, an arbitrary distinction. All Poets, all men, have some touches of the Universal; no man is wholly made of that. (*Works*, v, p. 82)

One hardly knows what to make of that passage; compared to it, Arnold's 'touchstone' theory is clarity and concreteness itself.

There is, however, more, for Carlyle is next intent on showing the difference between 'true Poetry' and 'true Speech not poetical'. He goes on to consider some things that have been mentioned by 'late German Critics', some of which, says Carlyle, 'are not very intelligible at first'. These critics say, for example, 'that the Poet has an *infinitude* in him; communicates an *Unedlichkeit*, a certain character of "infinitude," to whatsoever he delineates'. Carlyle goes on to 'clarify': 'This, though not very precise, yet on so vague a matter is worth remembering: if well meditated, some meaning will gradually be found in it' (*Works*, v, pp. 82, 83). Again, one thinks of Carlyle's harsh words about Coleridge's being abstract and wonders about the fairness of that criticism.

The most precise that Carlyle gets in his attempt to define 'true Poetry' is his notion of a poem's having 'musical thought'. Here is Carlyle:

> For my own part, I find considerable meaning in the old vulgar distinction of Poetry being *metrical*, having music in it, being a song. Truly, if pressed to give a definition, one might say this as soon as anything else: if your delineation be authentically *musical*, musical not in word only, but in heart and substance, in all the thoughts and utterances of it, in the whole conception of it, then it will be poetical; if not, not.—Musical: how much lies in that! A *musical* thought is one spoken by a mind that has penetrated into the inmost heart of the thing; detected the inmost mystery of it, namely the *melody* that lies hidden in it; the inward harmony of coherence which is its soul, whereby it exists, and has a right to be, here in this world. (*Works*, v, p. 83)

Then, as one by now knows and can expect, Carlyle expands his 'definition': 'Nay, all speech, even the commonest speech, has something of song in it: not a parish in the world but has its parish-accent;—the rhythm or *tune* to which the people there *sing* what they have to say!' (*Works*, v, p. 83).

Once again, one recognises the real basis of Carlyle's thought; it lies in matters other than aesthetic or poetic. He is interested, one can deduce, in the thoughts that are uttered, and his own thoughts go back to his own 'parish' or kirk, which had its own 'parish-accent'. Indeed, his mind also goes back to the 'assertive image' of the Universe.

> All deep things are Song. It seems somehow that very central essence of us, Song; as if all the rest were but wrappages and

> hulls! The primal element of us; of us, and of all things. The Greeks fabled of Sphere-Harmonies: it was the feeling they had of the inner structure of Nature; that the soul of all her voices and utterances was perfect music.

He then can conclude, with what one supposes for him makes a sensible definition, but leaves others as puzzled as ever: 'Poetry, therefore, we will call *musical Thought*' (*Works*, v, p. 83).

One finds the same approach in Carlyle's letters to various persons, the most prominent being Robert Browning, a good friend of Carlyle's. In a letter to Browning, Carlyle, who was reporting his 'hearty and spontaneous' approval of *Men and Women*, also told why he had been so long in writing about that volume. Browning had also asked Carlyle for any advice he might have. 'I really knew not what to say', Carlyle wrote, 'and hesitated always'. He goes on: 'I have renounced altogether the high thought of "advising," and the like. . . . Accept a few rough human words, then, such as the day gives; and do not consider them as pretending to be more than honest words, rough and ready, from a fellow-pilgrim well-affected to you'. Carlyle then goes on to tell Browning that there is 'an excellent opulence of intellect' in the two volumes, and that Browning has a 'pair of *eyes*' that will be busy 'inspecting human life this long while'. He also says that he has 'a fresh valiant manful character' and his poetry has 'a fine . . . most extraordinary power of expression'.

After these kind words Carlyle goes on to what he calls 'the shadow side of the Picture'. 'My friend', he writes Browning, 'it is what they call "unintelligibility!" That is a fact; you are dreadfully difficult to understand; and that is really a sin'. Carlyle concludes:

> I do not at this point any longer forbid you *verse*, as probably I once did. I perceive it has grown to be your dialect, it comes more naturally than prose;—and in prose too a man can be 'unintelligible' if he like! My private notion of what *is* Poetry—[here one gets ready for a definition, finally] Oh, I do hope to make *you*, one day, understand that; which hitherto no one will do: but it must not concern us at present. Continue to write in verse, if you find it handier.

Evidently Carlyle realises that he has not said very much to help poor Browning, for he then adds:

> And what more? Aye, what, what! Well, the sum of my idea is: If you took up some one *great* subject, and tasked all your powers upon it for a long while, vowing to Heaven that you *would* be plain to mean capacities, then—!—But I have done, *done*. Good be with you always, dear Browning; and high victory to sore fight! (*CMSB*, pp. 297–300)

Alexander Carlyle, who edited these letters, has a footnote in which he says that Carlyle had earlier clearly described what he understood poetry to be, and he quotes a section from *Heroes* that proves to be rather circumlocutory:

> Poetry, therefore, we will call *musical Thought*. The Poet is he who *thinks* in that manner. At bottom, it turns still on power of intellect; it is a man's sincerity and depth of vision that makes him a Poet. See deep enough, and you see musically; the heart of Nature *being* everywhere music, if you can only reach it. (*CMSB*, p. 299)

'It is a great mistake to say', says Alexander Carlyle, 'that Carlyle hated poetry. The fact is, . . . that it was only bad poetry that he disliked' (*CMSB*, p. 299). The point is, of course, that few accuse Carlyle of not liking poetry; the only question is what did he think poetry was?

In an article on Carlyle and Leigh Hunt, Sanders refers to Carlyle's various letters to Hunt, one of which contains Carlyle's reasons for liking Hunt's poetry, especially the 'genuine tone of *music*' that pervades 'all your way of thought'. Carlyle then goes on:

> This is what I call your vocation to Poetry: so long as this solicits you, let it in *all* forms have free course. Well for him that *hath* music in his soul! Indeed, when I try Defining (which grows less and less my habit), there is nothing that comes nearer my meaning as to poetry in general than this of *musical thought*. . . . To come a little to particulars: we all thought your *Rimini* very beautiful; sunny brilliancy and fateful gloom most softly blended, under an *atmosphere* of tenderness, clear and bright like that of Italian Pictures. Beautifully *painted*; what it wanted to be a *whole* (and a picture) I believe you know better than I.

Carlyle continues with another sentence or two, but the 'particulars' turn out to be his own reactions to the works rather than any particulars about the poetry. Indeed, Carlyle quickly shifts to talking about an article on Hunt's poetry some seventeen years ago, and he talks of a 'picture of a mother' that affected him and 'baulked the Reviewer' (*CL*, VII, pp. 8–29).

The cumulative result of Carlyle's various ineffectual attempts to 'define' poetry is not so much to undermine his influence on poets of his own age, but to indicate the complexity of his own thoughts and ideas and his real weakness in this one area. As in the case of Goethe's concept of Beauty, Carlyle seems to have known what he meant by *musical thought*, but nowhere does one find an adequate definition of it. He always placed the emphasis on the term *thought* rather than *musical*, and for him thought was identical with one's moral nature. They were the same under different terms, as he wrote in *Heroes*.

The truth remains that Carlyle did have a blind spot in this matter. We know, according to Allingham, that Browning 'never minded what Carlyle said of things outside his own little circle (drawing a circle in the air with his forefinger): what was it to me what he thought of Poetry or Music?'[2] Perhaps the most telling incident occurred at Craik's home, for it reveals much about Carlyle's own critical practice. 'He had been declaiming', we are told, 'against Wordsworth . . . , adding that from the *debris* of Robert Burns a thousand Wordsworths might have been made. We laughed at all this, especially when we found that he had never read, or, at least, had no recollection of "Laodamia" and various other things in which Wordsworth's finest powers are exhibited'. After more conversation of like nature, Carlyle finally said of Petrarch: 'All I have to say is, that there is one son of Adam who has no sympathy with his weak, washy twaddle about another man's wife'. At this point John Hunter, an Edinburgh lawyer present, interjected: 'Then I would say of you that you are to be pitied for wanting a perception which I have, and which I think, and the world in general will think, I am the richer for possessing; and I would just speak of what you have now uttered in these words:—Say, canst thou paint a sunbeam to the blind, / Or make him feel a shadow, with his mind?' Carlyle admitted Hunter was right. 'I ought to envy you', Carlyle told Hunter. 'I have no doubt you have pleasures and feelings manifold from which I am shut out, and have shut out myself, in consequence of the habit I have so long indulged of groping through the sepulchral caverns of our being' (*CFS*, p. 164). It was that same evening that Carlyle succeeded in shattering Hunt's 'fantastic framework of *agreeabilities*' in order to substitute his 'eternal principles of right and wrong, responsibility, awe of the Unseen' (*CFS*, p. 165; *CL*, XII, pp. 99–100). Typically, and in Carlylean fashion, matters were decided in terms of right and wrong.

The real standards by which a poet was to be judged are found in various of Carlyle's writings, notably his essay on the 'State of German Literature', the key ideas of which I have already touched on in various ways, in various comments in his *Journal* and letters and, most thoroughly, in his essay on the Poet as Hero. In his introductory comments in that essay and in his remarks on Dante and Shakespeare one finds Carlyle's most significant thoughts and statements on poetry and the poet. Not surprisingly, many of these ideas are already familiar ones, but it helps to see them stated in terms of specific figures. Not surprisingly, too, Carlyle begins with a Carlylean truism, one that is said over and over again in different ways and at different times: the great poet is simply a great man. 'Hero, Prophet, Poet,—many different names, in different times and places, do we give to Great Men. . . . I confess, I have no notion of a truly great man that could not be *all* sorts of men. . . . The grand fundamental character is that of Great Man; that the man be great' (*Works*, V, pp. 78–9).[3] One sees the typical Carlylean approach; if one states the word or idea enough, then one can begin to understand the meaning. No need for definition. The great poet is a great man; the great man is a great poet.

While this may sound a bit unfair to Carlyle, for the word 'man' carries a great deal of meaning in Carlylean coterie speech, the fact remains that for him there is a great deal of meaning in repetition. Indeed, one need read only a little of the essay to begin to realise how many times Carlyle uses the word, repeating 'man' many times in different places and in different contexts. Other familiar ideas also emerge. The Poet and the Prophet are first separated, then made into one. The Prophet has seized the moral side of things, the Poet the aesthetic side, or what the Germans, Carlyle is careful to say, call the 'Beautiful, and the like'. Soon, however, we hear: 'But indeed the two provinces run into one another, and cannot be disjoined'. When Shakespeare is being discussed, we know that although he is an Artist, ultimately the judgement will be that he is also moral. Words, Carlyle states, 'ought not to harden into things for us'. These divisions are 'at bottom but *names*'. 'Morality itself, what we call the moral quality of a man, what is this but another *side* of the one vital Force whereby he is and works'.

Carlyle's conclusions concerning Shakespeare are predictable, as are all his pronouncements on aesthetics and poetics: 'If I say therefore, that Shakespeare is the greatest of Intellects, I have said all concerning him'. He has said all, for Shakespeare has an 'unconscious intellect; there is more virtue in it that he himself is aware of'. Intellect and Morality are, one remembers, in Carlylean terms, the same. Predictably, too, Carlyle does not give us detailed discussion of Shakespeare's plays: 'We have no room to speak of Shakespeare's individual works; though perhaps there is much still waiting to be said on that head. Had we, for instance, all his plays reviewed as *Hamlet*, in *Wilhelm Meister*, is! A thing which might, one day, be done'. Carlyle then falls back on Schlegel: 'August Wilhelm Schlegel has a remark on his Historical Plays, *Henry Fifth* and the others, which is worth remembering. . . . There are really, if we look to it, few as memorable Histories'.

Instead, Carlyle takes his usual aesthetic stance; he talks of Shakespeare's prophetic strain and his human qualities, especially his triumph over circumstances.

> All his works seem, comparatively speaking, cursory, imperfect, written under cramping circumstances; giving only here and there a note of the full utterance of the man. . . . Alas, Shakespeare had to write for the Globe Playhouse: his great soul had to crush itself . . . into that and no other mould. It was with him, then, as it is with us all. No man works save under condition.

For Carlyle, both Shakespeare and Dante are intense, deep, sincere; however, Shakespeare, 'more perfect' than any other man, is a 'calmly *seeing eye*'. In the end Shakespeare is greater than Dante, 'in that he *fought truly*, and *did conquer*' (my italics). Then, reminding his readers of Shakespeare's 'prophetic' side, his 'unconscious intellect', Carlyle lapses into 'prophetic' vocabulary, mixing both the religious and critical strain:

But the man sang; did not preach, except musically. We called Dante the melodious Priest of Middle-Age Catholicism. May we not call Shakespeare the still more melodious Priest of a *true* Catholicism, the 'Universal Church' of the Future and of all times? . . . We may say without offence, that there rises a kind of universal Psalm out of this Shakespeare too; not unfit to make itself heard among the still more sacred Psalms. Not in disharmony with these with these, if we understand them, but in harmony! . . . For myself, I feel that there is actually a kind of sacredness in the fact of such a man being sent into this Earth. Is he not an eye to us all; a blessed heaven-sent Bringer of Light?

15

Carlyle and the Romantic Poets

What chance did the Romantic poets have in comparison to Shakespeare and Carlylean standards? There is one section in the essay on Shakespeare in which Carlyle actually compares him to Goethe. That Shakespeare did not suffer in this comparison is remarkable, for Goethe was the star to which Carlyle compared others. Needless to add, the Romantics did not do well in this exercise. In his study of Western philosophy Bertrand Russell reminds us that Carlyle, at one time, considered Byron 'the noblest spirit in Europe' and felt that, on his death, he had 'lost a brother'. He came afterwards to prefer Goethe, but we must remember, says Russell, that 'Byron was in his blood, whereas Goethe remained an aspiration'.[1] Perhaps that is too great a claim for Byron in terms of the impression he made on Carlyle, but the relationship of these two is indeed an interesting and complex one. On the one hand, as the editors of Carlyle's letters suggest, 'Close thy Byron; open thy Goethe' is too simple a formula; on the other, Carlyle, as Russell suggests, after an early attraction consistently rejected the notion of Byron as an important poetic or moral force, the two standing for the same thing in Carlyle's terms. In a letter to Jane in 1823, for instance, he talks of Goethe as a 'man of true culture and universal genius'. 'Wordsworth and Byron!' he tells her: 'They are as the Christian Ensign and Captain Bobadil before the Duke of Marlboro!' (*CL*, II, pp. 299, 300).

The Byron–Carlyle relationship revolves essentially around Carlyle's ideas on poets and poetry, and, as I have already suggested, on these terms Byron and the other Romantic poets did not, indeed could not, meet Carlylean standards. With Byron, however, there were special circumstances, which I shall shortly discuss. Byron was, of course, part of the 'literary world' that Carlyle, at the start of his own 'literary' career, had some notions about, and, as such, he was part of a world that Carlyle scorned.

Carlyle's contempt for this 'world' is contained in a letter to Jane dated 20 December 1824; he writes:

> Irving advises me to say in London; partly with a friendly feeling, partly with a half selfish one, for he would fain keep me near him. Along all his followers there is none whose intercourse can satisfy him. . . . Great part of them are blockheads, a few are fools; there is no rightly intellectual man among them. . . . On the whole, however, he is among the best fellows in London; by far the best that I have met with. Thomas Campbell has a far clearer judgement, infinitely more taste and refinement; but there is no living well of thought or feeling in him. . . . He is not so much a man, as the Editor of a Magazine: his life is that of an exotic; he exists in London, as most Scotchmen do, like a shrub disrooted, and stuck into a bottle of water. . . . Little Proctor here has set up house on the strength of his writing faculties. . . . He is a good-natured man, lively and ingenious; but essentially a Small.—Coleridge is sunk inextricably in the depths of putrescent indolence. Southey and Wordsworth have retired far from the din of this monstrous city. So has Thomas Moore. Whom have we left? The dwarf Opium-Eater . . . lives here in lodgings. . . . He carries a laudanum bottle in his pocket; and the venom of a wasp in his heart. . . . Hazlitt is *writing* his way thro' France and Italy: the ginshops and pawnbrokers bewail his absence. Leigh Hunt writes 'wishing caps' for the Examiner, and lives on the tightest of diets at Pisa. . . . Good Heavens! I often inwardly exclaim, and is *this* the Literary World? This rascal rout, this dirty rabble, destitute not only of high feeling or knowledge or intellect, but even of common honesty? The very best of them are ill-natured weaklings: they are not red-blooded *men* at all. (*CL*, III, pp. 232–35)

There are some very good reasons for Carlyle's scorn at this time, not the least of which have to do with his uneasiness about his own standing in the literary community. This was the second half of his first visit to London, and, as he told his brother, London was a nicer place to visit 'from time to time, than live in it' (*CL*, III, p. 219). Also, he was still looking about for a 'career', and literature was becoming more and more the obvious and only choice. He had done a great deal of writing already, and *Schiller* was being published serially in the *London Magazine*. 'Teaching', he wrote to Jane, 'I find is not the most amusing thing on earth; in fact with a stupid lump for a pupil it is about the most irksome'.

The letters during this period are mainly about his plans and his hopes, all of which include setting up an abode of his own and keeping busy. He had told his mother of his present situation:

> This book of mine must be printed and of course made ready for printing: til that is effected, I am fixed in London. I am just now gathering all my things around me, getting books and shoes and clothes and every thing put in order; with the intent of commencing strenuously and prudently in the great work of writing and doctoring. . . . I should like to stay here for a longer period; but if it will not, then also I know what to do. I will come and set up house with you in Scotland: I will have work to write, a little garden to cultivate, a horse to ride upon, and all the kind souls of Mainhill to love. (*CL*, III, p. 196)

He had written to Jane: 'To-morrow I commence a meditated plan of life and labour: I will study and write, and try if I can gather any touch of health and wisdom. . . . Here in my own quarters I am free as air, and except society have all I want: I am lonely, but I mean also to be busy. . . . A man that is not standing on his own feet in regard to economical affairs, soon ceases to be a man at all'. Then, significantly, he adds: 'Poor Coleridge is like the hulk of a huge ship; his mast and sails and rudder have rotted quite away' (*CL*, III, p. 199). The juxtaposition of Coleridge's state with his own is indicative of the way Carlyle often judged others; there was always, at bottom, only one criterion to judge anyone, writer, artist: Is he a *man*?

The connection of Carlyle's own plans and hopes and his aesthetic judgements of the Romantic poets, then, is a close one, for in some ways Carlyle saw himself in danger of becoming what they seemed to him to be. 'That I am one of the most pitiful and miserable of the sons of Adam', he wrote to Jane,

> is a fact with which I was long ago familiar: how to help the evil, to grow less pitiful and miserable is the question I am now debating. . . . Life with all its difficulties, Mr. C., and this very sickness the crowning curse of all, is the problem given you to solve; the chaos out of which your understanding (if any) is to

> bring out order and happiness and beauty: you are now free . . .; accomplish this solution; regulate this chaos; or go down to the Devil, and break some hearts that are dearer to you than existence—whichever you prefer. (*CL*, III, p. 200)

A little later he is telling Jane:

> I must settle myself down within a reach of Edinburgh or London: I must divide my time between mental and bodily exercises. . . . Had I land of my own, I should instantly be tempted a become a—farmer! Laugh outright! But it is very true. . . . In the intermediate hours, I could work at literature, thus *compelled* to live according to the wants of Nature. . . . It is no part of my plan to eat the bread of idleness, so long as I have the force of a sparrow left in me to procure the honest bread of industry. . . . It is the law in Yarmouth that 'every herring hang by its own head'; . . . that judicious principle, I think, should also govern life. (*CL*, III, pp. 214–15)

How would Carlyle react to a poet whose writing contained a volume entitled *Hours of Idleness*? One needs, of course, to give Carlyle credit for an aesthetic sense that goes beyond this level, but the fact remains that Byron's character was as significant to Carlyle as his work when it came to judge Byron as poet. 'Carlyle', writes Jerome McGann, 'dismissed nearly all of Byron's work before *Don Juan* as largely trumped-up attitudinizing. What Carlyle meant was that Byron in reality was not like the Giaour, or Conrad, or Childe Harold, and that consequently these were "insincere" representations of himself—not accordant with the truth of fact'.[2] Sincerity, we recall, was one of the Carlylean standards for being a Poet. Typically, Carlyle never gives any detailed discussion of Byron's poetic techniques or even his poetic successes or failures; he talks either of his unrealised potential or his character flaws. The truth is that Carlyle is influenced by considerations other than Byron's poetic skill or art; he sees Byron at various times as either a potential rival or as a rival to his one great hero-artist, Goethe. There was also the Byron who served as an example of the dangers to which Carlyle himself was susceptible: pride and selfishness. These, rather than strict aesthetic considerations, set the tone for his remarks on Byron.

Although he tends to underestimate Carlyle's early admiration for Byron, claiming that he was simply 'willing to go along with Jane' rather than hurt her feelings, Sanders is correct in emphasising the importance of the 'tug-of-war' that developed over the comparative importance of Goethe and Byron and the extent of the debt that Byron owed to Goethe. In fact, with the increasing importance of Goethe to Carlyle, there was a corresponding decrease in Carlyle's estimate of the English poet. Also, the more he came to realise that he would never become the Artist that Goethe was, the more Carlyle came to emphasise the moral aspect of the Poet, and the more he tended to condemn Byron. Correspondingly, as his admiration of German literature grew, the less he found admirable in Byron; and he soon resorted to the only possible position left: Byron died young, full of promise. Thus, while he could recommend Byron's poetry to his brother, and he could salute Byron on his death as the 'noblest spirit in Europe', he could also find 'something psychologically and spiritually unhealthy in Byron's poetry' (*CFS*, p. 68).

Some of the passages are interesting in the way they reveal Carlyle's own poetic as well as his own biases; he writes to William Graham, who had suggested that Carlyle try writing poetry in 'competition' with Byron:

> Alas! my dear Sir, if discontented thoughts and reckless familiarity with whatever is at first sight more appalling in our inexplicable destiny, were all that went to form Giaours and Childe Harolds, there would indeed be a plentiful supply of that commodity. The corroding strife of will against Necessity, the vain tho' desperate efforts we make to reconcile the world within and the world without, are not confined to Byron: thousands feel this deeply; but the magic voice that gives it utterance, and clothes it all with splendour and beauty are the lot of one or two. [One imagines Carlyle here thinking of Goethe and Shakespeare.] I might write 'last speeches' and 'dying words': poetry—alas!—upon the whole, I do not regret this deficiency. Poets such as Byron and Rousseau are like opium eaters [poor DeQuincey comes to mind]; they raise their minds by brooding over and embellishing their sufferings, from one degree of fervid exaltation and dreamy greatness to another, till at length they run *amuck* entirely and whoever meets them would do well to run them thro' the body. Peace to the unfortunates? They find repose at last. (*CL*, I, pp. 315–16)

The reaction of Carlyle seems strangely and unusually strong for what is a rather mild statement by one who admired him. There are, as I have suggested, reasons other than aesthetic for Carlyle's response to Byron's poetry. One can see his condemnation of Byronic character, wild, undependable, almost insane. There is the suggestion that Carlyle has been unable to reach the success that Byron has. There is an implicit defence of Goethe. There is also a great deal of irony here, for Carlyle was, indeed, to write, under various guises, many 'last speeches' and 'dying words'; one thinks only of the *French Revolution* and *Cromwell*. There are references to Byronic characters, but no specific comments on the poetry.

Also typical of his later remarks on Byron are those that reflect his famous plea to close one's Byron and open one's Goethe. Byron becomes the 'puking and sprawling' Byron, the 'sulky' Byron; he becomes the 'Sulking Dandy'. Carlyle's 'rejection' of Byron, in short, is based on his own 'moral' poetic, one that reflects his own approach to writing, one that depends on personality as much as on theory, on one's humanity as much as on one's artistic ideas. The best illustration of Carlyle's position is seen in the episode with Napier over his (Carlyle's) writing an article on Byron for the *Edinburgh Review*, of which Napier was then editor; in 1830 he writes:

> Occasionally of late I have been meditating an Essay on *Byron*; which, on appearance of Mr Moore's Second Volume, now soon expected, I should have no objection to attempt for you. Of Mr Moore himself I should say little; or rather perhaps, as he may be a favourite of yours, Nothing: neither would my opinion of Byron prove very heterodox; my chief aim would be to *see* him and show him, not, as is too often the way, (if I could help it) to write merely 'about him and about him.' For the rest, tho' no Whig in the strict sense, I have no disposition to run *amuck* against any set of men or of opinions; but only to put forth certain Truths that I feel in me, with all sincerity; for some of which this *Byron*, if you liked it, were a fit enough channel. Dilettantism, and mere toying with Truth, is, on the whole, a thing which I cannot practice: nevertheless real Love, real Belief, is not inconsistent with Tolerance of its opposite; nay is the only thing consistent there with, for your Elegant Indifference is at heart only *idle*, selfish, and quite *in*tolerant. At

> all events, one can and should ever *speak quietly*; loud hysterical vehemence, foaming, and hissing least of all beseems him that is convinced, and not only *supposes*, but *known*. (*CL*, v, p. 196)

In contrast to the tone of this letter, which reveals Carlyle's 'blood' relationship, in Russell's terms, to Byron, for even the vocabulary used by Carlyle demonstrates his determination to be 'tolerant' and understanding, the next letter to Napier on this subject (1832) is startling. Carlyle no longer wishes to write a *Byron* essay. He tells Napier some time later, in a letter from which I have earlier quoted, that he will do it, but it will be 'without inward call'. He then gives some reasons for his disenchantment with Byron: 'No genuine productive thought was ever revealed by him to mankind; indeed no clear undistorted vision into anything, or picture of anything; but all had a certain falsehood, a brawling theatrical insincere character.' Carlyle drives home those points about Byron that really matter to him now, and have become very important in judging poets.

> The man's moral nature too was bad, his demeanour, as a man, was bad. What was he, in short, but a huge *sulky Dandy*; of giant dimensions, to be sure, yet still a Dandy; who sulked, as poor Mrs Hunt expressed it [,] 'like a schoolboy that had got a plain bunn given him instead of a plum one.' His Bunn was nevertheless God's Universe with what Tasks are there; and it had served better men than he. (*CL*, vi, p. 149)

Needless to say, Napier decided not to ask Carlyle to do the essay. He recognised, as we must, the various elements that Carlyle was now using to judge Byron; rather than discuss Byron's work and art, here was Carlyle condemning him for being immoral, sulking, selfish, and insincere, of not being a real man.

There is one obvious reason for Carlyle's change of heart, one which involves his close relationships with the Hunts. The clue to his feelings towards Byron on this level, which can hardly be called 'literary', is revealed by his reference to 'poor Mrs Hunt', whom he had come to know only a short time before his letter to Napier on 28 April 1832. The entire 'episode' deserves a brief summary, only because it helps shed light on the complexity of

Carlyle's approach towards literary criticism and his judgement of writers as 'men' as well as 'literary' figures.[3]

The chronology is simple enough. In 1830, as I have indicated, Carlyle wrote to Napier and suggested an article on Byron, his opinion of whom would not prove 'very heterodox'. He then met Leigh Hunt for the first time in London on Wednesday, 22 February 1832, 'just a few weeks', Sanders tells us, 'before the Carlyles returned to Craigenputtoch'. Sanders then adds: 'The meeting seems to have pleased everyone who was there, and soon the Carlyles met Marianne, Mrs. Hunt, and there was visiting back and forth' (*CFS*, p. 97). It does not take much stretching of the imagination to venture the guess that Mrs Hunt soon was telling the Carlyles of the experiences she, her husband and their seven children had had when they had journeyed to Italy in 1822 to join Byron and Shelly in the ill-fated venture with the *Liberal*. Accounts of that time vary, but most agree that Byron's treatment of the Hunts was not the most courteous, and they also are unanimous in telling of Mrs Hunt's lack of 'respect' for Byron, both his person and rank.

Monkhouse in his *Life* of Hunt writes that Byron was 'irritable' on the subject of his promises to Leigh Hunt. He goes on to describe the situation: 'Williams, in his last letter to his wife, expresses his opinion that Byron had treated Hunt vilely, and . . . adds, "Lord B.'s reception of Mrs. H. was . . . most shameful. She came into his house sick and exhausted, and he scarcely deigned to notice her; was silent, and scarcely bowed. This conduct cut H. to the soul."'[4] On the subject of Mrs Hunt's behaviour he is also explicit:

> Then there was the serious difficulty of the ladies. Hunt's freely-spoken opinions about marriage and the relations of the sexes, prevented him from expressing, perhaps, from feeling, any objection to taking up his abode with Byron and his mistress; but it was very difficult with Mrs. Hunt, whose opinions were not so 'advanced' as her husband's. . . . Though compelled to live under the same roof with this strange family party, and to eat the bread of Byron, Mrs. Hunt kept to her own apartments, her ill-health affording an efficient excuse. Professor Nichol says that she does not seem to have been a very judicious person. 'Trelawny here,' said Byron one day, 'has been speaking against my morals.' 'It is the first time I ever

> heard of them,' she replied. This may have been injudicious, but it was well-deserved, and is about the only healthy utterance to be found in the records of this miserable episode in Hunt's life. (Monkhouse, p. 159)

In his own study of the Hunts and Byron, Barnette Miller also talks of Mrs Hunt's dealings with Byron.

> Mrs. Hunt [he writes] seems to have widened further the breach between the two men. She did not speak Italian and the Countess Guiccioli . . . did not speak English. . . . This, Hunt later says, was the first cause of diminished cordiality between Byron and himself. The Hunt children were a further cause of trouble. Byron wrote of them to Mrs. Shelley: 'They were dirtier and more mischievous than Yahoos. What they can't destroy with their feet they will with their fingers.'

Miller also records the source of the statement often quoted by Carlyle:

> She used no tact in her dealings with Lord Byron. She let him see that she had no respect for rank or titles. She even went beyond the limits of courtesy in her remarks to him. . . . Of his portrait by Harlowe she said 'that it resembled a great schoolboy, who had had a plain bun given him, instead of a plum one,' a facetious speech indiscreetly repeated by Hunt to Byron. (Miller, p. 108)

It should come as no surprise then, to see Carlyle's reluctance to accept Napier's request in 1832 for an encyclopaedia 'piece' on Byron, especially after hearing from the Hunts, particularly Mrs Hunt, about Byron's treatment of her and, one assumes, his 'immoral' behaviour. Carlyle had written in his first letter that his chief aim would be 'to *see*' Byron. In the second letter, however, after the relatively short period of knowing the Hunts, he does all he can do to wash his hands of any writing about Byron. His words reflect the Hunt–Byron situation; indeed, this affair helps explain Carlyle's vehemence: 'In my mind', he tells Napier, 'Byron has been sinking at an accelerated rate, for the last ten years, and has now reached a very low level: I should say *too* low, were there not a *Hibernicism* involved in the expression.' Carlyle evidently saw this 'sinking' as an 'emblem' of Byronic Dandyism and indolence, for how else can one explain the force of his 'personal' denunciation of Byron: 'I love him not; I *owe* him nothing; only pity, and forgiveness: he taught me nothing that I had not again to forget' (*CL*, VI, p. 149; *2NB*, pp. 267–8).

There is, however, another level at which Carlyle's rejection of Byron as a man of letters and poet can be seen. By 1832 Carlyle had come to believe in certain 'aesthetic' principles, and these clearly form the basis of his own attitude towards Byron and the other Romantics. One could make a number of claims other than the Hunts to try to account for this apparently violent shift in Carlyle's attitude towards Byron; after all, he was the one who had approached Napier in 1830. For one thing, Carlyle's father had died in January and Carlyle had written his reminiscence in the week following his father's death. As we know, Carlyle admired and loved his father first and foremost as a *man*, one who had served as an example to him, especially as believer and a conqueror over suffering. To Carlyle his father must have seemed in every respect the very opposite of Byronism. For another thing, Carlyle had finished *Sartor* in 1831, and the underlying ideas in it were anti-Byronic on grounds similar to those expressed in the letter to Napier. Third, and certainly an influence that cannot be ignored, was the death of Goethe, on which ocassion Carlyle had written another form of 'reminiscence': 'Death of Goethe' and 'Goethe's Works', both published in 1832.

One need only read Carlyle's tributes to Goethe to sense what memories and thoughts the death of his hero-artist had brought to him. Indeed, Carlyle falls back on his assertive image: 'If his course, as we may say of him more justly of any other, was like the Sun's, so also was his going down. For indeed, as the material Sun is the eye and revealer of all things, so is Poetry, so is the World-Poet in a spiritual sense' (*Works*, XXVII, p. 375). Later Carlyle once again refers to the influence of this World-Poet:

> Goethe, it is commonly said, made a New Era in Literature; a Poetic Era began with him. . . . Were the Poet but a sweet sound and singer, solacing the ear of the idle with pleasant songs; and the new Poet one who could sing his idle pleasant song to a new air,—we should account him a small matter, and his performance small. But this man, . . . was a Poet in such a sense as the late generations have witnessed no other. . . . The

> true Poet is ever, as of old, the Seer; whose eye has been gifted to discern the godlike Mystery of God's Universe, and decipher some new lines of its celestial writing; we can still call him a *Vates* and Seer. . . . The true Sovereign of the world, . . . is he who lovingly *sees* into the world; the 'inspired Thinker,' whom in these days we name Poet.

Carlyle then turns to Goethe's *Works* and calls them 'Pure works of Art'. He concludes:

> The corner-stone of a new social edifice for mankind is laid there. . . . To live, as he counselled and commanded, not commodiously in the Reputable, the Plausible, the Half, but resolutely in the Whole, the Good, The True. (*Works*, XXVII, pp. 376–7, 381, 384)

It is no coincidence, either, that in his essay 'Goethe's Works' he takes Byron to task:

> The Self-worshipper, again, has no seasons of light, which are not of blue sulphur-light; hungry, envious pride, not humility in any sort, is the ashy fruit of his worship; his self-god growls on him with the perpetual wolf-cry, Give! Give! and your devout Byron, as the Frau Hunt, with a wise simplicity . . . , once said, 'must sit sulking like a great schoolboy, in pet because they have given him a plain bun and not a spiced one.' (*Works*, XXVII, p. 397)

Certainly in composing these notices Carlyle must have thought of all that German literature stood for; and the contrast between the German poets, especially Goethe, and the English ones, especially Byron, perhaps Coleridge, must have been overwhelming. In his earlier essay on the 'State of German Literature' (1827) he had enthusiastically endorsed the German poets for those same qualities that he had praised in *Heroes*, and we find those same sentiments in 'Goethe's Works'. In the earlier (1827) essay he had praised Goethe and Schiller for their ability to take the contradictions of their time and, through their clear eye and loving heart, enamel into beauty the age in which they lived: 'As the first and indispensable condition of good poets, they are wise and good men: much they have seen and suffered, and they have conquered all this, and made it all their own; they have known life in its heights and depths, and mastered it in both, and can teach others what it is, and how to lead it rightly' (*Works*, XXVI, p. 66).

Byron is nothing in comparison: 'Our Byron was in his youth but what Schiller and Goethe had been in theirs. . . . With longer life, all things were to have been hoped for from Byron: for he loved truth in his inmost heart, and would have discovered at last that his Corsairs and Harold were not true. It was otherwise appointed' (*Works*, XXVI, p. 69). That was in 1827; in 1832 Carlyle is not so kind to Byron. He is dismissed as a son of Chaos. Carlyle uses what amounts to a 'coterie' image for his readers, and he indicates how much Byron has fallen in his estimation: 'Woe to the land where . . . no prophet arises; but only censors, satirists and embittered desperadoes, to make the evil worse; at best but to accelerate a consummation, which in accelerating they have aggravated!' To make certain that his readers know just who these satirists and 'embittered desperadoes' are, Carlyle names names: 'Old Europe had its Tacitus and Juvenal; but these availed not. New Europe too has had its Mirabeaus, and Byrons, and Napoleons, and innumerable red-flaming meteors, shaking pestilence from their hair; and earthquakes and deluges, and Chaos come again; but the clear Star, day's harbinger (*Phosphorus*, the bringer of *light*), had not yet been recognised' (*Works*, XXVII, p. 435).

Byron, in fact, is not in bad company, for one remembers Carlyle's ambivalent attitude towards both Napoleon and Mirabeau. However, no one stands up to Goethe, the bringer of light, the Day-Star. Byron is simply one of the Power-men, the *Kraftmanner*. 'They dealt in sceptical lamentation', states Carlyle,

> mysterious enthusiasm, frenzy and suicide: . . . in reflection, as in action, they studied to be strong, vehement, rapidly effective; of battle-tumult, love-madness, heroism and despair, there was no end. . . . Beauty, to their mind, seemed synonymous with Strength. All passion was poetical, so it were but fierce enough. Their head moral virtue was pride; their *beau ideal* of manhood was some transcript of Milton's Devil. Often . . . instead of 'patronising Providence,' did directly the opposite; raging with extreme animation again Fate in general, because it enthralled free virtue; and with clenched hands, or sounding shields,

> hurling defiance towards the vault of heaven. (*Works*, XXVI, pp. 68–9)

One could understand why Jane so enthusiastically admired Byron and why he had been called by Carlyle himself 'a noble spirit'. However, whenever Carlyle compared Byron (or anyone, except Shakespeare) with Goethe, the conclusion was predictable. Goethe was simply the universal man. One recognises, in his tribute to his hero, even in spite of the old, by now familiar terminology we have come to expect, the genuine admiration and love that Carlyle had for Goethe, who after all, had saved his life. In contrast to the Power-man that Byron was, here is Goethe:

> Of Goethe's spiritual Endowment, looked at on the Intellectual side, we have (as indeed lies in the nature of things, for moral and intellectual are fundamentally one and the same) to pronounce a similar opinion; that it is great among the very greatest. As the first gift of all, may be discerned here utmost Clearness, all-piercing faculty of Vision; whereto, as we ever find it, all other gifts are superadded; nay, properly they are but other forms of the same gift. A nobler power of insight than this of Goethe you in vain look for, since Shakespeare passed away.

Carlyle then lists the similarities of the two greatest Poets he had known; Shakespeare, too, was 'a Thinker in the highest of all senses: he is a poet'. Carlyle concludes with what for him can only be the highest possible praise:

> For Goethe, as for Shakespeare, the world lies all translucent, all *fusible* we might call it, encircled with WONDER; the Natural in reality the Supernatural, for to the seer's eye both become one. What are the *Hamlets* and *Tempests*, the *Fausts* and *Mignons*, but glimpses accorded us into this translucent, wonder-encircled world; revelations of the mystery of all mysteries, Man's Life as it actually is? (*Works*, XXVII, pp. 436–7)

Thus, Carlyle comes full circle; his poetic becomes another form of his view of life itself. A Poet is one who, as any real hero, sees into the heart of the Universe, the Wholeness of it, the natural in reality the Supernatural. The Poet, above all, has to be Moral in order to have this Vision, a Vision allowed only to a few. Byron certainly did not, although he did have a certain nobility of spirit that Carlyle recognised, reluctantly it is true, and he also 'loved truth in his inmost heart'. However, he was, unfortunately, a huge sulky Dandy, who had revealed 'no genuine productive Thought' to mankind. Most damning of all, his 'moral nature' was bad.

This attitude also determined his approach towards Coleridge, the Romantic figure whom one would think Carlyle would understand best. It was as man and philosopher, chiefly, that Carlyle found Coleridge disgusting, and that is not too strong a word. Given his own religious position, a Calvinist without the theology, it is not surprising that Carlyle would find Coleridge's views unsatisfactory. 'Coleridge's championing of the Church of England', writes Sanders, 'was a very real issue between the two men' (*CFS*, p. 48). Sanders traces some of this, particularly in conjunction with John Sterling's enthusiastic support of Coleridge; and while he does not mention it, it is evident that Carlyle felt that Sterling, who had been the first real 'disciple' he had gained, was being unfaithful. In this connection, it is fascinating to read Carlyle's biography of Sterling, in which he often downplays, or attempts to, the influence of Coleridge on Sterling, and his marginalia on Sterling's works.

Duffy confirms Carlyle's objections to Coleridge's religious views; indeed, one can infer from the question and answer that Carlyle saw a very close relationship between Coleridge's poetry and his religious views. Duffy writes: 'I said I thought the stronger man [Browning] would find it hard to match "Christabel," or "The Ancient Mariner," or to influence men's lives as they had been influenced by "The Friend," or "The Lay Sermon" in their day'. Duffy continues:

> Not so, Carlyle said; whatever Coleridge had written was vague and purposeless, and, when one came to consider it, intrinsically cowardly, and for the most part was quite forgotten in these times. He had reconciled himself to believe in the Church of England long after it had become a dream to him. For his part he had gone to hear Coleridge when he first came to London with a certain sort of interest, and he talked an entire evening, or lectured, for it was not talk, on whatever came uppermost in his mind. There were a number of ingenious flashes and

> pleasant illustrations in his discourse, but it led nowhere, and was essentially barren. When all was said, Coleridge was a poor, greedy, sensual creature, who could not keep from his laudanum bottle though he knew it would destroy him. (Duffy, pp. 59–60)

Duffy persists in 'defending' Coleridge against Browning, and he recites a sonnet by Coleridge that, Duffy says, 'might be confidently placed beside the best sonnets of Milton and Wordsworth'. After Carlyle listened to Duffy recite the sonnet, he replied: 'Yes, he said there were bits of Coleridge fanciful and musical enough, but the theory and practice of his life as he lived it, and his doctrines as he practised them, was a result not pleasant to contemplate' (Duffy, pp. 61–2).

Carlyle judged Coleridge the man as a failure, and this was enough to condemn him in all his other pursuits; his remarks are essentially cruel and spiteful. It is true that Carlyle occasionally quotes Coleridge or alludes to some of his statements in various works, but on the whole his attitude towards the older Romantic is unforgiving and pitiless in its scorn. An entry for 26 May 1835 sets the tone: 'Coleridge's "Table Talk" . . . insignificant for most part, a helpless Psyche overspun with Church of England cobwebs; a weak, diffusive, weltering ineffectual man' (Froude, III, p. 45). Other comments are not much kinder. He writes to Jane of Coleridge's 'putrescent indolence'; and a short time later he tells his brother: 'Coleridge is a mass of richest spices, putrified into a dunghill: I never hear him *tawlk*, without feeling ready to worship him and toss him in a blanket' (*CL*, III, pp. 233, 261).

After Coleridge's death he writes to his mother, almost as an after-thought, it would seem, since it is the penultimate paragraph: 'Coleridge, a very noted Literary man here, . . . died about a week ago, at the age of 62. An Apothecary had supported him for many years: his wife and children shifted elsewhere as they could. He could earn no money, could set himself steadfastly to no painful task [both damning weaknesses in Carlyle's view]; took to opium and poetic and philosophic dreaming. A better faculty has not been often worse wasted'. He writes to Emerson a short time later and adds in a postscript: 'How great a Possibility, how small a realized Result! They are delivering Orations about him, and emitting other kinds of Froth, *ut mos est*. . . . What hurt can it do?' (*CL*, VII, pp. 261, 267).

The thoughts expressed in the letter to his mother reflect what were for Carlyle, as I have suggested, Coleridge's most serious flaws. He had wasted his life; more seriously, he had refused to fight back, to overcome, as had Goethe, and Carlyle himself, suffering and hardship. His attitude is demonstrated in an entry (part of which I have already quoted) for 26 May 1835. Coleridge had been dead for some ten months. He is commenting on Coleridge's *Table Talk*:

> insignificant yet expressive of Coleridge: a great possibility that has not realised itself. Never did I see such apparatus got ready for thinking, and so little thought. He mounts scaffolding, pulleys, and tackle, gathers all the tools in the neighbourhood with labour, with noise, demonstration, precept, abuse, and sets—three bricks. I do *not* honour the man. (Froude, III, p. 46)

Carlyle was obviously thinking of his father, who built things to last; of course he could not honour the man. Coleridge was no James Carlyle or Goethe or Shakespeare. He was, as Carlyle says in the same note, 'ineffectual, . . . a lax, languid, impotent *character*' (Froude, III, p. 46).

'I pity him (with the opposite of contempt)', Carlyle states, but if one reads the letters and the portrait of Coleridge in his *Sterling* one finds little pity and much contempt. Sanders is perhaps overly cautious when he writes that there is balance and restraint in that portrait; it is, as he says, 'one of the finest passages of prose in Victorian literature', but it is on balance a damning portrait. Indeed, one could, on the basis of it, see some justification in McFarland's calling it a 'malefic portrait', and even, to some extent, his remarks concerning Carlyle's 'excessive spitefulness' and his 'sensitivity and envy'.[5] One need only read not the portrait but the letter which Froude says is the original of the 'malefic' portrait in *Sterling*. Carlyle writes to his brother:

> Besides Irving I have seen many other curiosities. Not the least of those I reckon Coleridge, the Kantean metaphysician and quondam Lake poet. . . . Figure a fat flabby incurvated personage, at once short, rotund and relaxed, with a watery mouth, a snuffy nose, a pair of strange brown timid yet earnest looking eyes, a high tapering brow, and a great bush of grey hair—you will have some faint idea of Coleridge. He is a kind,

> good soul, full of religion and affection, and poetry and animal magnetism. His cardinal sin is that he wants *will*; he has no resolution, he shrinks from pain or labour in any of its shapes. His very attitude bespeaks this: he never straightens his knee joints, he stoops with his fat ill shapen shoulders, and in walking he does not tread but shovel and slide—my father would call it *skluiffing*. He is also always busied to keep . . . the water of his mouth from overflowing; and his eyes have a look of anxious impotence; he *would* do with all his heart, but he knows he dare not.

Carlyle proceeds to describe Coleridge's talk, but he begins by indicating that he was not expecting much, and he did not receive much:

> The conversation of the man is much as I anticipated. A forest of thoughts; some true, many false, most part dubious, all of them ingenious in some degree, often in high degree. But there is no method in his talk; he wanders like a man sailing among many currents, whithersoever his lazy mind directs him—; and what is more unpleasant he preaches, or rather soliloquizes: he cannot speak; he can only '*tal-k*' (so he names it).

Carlyle summarises with what amounts to an understatement: 'Hence I found him unprofitable, even tedious'. 'I reckon him', he concludes, 'a man of great and useless genius—a strange not at all a great man' (*CL*, III, pp. 90–1; 24 June 1824).

A letter to his friend Murray, two months later, simply elaborates details: 'Coleridge is a steam-engine of a hundred horses power—with the boiler burst. His talk is resplendent with imagery and the shows of thought; you listen as to an oracle, and find yourself no jot the wiser. He is without beginning or middle or end'. Carlyle next gives the physical description: 'A round fat oily yet impatient little man, his mind seems totally beyond his controul; he speaks incessantly, not thinking or imagining or remembering, but combining all these processes into one; as a rich and lazy housewife might mingle her soup and fish and beef and custard into one unspeakable mass and present it trueheartedly to her astonished guests' (*CL*, III, p. 139). To talk of the *Sterling* portrait as being balanced and moderate, then, is possible, but one has to make much, as Sanders does, of elements other than

Carlyle's own words about Coleridge, aspects such as Gillman's garden, in Sanders's words, the 'frame for his picture' (*CFS*, p. 57). When one reads Carlyle's own words as they refer to Coleridge there is one inescapable conclusion; it is, indeed, a 'malefic' portrait.[6] His 'express contributions to poetry, philosophy, or any specific province of human literature or enlightenment, had been small'. 'He was *thought to hold* . . . the key of German and other Transcendentalisms' (my italics). He could still, after Hume and Voltaire, 'profess himself an orthodox Christian, and say and point to the Church of England, with its singular old rubrics and surplices at Allhallowtide, *Esto perpetua*'. 'A life heavy-laden, half-vanquished, still swimming painfully in seas of manifold physical and other bewilderment'. Brow and head were 'round, and of massive weight', but the face was 'flabby and irresolute'. 'His talk, alas, was distinguished, like himself, by irresolution: it disliked to be troubled with conditions, abstinences, definite fulfillments;—loved to wander at its own sweet will'. 'In general he seemed deficient in laughter; or indeed in sympathy for concrete human things either on the sunny or on the stormy side'. Finally: 'The moaning singsong of that theosophico-metaphysical monotony left on you, at last, a very dreary feeling'. Carlyle was delighted when his brother wrote to tell him that he had heard the phrase *Krankhafte Dunkelheit* applied to Coleridge. 'I have amused several with it', Carlyle wrote his brother later, 'to whom also it is *treffend*', which is translated as 'pertinent' (*CL*, VIII, p. 174).

Byron was too proud and selfish, Coleridge too irresolute and lazy. Both, somehow, had not realised their potential, chiefly because they could not overcome pain and suffering, hardly, one thinks, considerations for judging fellow-writers. They were not men. These flaws were essentially the same ones found in the other Romantics. Wordsworth, Shelley and Keats were dismissed in terms that amounted to the same thing. Of the three, Wordsworth stood highest, although he also was 'essentially a small man'. Allingham reports that Carlyle 'ran down Keats and Shelley: "Keats wanted a world of treacle!"' Another time Allingham asked Mrs Carlyle her husband's opinion of Keats. 'I brought her *Isabella* and *The Eve of St. Agnes* (I was too knowing to try her with *Endymion*). She wrote me a letter—"Almost any young gentleman with a sweet tooth might be expected to write such things. *Isabella* might have been written by a seamstress who had eaten something too rich for supper and slept upon her back"' (Allingham, pp. 205, 310).

If Keats wanted treacle, then Shelley, so far as Carlyle was concerned, seemed to be a combination of the worst traits of Byron and Coleridge, morbidity and violence. In responding to Browning, after reading his introduction to the letters (which turned out to be false), Carlyle, knowing Browning's feelings for Shelley and his poetry, wrote to tell his friends his true feelings. He was trying to be kind, it is obvious; again, the tone and approach are recognisable:

> In fact, I am not sure but you would excommunicate me,—at least lay me under the 'lesser sentence,' for a time,—if I told you all I thought of Shelley! Poor soul, he has always seemed to me an extremely weak creature, and lamentable much more than admirable. Weak in genius, weak in character (for these two already go together); a poor, thin, spasmodic, hectic, shrill and pallid being;—one of those unfortunates, of whom I often speak, to whom 'the talent of *silence*,' first of all, has been denied. The speech of such is never good for much. Poor Shelley, there is something void, and Hades-like in the whole inner world of him; his universe is all vacant azure, hung with a few frosty mournful if beautiful stars [the negative assertive image is damning]; the very voice of him (his style, &c), shrill, shrieky, to my ear has too much of the *ghost*! (*CMSB*, p. 292)

In another reference to Shelley Carlyle said that he knew 'no more *urned* books' than his. Continuing in that vein, he told Milnes: 'It is like the writing of a ghost, uttering infinite wail into the night, unable to help itself or anyone else' (*CL*, I, p. xxxviii).

In a note Alexander Carlyle states that Browning later told Carlyle that 'he agreed with him about Shelley and his poetry'. He adds: 'Emerson held an equally poor opinion of Shelley, saying that he could see nothing in his poetry but some pretty verses in *The Skylark* and *The Cloud*' (*CMSB*, p. 292). Emerson probably read the poetry, but one wonders just how much of Shelley's poetry Carlyle had really looked at. In his comments are the usual absence of any detailed criticism; instead are found the usual principles invoked by Carlyle. In the place of details Carlyle supplies 'his style, &c'; Shelley's greatest weakness is, as one comes to expect, his character. Character and genius 'always go together', just as intellect and morality are really the same. The depth of Carlyle's disgust with Shelley may be seen in the figure he uses to dismiss him utterly and finally: 'Hades-like, his universe all vacant azure'. His 'assertive image' would be a signal to those who knew how to read him.

Of the major Romantics, one would think that Carlyle would be most sympathetic to Wordsworth, and, in some respects, this conjecture would be a true one. Carlyle saw in Wordsworth a few redeeming qualities, although on the whole he was unable to respond to his poetry in any positive way. He condemned Wordsworth for being egotistical, for being interested only in those who where, in Carlyle's words, 'real worshippers' (*Reminiscences*, p. 363). He condemned him, too, or at least found him 'wanting' as a poet:

> A man recognisably of strong intellectual powers, strong character; given to meditation, and much contemptuous of the *un*meditative world and its noisy nothingness; had a fine limpid style of writing and delineating [although his father, Carlyle later writes, was better], in his small way; a fine limpid vein of melody too in him (as of an honest rustic *fiddle*, good, and well handled, but *wanting* two or more of the *strings*, and not capable of much!)—in fact, a rather dull, hard-tempered, unproductive and almost wearisome kind of man; not adorable, by any means, as a great Poetic Genius, much less as the Trismegistus of such; whom only a select few could even read, instead of misreading, which was the opinion his worshippers confidently entertained of him!

Then Carlyle adds, as he so often did of others, his *real* view of his great predecessor:

> Privately I had a real respect for him withal, founded on his early Biography, which Wilson of Edinburgh had painted to me as of antique greatness signifying: 'Poverty and Peasanthood, then, be it so. But we consecrate ourselves to the Muses, all the same, and will proceed on those terms, Heaven aiding!' (*Reminiscences*, p. 357)

Carlyle's attitude towards Wordsworth, then, was, as one would expect, based on the appreciation of Wordsworth's character, most particularly his view of Nature (closer to Carlyle's than any of the other Romantics) rather than on any particular knowledge of or views about his poetry. In a letter to his brother he describes meeting Wordsworth: 'I did not expect much; but got mostly what I expected'. Wordsworth has, Carlyle tells him, 'a fine shrewdness and naturalness . . .; one finds also a kind of *sincerity* in his speech. . . . A genuine man (which is much) but also essentially a *small* genuine man'. What served to put off Carlyle, apparently, was Wordsworth's great love of self and his desire to be admired.

> I fancy . . . he has fallen into the garrulity of age, and is not what he was: also that his environment (and rural Prophethood) has hurt him much. He seem impatient that even Shakspeare [*sic*] should be admired. . . . The shake of hand he gives you is feckless, egoistical; I rather fancy he *loves* nothing in the world so much as one could wish. When I compare that man with a great man,—alas, he is like dwindling into a contemptibility. (*CL*, VIII, pp. 80–1)

He writes to Mill about this same time: 'I have seen Wordsworth again, and find my former interpretation of him strengthened. He seems to me a most *natural* man (a mighty point in these days); and flows on there, delivering what is really in him, platitudes or wisdoms as the case maybe. A really *earth*born *well*, not an artificial *jet d'eau*: let us be satisfied with the "day of small things."' (*CL*, VIII, pp. 87–8).

Of Wordsworth's poetry, there is very little said, and that is derogatory. I have already quoted Carlyle's remarks about Wordsworth 'from the *debris* of Robert Burns a thousand Wordsworth's might have been made'. Other remarks are equally derisive. He notes: 'Went on Sunday with Wordsworth's new volume to Kensington Gardens; got through most of it there. A picture of a wren's nest, two pictures of such almost all that abides with me'. By now we know what to expect: 'A genuine but a small diluted man. No other thing can I think of him; they must sing and they must say whatsoever seems good to them' (Froude, II, p. 45). Time and time again one waits for some specific remarks on Wordsworth's poems, but in vain; there is nothing of that nature. Inevitably all remarks and comments come back to Wordsworth's character, small but genuine. Even in the Paper on

Wordsworth, we find the briefest commentary on the poetry, and this is general: 'But to my private self his divine reflections and unfathomabilities seem stinted, scanty; palish and uncertain;—perhaps in part a feeble *reflex* (derived at second hand through Coleridge) of the immense German fund of such?—and I reckoned his Poetic Storehouse to be far from an opulent or well furnished apartment!' (*Reminiscences*, p. 358).

What, then, can we say of Carlyle's poetic, particularly one that can be gathered from his views towards the Romantic generation? It is, not surprisingly, consistent with his views towards other figures. To read Carlylean criticism for specific comments is, as Johnson said, to read Richardson for the story. Byron is inferior to Burns. Why? Both are 'missionaries to their generation', but Burns came nearer to accomplishing the goal of teaching that generation 'a higher Doctrine' and a 'purer Truth'. Why? Burns, unlike Byron, 'the gifted Peer', Burns, 'the gifted Ploughman', had 'partially prevailed' in his struggle towards clear Manhood, while Byron, who 'must shoot-out in wild efforts', must 'die at last in Boyhood, with the promise of his Manhood still but announcing itself in the distance' (*Works*, XXVIII, p. 140).

Wordsworth and Coleridge are inferior to Shakespeare and Goethe, of course, but even in some ways to his father, James, who could build better than Coleridge and paint 'human portraiture' even better than Wordsworth. 'My Father's', he writes, 'in rugged simple force, picturesque ingenuity, veracity and brevity, were, I do judge, superior to even Wordsworth's as bits of human Portraiture'. It is the 'human' element that is, of course, important to Carlyle. He continues: 'And intermixed here and there with flashes of the *Poetical* and soberly Pathetic . . . , which the Wordsworth Sketches, mainly of distant and indifferent persons, altogether wanted' (*Reminiscences*, p. 362). Keats and Shelley, as we have seen, had nothing in their characters or writings to have them come under serious consideration as Poets in the Carlylean sense. Character and genius go together, as Carlyle believed, and both failed on that criterion.

Carlyle's criteria, then, concern character and human nature rather than formal aesthetic principles. His poetic heroes are Goethe, Shakespeare, and Burns, and they all, especially the first two, had those gifts of character that were important. His father, too, he included. All these had the gifts of insight, the ability to 'read' the secret of the Universe. 'At bottom', he had written, 'it turns still on power of intellect; it is a man's sincerity and depth of vision that makes him a Poet' (*Works*, v, p. 84). Of course, Intellect and Morality are essentially the same, so the Poet must be Moral. In short, as we have seen, the great poet is simply a great man.

The clue seems to be not so much musical thought, which is never fully explained nor defined, but perseverance of character and the overcoming of obstacles. As Carlyle explains in the '*Corn-Law Rhymes* Review':

> So too with the spirits of men: they become pure from their errors by suffering for them; he who has battled, were it only with Poverty and hard toil, will be found stronger, more expert, than he could stay at home from the battle. . . . In which sense, an observer . . . has said: Had I a man of clearly developed character (clear, sincere within its limits), of insight, courage and real applicable force of head and of heart, to search for; and not a man of luxuriously distorted character, with haughtiness for courage, and for insight and applicable force, speculation and plausible show of force,—it were rather among the lower than among the higher classes that I should look for him. (*Works*, XXVIII, p. 141)

One can simply substitute the word 'poet' for 'man' and one has the heart of Carlyle's poetic. Indeed, how else could his father be classified among the great poets of the world? Here is Carlyle's praise of his father, a man with all the qualities above, a Poet who ranks with the great Carlylean poets, certainly above all the Romantics, all of whom had, for one reason or another, characters that were distorted; his words are very moving, if somewhat lacking in any clearly stated poetic:

> Oh my brave, dear, and ever-honoured Peasant Father, where among the Grandees, Sages, and recognised Poets of the world, did I listen to such sterling speech as yours,—golden product of a heart and brain all sterling and royal! That is a literal *fact*;—and it has often filled me with strange reflections, in the whirlpools of this mad world! (*Reminiscences*, p. 362)

A Coleridge could put only three bricks together, while his father had built houses of stone. That was enough for Carlyle.

16

Carlyle and Art: Symbol, Emblem and Image

While there are many who would quarrel over Carlyle's ideas, few would deny his claim as artist; and one significant 'artistic' device upon which he relied was the use of emblems or symbols, a device that again reflects his view of the whole. In analysing Teufelsdröckh's statement that all visible things are symbols of more important invisible ideas or forces, Georg Tennyson writes:

> The sentence, with its three independent clauses, states this idea from several vantage points, turns, as it were, the jewel to different lights. . . . By the conclusion of the sentence Carlyle has moved to a philosophic . . . vocabulary—Matter, Idea—which lends authority to the statement that began with common language. Moreover, Carlyle, by the end of the sentence, has made a more inclusive statement than the one he began with.[1]

Carlyle's method, then, reflects his own religious, philosophic, and aesthetic thought: it straddles two worlds, the common and the philosophic, the real and the ideal. Newton and Goethe were simply two sides of a single concept, each necessary to the other. Newton's universe was the Word; Goethe's the Idea: Newton's the photograph or Emblem; Goethe's the Reality.

One more point might be made concerning Carlyle's notions of style and language. Again, Tennyson is helpful. In discussing Carlyle's use of the term *body forth,* he characterises it as the Carlylean equivalent of the author's placing 'his inner vision in a form that does justice to it', projecting something that 'comes from within rather than mirroring that which is outside' (Tennyson, p. 89). Carlyle certainly had something like that in mind as he wrote of Novalis's ideas about Nature and the Deity. 'To live in that Light of Reason', Carlyle had written in his explanation of Novalis's thought, 'to have, even while here and encircled with this Vision of Existence, our abode in that Eternal

City, is the highest and sole duty of man. These things Novalis figures to himself under various images' (*Works*, XXVII, p. 29).

Carlyle is obviously expressing his own ideas; and his own attempt at presenting Novalian imagery, to 'encircle' his own 'Vision of Existence', may be seen in his 'assertive image', a device best exemplified in the 'Mountains were not new to him' passage in *Sartor Resartus*, discussed below. This image encompasses not only his positive views of German idealism, its substantive aspect, but also its 'aesthetic' one, particularly its integrative ability to depict the 'real' world and render it 'holier' to our eyes, to make it once more become 'a solemn temple'. 'The end of Poetry', Carlyle had insisted, 'is higher: she must dwell in Reality, and become manifest to men in the forms among which they live and move. . . . The Nineteenth Century stands before us, in all its contradiction and perplexities; barren, mean and baleful, as we have all known it, yet here no longer mean or barren, but enamelled into beauty in the poet's spirit' (*Works*, XXVI, p. 66). This image also encompasses and reflects his earlier readings and experiences as well as the other aspects of his overall faith: his strong belief in the primacy of the Divine, his reliance on biblical truths, his incorruptible ethical sense, his confidence, however tentative, in some Divine plan, and his ultimate trust in the unity of the universe.

In the context of this 'emblem', Carlyle's many references to Nature became especially significant, taking on meanings far beyond what they seem to signify on first reading. They often contain, directly and indirectly, those views he had gained from the German writers and the other important influences in his early years: the sense of the wholeness of the universe, the integration of the ideal with the practical, the clear eye and the loving heart, the importance of suffering and the sense of wonder at the mystery of man and the universe itself. These references to Nature do more, however; they often provide a frame of reference by which to judge the reliability of his statements. Often this image conveys his meaning more directly than the words themselves; indeed, it sometimes provides an ambivalence or ambiguity to statements made with absolute directness. To learn to read this assertive image is to learn to recognise those moments when Carlyle is suggesting ideas with far less certainty than readers often take him to be doing; as a result, when one learns to decipher it one finds Carlyle a far more complex writer and person than he is often thought to be. At times, in fact, the assertive image undercuts or mitigates the 'message' that the 'prophet' seems to be proclaiming; and this phenomenon is especially true of his writings dealing with Nature in its various facets.

Finally, it is possible to view this 'natural' assertive image as a reflection of the 'Carlylean' view of Nature, one uniquely his, reflecting, of course, his early reading and his own kind of idealism. Rejecting pantheism, Carlyle viewed Nature as a reflection of the Divine, and as a voice of the Divine, a force through which He proclaimed His power and the means by which He illustrated His laws. Carlyle's Calvinism would support this position: the world was no playground but a place for earnest labour and suffering. His use of 'natural' imagery in this respect also illustrates dramatically what has been characterised as the abandonment by many Victorians of 'an unqualified belief in the kind of pantheism' found in Wordsworth's youthful Nature poetry.[2] Carlyle's assertive 'natural' images, are his attempts to illustrate the Universe as a 'self-subsistent universally connected Whole' and to bring, in Novalian fashion, into true poetic relation the spiritual and material world.

One passage that serves to epitomise Carlyle's attitude towards 'Romantic' nature is found in *Sartor Resartus* as the Professor is talking of view-hunters, those who enjoy 'luxuriating in [their] feelings as [they discover] beautiful and picturesque natural landscapes' (*CFS*, p. 62). One remembers Wotton Reinfred's discussion of the subject:

> One thing, at least, you have on many times occasion to observe: No topic sooner or more painfully wearies us than description of scenery. Your view-hunter is the most irksome of all articulate-speaking men. . . . If long-winded he is generally in part insincere: there is cant in his raptures; he is treating us not with his subject, but with his own false vainglorious self. At best, it is sensations not thoughts that he is describing; and no sensations, except our own, can long fix our attention. (*LW*, p. 53)

In *Sartor* Carlyle writes:

> 'Some time before Small-pox was extirpated,' says the Professor, 'came a new malady of the spiritual sort on Europe: I mean the

> epidemic, now endemical, of View-hunting. Poets of old date, being privileged with Senses, had also enjoyed external Nature; but chiefly as we enjoy the crystal cup which holds good or bad liquor for us; that is to say, in silence, or with slight incidental commentary: never, as I compute, till after the *Sorrows of Werter*, was there man found who would say: "Come let us make a Description! Having drunk the liquor, come let us eat the glass! Of which endemic the Jenner is unhappily still to seek." Too true!' (*Works*, I, pp. 123–4)

The significance of this passage is found in the way it demonstrates Carlyle's complete rejection of sentimental indulgence in natural scenery and conveys his own attitude towards external Nature as the 'garment' of God.

Carlyle's employment of the assertive image ranges from a simple sentence to the elaborate description, already cited, of the mountains in *Sartor Resartus*. His dependence on it soon becomes evident to any reader. There are references to the heavens, the starry vault, the constellations doing their rounds; allusions to the 'celestial city' or the 'everlasting city' also appear in conjunction, as would seem appropriate, with mountain imagery. The crucial point is that Carlyle used the image, as he would himself perhaps say, 'organically' rather than 'mechanically'; it is not 'decorative'. Tillotson, therefore, is a little misleading when he states that 'the universe helped Carlyle to add bugles to his orchestra', the implication being that Carlyle simply used references to it for effect. He goes on, again suggesting a bit of Carlylean rococo in his use of the image:

> With it at call he was not at too great a disadvantage beside the prophets of the Old Testament, who could call on God confidently, as on a father. Like any of them, he could thunder: 'Sooty Manchester,—it too is built on the infinite Abysses; overspanned by the skyey Firmaments . . .' Industrialists in Lancashire could be counted on to attend to words like those. . . . Having gazed for help at the stars he finally circled back to man.[3]

These comments suggest too strongly, and unfairly, a rhetorical strategy on Carlyle's part in his 'dependence' on the Universe. The pervasiveness of the image and the 'naturalness' with which he uses it suggest otherwise. In a letter to his brother John in 1828, for instance, he writes, 'I walk often under cloud of night . . . conversing with the void heaven, in the most pleasant fashion' (*CL*, IV, p. 421). Another time he tells Mill: 'There is something infinitely sanative in the sight, face to face, of this great universe,—*God's* universe, as one's whole heart may discern it to be. A divine old universe, our old mysterious Mother; of which all that can be preached and prated, in the modern and in the ancient time, is but a mockery in comparison to the *un*speakable meanings of it' (*CSMB*, p. 178). One finds the same impulse in his writings. 'O ye kind Heavens', he writes in *The French Revolution*, 'azure, beautiful, eternal behind your tempests and Time-clouds, is there not pity in store of all!'

His heavy dependence on this device is evident everywhere in his works. The following is found in *Sartor Resartus*:

> *Ach Gott*, when I gazed into these Stars, have they not looked-down on me as if with pity, from their serene spaces; like Eyes glistening with heavenly tears over the little lot of man! Thousands of human generations, all as noisy as our own, have been swallowed-up of Time, and there remains no wreck of them any more; and Arcturus and Orion and Sirius and the Pleiades are still shining in their courses, clear and young, as when the Shepherd first noted them in the plain of Shinar. (*Works*, I, pp. 145–6)

In his early essay 'On History' he relies on the same kind of emblem:

> But the Artist in History may be distinguished from the Artisan in History. . . . The simple husbandman can till his field, and by knowledge he has gained of its soil, sow it with the fit grain, though the deep rocks and central fires are unknown to him: his little crop hangs under and over the firmament of stars, and sails through whole untracked celestial spaces, between Aries and Libra; nevertheless it ripens for him in due season, and he gathers it safe into his barn. (*Works*, XXVII, p. 90)

Carlyle then carefully explains what the emblem signifies, just what the reader is expected to conclude from the image, and what, in his later essays, he assumed the reader would get and often did not bother to explain:

> As a husbandman he is blameless in disregarding those higher wonders; but as a thinker, and faithful inquirer into Nature, he were wrong. . . . However, that class of cause-and-effect speculators, with whom no wonder would remain wonderful, but all things in Heaven and Earth must be computed and 'accounted for'; and even the Unknown, the Infinite in man's Life, had under the words *enthusiasm, superstition, spirit of the age* and so forth . . . have now wellnigh played their part in European culture. (*Works*, XXVII, p. 90)

The careful reader learns to recognise these images or emblematic messages, short or long, and to read them as a 'faithful inquirer' rather than a cause-and-effect speculator. This device serves to alert readers to those passages that deserve particular attention. In one of his earlier essays, at a strategic place, he transmits this message:

> Art indeed is Art; yet Man also is Man. Had the *Transfiguration* been painted without human hand; had it grown merely on the canvas, . . . it were a grand Picture doubtless; yet nothing like so grand as *the* Picture, which, on opening our eyes, we everywhere in Heaven and on Earth see painted; and everywhere pass over with indifference,—because the Painter was not a Man. . . . The Vatican is great; yet poor to Chimborazo of the Peak of Teneriffe; its dome is but a foolish Big-endian or Little-endian chip of an egg-shell, compared with that star-fretted dome where Arcturus and Orion glance forever; which latter, notwithstanding, who looks at, save perhaps some necessitous star-gazer bent to make Almanacs. (*Works*, XXVIII, p. 46)

In one of his later essays 'Shooting Niagara', regarded by many critics as one of the least attractive and defensible for many reasons, he resorts to this device again and again. There are frequent references to Heaven and Earth and to God's Universe. At a particularly significant point in the essay at which he refers to the 'perennial Miracle of Man' and his connection to his Maker, who is Eternal in the Heavens, Carlyle again falls back on Kant and what he calls '*visible* Infinities': '"Two things," says the memorable Kant, deepest and most logical of Metaphysical Thinkers, "Two Things strike me dumb: the infinite Starry Heaven; and the Sense of Right and Wrong in Man" ' (*Works*, XXX, p. 29). At another important place in the essay he describes his 'Practical hero, Aristocrat by nature', standing face to face and hand to hand, all his days, 'in life-battle with Practical Chaos . . . slowly coercing it into Cosmos' (*Works*, XXX, pp. 45–6).

These 'emblematic' messages occur throughout *Cromwell* and *Frederick*, although in these they are, in fact, because of the nature of the works themselves, flashed only from time to time. Also, as one might expect, Carlyle reserves the best of them for his heroes. Frederick, Carlyle describes at the very beginning: ' "Those eyes," says Mirabeau, "which, at the bidding of his great soul, fascinated you with seduction or with terror. . . ." Most excellent potent brilliant eyes, swift-darting as the stars, stedfast as the sun; gray, we said, of the azure-gray colour; large enough, not of glaring size; the habitual expression of them vigilance and penetrating sense, rapidly resting on depth' (*Works*, XII, p. 2). Cromwell's true nature must be recognised too. In his 'elucidation' of a letter of Cromwell's Carlyle chides the Reverend Mark Noble, who was able to find in the letter only that 'Oliver was once a very dissolute man', and concludes:

> O my reverend imbecile friend, hadst thou thyself never any moral life, but only a sensitive and digestive? Thy soul never longed towards the serene heights, all hidden from thee; and thirsted as the hart in dry places where no waters be? It was never a sorrow for thee that the eternal pole-star had gone out, veiled itself in dark clouds. (*Works*, VI, p. 102)

At another point in his *Cromwell* Carlyle comments on a letter in which Cromwell has cited Psalm 85: 'What a vision of celestial hope is this! vista into Lands of Light; God's Will done on Earth; this poor English Earth an Emblem of Heaven. . . . O Oliver, I could weep,—and yet it steads not. Do not I too look into "Psalms," into a kind of Eternal Psalm, unalterable as adamant,—which the whole world yet will look into?' (*Works*, VII, p. 308). In this same letter Cromwell's reference to 'Luther's Psalm' sets Carlyle's 'emblematic' imagination off once more: 'Psalm Forty-sixth; of which Luther's Paraphrase, *Eine feste Burg ist unser Gott*, is still very celebrated'. Carlyle then elucidates: 'We shall not again hear a Supreme Governor talk in this strain: the dialect of it is very obsolete. . . . The spirit of it will have to revive itself again; and shine out in *new* dialect and vesture, in infinitely wider compass, wide as God's known Universe *now* is,—if it please Heaven!' (*Works*, VIII, pp. 309, 311). In describing the discipline of the Prussian Army under Frederick, Carlyle cannot resist: 'Never will Valori forget the discipline of these Prussians, and how they marched. . . . Wholly in order, wholly silent. . . . Steady a Time; and, except that their shoes are not of felt, silent as he. The Austrian watchfires grow silent manifold to leftward yonder; [then the inevitable 'emblem'] silent overhead are the stars:—the path of all duty, too, is silent . . . for every well-drilled man' (*Works*, XVI, p. 118).

Carlyle's final tributes to both men are phrased in emblematic speech. Of Cromwell he writes:

> Truly it is a great scene of World-History, this in old Whitehall: Oliver Cromwell drawing nigh to his end. The exit of Oliver Cromwell and of English Puritanism; a great Light, one of our few authentic Solar Luminaries, going down now amid the clouds of Death. Like the setting of a great victorious Summer Sun; its course now finished. (*Works*, IX, p. 201)

On Frederick's death:

> Yes, reader;—and what is well worth your attention, you will have difficulty to find, in the annals of any Creed, a King or man who stood more faithfully to his duty; and, till the last hour, alone concerned himself with doing that. . . . One day, sitting for a while out of doors, gazing into the Sun, he was heard to murmur, 'Perhaps I shall be nearer thee soon:' . . . There is traceable only a complete superiority to Fear and Hope. (*Works*, XIX, p. 291)

While one may disagree with those who claim *Sartor Resartus* to be the greatest of Carlyle's works, there is much evidence to show that *Sartor* is the work that contains the most brilliant examples of his emblematic manner. In 'The Everlasting Yea', for instance, there are at least two that illustrate most effectively his art in this respect. The first, in fact, might be dismissed as either Carlylean rhetorical fancy or simply an attempt at an imitation of the Book of Revelation; however, since it is 'emblematic', one knows immediately that Carlyle wants it to be given much weight. Indeed, as Harrold points out, the Novalian influence is particularly evident in this passage; and, as one reads it, one is in fact reminded of Carlyle's praise of Novalis as poet as well as philosopher.

Here is the first passage, which the 'editor' has transcribed in its entirety:

> Beautiful it was to sit there, as in my skyey Tent, musing and meditating; on the high table-land, in front of the Mountains; over me, as roof, the azure Dome, and around me, for walls, four azure-flowing curtains,—namely, of the Four azure Winds, on whose bottom-fringes also I have seen gilding. And then to fancy the fair Castles that stood sheltered in these Mountain hollows; with their green flower-lawns, and white dames and damosels, lovely enough; or better still, the straw-roofed Cottages, wherein stood many a Mother baking bread, with her children round her;—all hidden and protectingly folded-up in the valley-folds; yet there and alive, as sure as if I beheld them. Or to see, as well as fancy, the nine Towns and Villages, that lay round my mountain-seat, which, in still weather, were wont to speak to me (by their steeple-bells) with metal tongue; and, in almost all weather, proclaimed their vitality by repeated Smoke-clouds; whereon, as on a culinary horologe, I might read the hour of the day. . . . Not uninteresting! For you have the whole Borough, with all its love-makings and scandal-mongeries, contentions and contentments, as in miniature, and could cover it all with your hat.—If, in my wide Wayfarings, I had learned to look into the business of the World in its details, here perhaps was the place for combining it into general propositions, and deducing inferences therefrom. (*Works*, I, pp. 149–50)

It also comes as no surprise, then, that at the point of *Sartor* that Harrold calls its 'first great climax' Carlyle employs this same type of image and invokes the everlasting Luminaries, the skyey vault, and a heaven-encompassed World. As the 'hour of Spiritual Enfranchisement' approaches, Carlyle writes:

> But it is with man's Soul as it was with Nature: the beginning of Creation is—Light. Till the eye have vision, the whole members

> are in bonds. Divine moment, when over the tempest-tost Soul, as once over the wild-weltering Chaos, it is spoken: Let there be Light! Ever to the greatest that has felt such a moment, is it not miraculous and God-announcing; even as, under simpler figures, to the simplest and least. The mad primeval Discord is hushed; the rudely-jumbled conflicting elements bind themselves into separate Firmaments: deep silent rock-foundations are built beneath; and the skyey vault with its everlasting Luminaries above: instead of a dark wasteful Chaos, we have a blooming, fertile, heaven-encompassed World.

Predictably, Carlyle turns from the skyey-vault to the human world, and proclaims one of his favourite doctrines: the Gospel of Work:

> I too could now say to myself: Be no longer a Chaos, but a World, or even Worldkin. Produce! Produce! Were it but the pitifullest infinitesimal fraction of a Product, produce it, in God's name! 'Tis the utmost thou hast in thee: out with it, then, Up, up! Whatsoever thy hand findeth to do, do it with they whole might. Work while it is called Today; for the Night cometh, wherein no man can work. (*Works*, I, p. 157)

In much the same way his 'emblematic' descriptions of the mountains in *Sartor Resartus* and of the prospect from Arthur's Seat (contained in a letter to his brother) resonate with intimations of the supernatural within the natural. The seeming realistic 'natural' descriptions reflect those same qualities he was always praising: order, power, beauty, action, wonder. Much is left unsaid in the letter, but one sees the same emblematic thrust found in much more detail in the longer mountain passage. He writes to his brother:

> [The wet weather] prevented me from breathing the air of Arthur's seat, a mountain close beside us where the atmosphere is pure as a diamond, and the prospect grander than any you ever saw. The blue majestic, everlasting ocean, with the Fife hills swelling gradually into the Grampians behind it on the north; rough crags and rude precipices at our feet ('where not a hillock rears its head unsung') with Edinburgh at their base, clustering proudly over her rugged foundations, and covering

> with a vapoury mantle the jagged, black, venerable masses of stonework, that stretch far and wide and shew like a city of fairy-land—There's for you, man! I saw it all last evening—when the sun was going down—and the moon's fine crescent (like a pretty silver creature as it is) was riding quietly above me. Such a sight does one good. (*CL*, I, pp. 338–9)

The presence of the everlasting luminaries, rough crags and precipices, masses of stonework, rugged foundations and city of fairy-land (usually the celestial city) supports the notion that Carlyle has either just told or is going to tell his brother something rather serious, and, in fact, he has just been lamenting his idleness, 'with no hand in the game of life, where I have yet so much to win. . . . I must do or die, . . . and Edin*r* with all its drawbacks is the only scene for me. . . . In summer I must endeavour most sternly, for this state of things cannot last' (*CL*, I, p. 338).

The mountain passage in *Sartor Resartus*, as I have already suggested, has much wider and deeper implications, although its emblematic procedure is the same. Here is the first part of the passage:

> Mountains were not new to him; but rarely are Mountains seen in such combined majesty and grace as here. . . . In fine vicissitude, Beauty alternates with Grandeur: you ride through stony hollows, along strait passes, traversed by torrents, overhung by high walls of rock; now winding amid broken shaggy chasms, and huge fragments; now suddenly emerging into some emerald valley, where the streamlet collects itself into a Lake, and man has again found a fair dwelling, and it seems as if Peace had established herself in the bosom of Strength. (*Works*, I, p. 122)

As other passages of this kind, this one occurs at an important point in the novel. It comes just before 'the Everlasting No' and contributes to the irony and the pathos of that chapter. It comes, too, just before Teufelsdröckh turns 'pilgrim', just before he leaves his native Entepfuhl, and just before the remarks on 'view-hunting', the new malady of the spiritual sort. The contrast is thus clearly depicted, and the difference between 'eating the glass' and the 'silent experience', the communion with Nature that the Wanderer experiences immediately before Herr Towgood and Blumine appear, is especially effective.

In this context one is able to see certain principles of organisation emerging from the description; it follows, in some ways, Carlyle's approving evaluation of what the German poets were able to accomplish with their clear eye and loving heart. The rocks, rugged, gigantic, once bare, are now covered with a garment of foliage or verdure. The Wanderer proceeds through the 'wilds of Nature', where 'Beauty alternates with Grandeur'; next Carlyle presents specific, concrete details: stony hollows, strait passages, traversed by torrents, high walls of rock, broken shaggy chasms, huge fragments. All of a sudden the Wanderer enters 'some emerald valley, where the streamlet collects itself into a lake, and man has again found a fair dwelling, and [here occurs Carlyle's notion of a reconciliation] it seems as if Peace had established herself in the bosom of Strength'. The Carlylean and the Divine characteristics have emerged as the natural and supernatural have coalesced. Whatever one's reaction to the success or failure of the passage, it seems clear that in this instance there is no simple view-hunting. Echoes of his German and scientific readings, his own religious faith and his family heritage are apparent, with the 'pilgrim' wandering through the valley and hills, struggling towards the 'fair dwelling'.

Carlyle, however, is not done, for Teufelsdröckh, at this stage of the novel, is still a 'son of Time'; he goes on to indicate what the possibilities are, even for the poor pilgrim. The Wanderer rides into the Valley, emerges aloft, and finds himself 'again lifted into the evening sunset light', where he pauses and gazes round. Once more Carlyle speaks 'emblematically', one might say 'poetically', stressing the concrete as well as the transcendental. His aim is to demonstrate, through what for him represents some quintessential 'natural description', that which he has been attempting to put forward as the essence of Novalis' ideas about Nature and the Deity; the conclusion of the mountain passage in *Sartor*, I think, is Carlyle's own attempt at such an image or emblem:

> The mountain-ranges are beneath your feet, and folded together: Only the loftier summits look down here and there as on a second plain; lakes also lie clear and earnest in their solitude. No trace of man now visible; unless indeed it were he who

fashioned that little visible link of Highway, here, as would seem, scaling the inaccessible, to unite Province with Province. But sun-wards, lo you! how it towers sheer up, a world of Mountains, the diadem and centre of the mountain region! A hundred and a hundred savage peaks, in the last light of Day; all glowing, of gold and amethyst, like giant spirits of the wilderness; there in their silence, in their solitude, even as on the night when Noah's Deluge first dried! Beautiful, nay solemn, was the sudden aspect to our Wanderer. He gazed over those stupendous masses with wonder, almost with longing desire; never till this hour had he known Nature, that she was One, that she was his Mother and divine. As the ruddy glow was fading into clearness in the sky, and the Sun had now departed, a murmur of Eternity and Immensity, of Death and of Life, stole through his soul; and he felt as if Death and Life were one, as if the Earth were not dead, as if the Spirit of the Earth had its throne in that splendour, and his own spirit were therewith holding communion. (*Works*, I, pp. 122–3)

17

Wonder, Metaphor and Fact

The unique character of the Carlylean–Novalian image reflected in the mountain passage cited above becomes even clearer when one remembers Carlyle's sense of wonder, a word he uses often implicitly and explicitly. He had written not only of mighty glimpses into the 'spiritual Universe' and the possibility of 'supernatural (really natural) influences'; he had also talked of every living man being a 'living mystery: he walks between two Eternities and two Infinitudes'. Perhaps Carlyle's attitude is summed up best by his statement: 'Wonderful Universe! Were our eyes but opened, what a "secret" were it that we daily see and handle, without heed!' (*2NB*, p. 142). Carlyle's sense of wonder and his constant use of the word 'miracle' are connected, of course, with his emphasis on the 'Spiritual Force' behind the laws of Nature, and these concepts also reflect his attitude towards art. His ideas and his way of expressing them metaphorically are linked.

Indeed, the emphasis on the 'wonderful' is particularly significant, for it helps explain his reliance on metaphor. 'He was unobtrusive, but when asked for his opinion he gave it in his metaphoric manner' (Froude, III, p. 9). 'As to this metaphorical talent', Carlyle himself wrote in his *Journal* (1822) 'it is the first characteristic of genius. . . . It denotes an inward eye quick to perceive the relations & analogies of things; a ready memory to furnish them when occasion demands; and a sense of propriety & beauty to select what is best, from the immense store so furnished' (*2NB*, p. 30). 'What am I but a sort of Ghost?' he noted another time. What a miracle is all existence', he wrote to Jane in 1835 (Froude, III, p. 20); while in his *Journal* for 1836 we find: '[Life] is fearful and wonderful to me' (*2NB*, p. 73).

One of the most moving passages is his description of Mrs Welsh's grave in 1843:

> Nobody knew me. I sate two minutes in Thornhill Street, unsuspected by all men, a kind of ghost among men. The day was windless: the earth stood still: grey mist rested on the tops of the green hills, the vacant brown moors: silence as of eternity rested over the world. It was like a journey through the kingdoms of the dead, one Hall of Spirits till I got past Crawford. . . . I was as a spirit in the land of spirits, called land of the living. (Froude, III, p. 323)

At times this sense of wonder, this inward eye, and the metaphoric expression come together felicitously: 'Then sawest thou that this fair Universe . . . is in very deed the star-doomed [*sic*] City of God;[1] that through every star, through every grass-blade, and most through every living soul, the glory of a present God still beams. But Nature, which is the Time-vesture of God, and reveals Him to the wise, hides Him from the foolish' (*Works*, I, p. 210).

There are times when this metaphorical thought becomes translated into what for Carlyle does indeed become fact, and this 'leap' or insight constitutes the basis for the climactic chapter in *Sartor*, 'Natural Supernaturalism'. This chapter is filled with 'Natural' imagery taken from the heavens, and it becomes, in Carlylean 'coterie' writing, the key to Carlyle's 'prophetic' vision. The following is typical: 'Are we not Spirits, that are shaped into a body, into an Appearance; and that fade away again into air and Invisibility? This is no metaphor, it is a simple scientific *fact*; we start out of Nothingness, take figure and are Apparitions; round us, as round the veriest spectre, is Eternity; and to Eternity minutes are as years and aeons' (*Works*, I, p. 211). Another incorporates the cosmological:

> We speak of the Volume of Nature: and truly a volume it is,—whose Author and Writer is God. To read it! Dost thou, does man, so much as well know the Alphabet thereof? With its words, Sentences, and great descriptive Pages, poetical and philosophical, spread out through Solar Systems, and Thousands of Years, we shall not try thee. It is a Volume written in celestial hieroglyphs, in the true Sacred-writing of which even Prophets are happy that they can read here a line and there a line. . . . That Nature is more than some boundless Volume of such Recipes, or huge, well-nigh inexhaustible Domestic-Cookery Book, of which the whole secret will in this manner one day evolve itself, the fewest dream. (*Works*, I, pp. 205–6)

Perhaps one of the finest examples of Carlyle's 'metaphoric manner' reveals his ability to bring together 'organically' the natural and supernatural, the basis of his unique ability to evoke a sense of wonder. The passage is indeed a *tour de force* but it retains a Carlylean 'solidity' and 'factualness' that keep it from evaporating into Emersonian 'moonshine':

> Were it not wonderful, for instance, had Orpheus, or Amphion, built the walls of Thebes by the mere sound of his Lyre? Yet tell me, Who built these walls of Weissnichtwo; summoning out all the sandstone rocks, to dance along from the *Steinbruch* (now a huge Troglodyte Chasm, with frightful green-mantled pools); and shape themselves into Doric and Ionic pillars, squared ashlar houses and noble streets? Was it not the still higher Orpheus, or Orpheuses, who, in past centuries, by the divine Music of Wisdom, succeeded in civilising Man? Our highest Orpheus walked in Judea, eighteen-hundred years ago: his sphere-melody, flowing in wild native tones, took captive and ravished souls of men; and, being of true sphere-melody still flows and sounds, though now with thousandfold accompaniments, and rich symphonies, through all our hearts; and modulates, and divinely leads them. Is that a wonder, which happens in two hours; and does it cease to be wonderful if happening in two million? Not only was Thebes built by the music of an Orpheus; but without the music of some inspired Orpheus was no city ever built, no work that man glories in ever done. (*Works*,I, pp. 209–10)

'The man who cannot wonder', Carlyle wrote, 'who does not habitually wonder (and worship), were he President of inumerable Royal Societies, and carried the whole *Mécanique Céleste* and *Hegel's Philosophy*, and the epitome of all Laboratories and Observatories . . . in his single head,—is but a Pair of Spectacles behind which there is no Eye' (*Works*, I, p. 54). It is this sense of wonder that drove Carlyle to write and speak in emblems. His praise of Goethe as prophet and literature as 'religion' was due to these concepts of his, concepts ultimately aesthetic as well as substantive. In the chapter entitled 'Organic Filaments', for instance, he could make what seemed to many extravagant and 'heretical' claims for literature:

> 'But there is no Religion?' reiterates the Professor. 'Fool! I tell thee, there is, Hast thou well considered all that lies in this immeasurable froth-ocean we name LITERATURE? Fragments of a genuine Church-*Homiletic* lie scattered there, which Time will assort: nay fractions even of a *Liturgy* could I point out. And knowest thou no Prophet, even in this vesture, environment, and dialect of this age? None to whom the Godlike has revealed itself, through all meanest and highest forms of the Common; and by him been again prophetically revealed: in whose inspired melody, even in these rag-gathering and rag-burning days, Man's Life again begins, were it but afar off, to be divine? Knowest thou none such? O know him, and name him—Goethe.' (*Works*, I, pp. 201–2)

In evaluating the Carlylean assertive image, then, one needs to think not so much in terms of rhetorical flourishes as in his own concept of inspired melody, fragments of a genuine Church-Homiletic. The eye rather than the spectacles assumes importance, and the ability to see is the ability to think and write metaphorically and emblematically. One is reminded of Conrad's famous 'Preface' to *The Nigger of the Narcissus* and Emerson's naked eyeball. The inward eye that perceives relations and analogies assures metaphorical talent, but all is guided by a 'sense of propriety and beauty to select what is best, from the immense store so furnished'.

Metaphors become 'Fact' for Carlyle, and this very strong belief leads to some interesting consequences in reading his works. Sanders, whose various studies of Carlyle are indispensable, begins one of his essays by citing from Allingham a quotation by Carlyle on the stars: 'I care very little about the stars. I look round upon my fellow-creatures' (*CFS*, p. 3). Sanders then goes on to show that this illustrates a conflict in Carlyle's nature, between his interest in man and his strongly antisocial tendencies, 'a conflict that also proved to be lifelong'. Looked at from the perspective of 'natural supernaturalism' however, there would, in fact, be no conflict at all; one could indeed state that in a Carlylean sense the world of stars was the world of man. Harrold seems unable to avoid the same trap when commenting on the later Carlyle. 'By the time Carlyle began the writing of *Cromwell* (late in 1843)', he writes,

> His universe had become considerably simplified. His old preoccupations with space, time, reason, organism, symbolism, 'revelation,' had all become merely the background, or the premise, of his more specific concerns. . . . God had become less the Divine idea and more the Maker, less the Being whom Faust dared not name, and more the Jehovah of eternal law and wrath, namable by Carlyle in scores of passages in thundering rhetoric. (Harrold, p. 236)

Once again, as in Tillotson, we find the suggestion that Carlyle came to depend on rhetoric, the bugles; whereas one could make the case that he simply expected his readers to recognise his assertive images and let these carry the weight of his 'old preoccupations'. Carlyle, after his early writings, expected the emotive power of the familiar imagery, the logical arguments so often made through it and the 'true-melody' to carry the burden of his message. One has to keep in mind that Carlyle always relied on coterie speech, and his writing was no different.

His approach in *Reminiscences* reflects this reliance. His father was 'looking towards "a city that *had* foundations" '. A letter to his sister reveals the same blending of the natural and the supernatural, the human and divine:

> The horse . . . carries me out into the clear afternoon air, the bright greenness of the world; shews me how like Elysium it is. . . . I go little into the Town; call on nobody there; . . . Our old wooden Battersea Bridge takes me over the River . . .; in ten minutes' swift trotting I am fairly away from the Monster and its bricks; all lies behind me like an enormous world-filling *pfluister*, infinite potter's furnace,—sea of smoke, with steeples, domes, gilt crosses, high black architecture swimming in it: really beautiful to look at from some knoll top, while the sun shines on it. I plug away, away, some half-dozen miles out. The Monster is then quite buried,—its smoke rising like a great dusky-coloured mountain, melting into the infinite clear sky: all is green, musical, bright; one feels that it is God's world this, and not an infinite Cockneydom of *stoor* and din after all! (*CL*, XII, p. 168)

The emblematic statements are limitless. 'The general sum of human Action is a whole Universe. . . . History strive[s] . . . to secure for us some oversight of the Whole' (*Works*, XXVII, p. 95). 'Behind us, . . . lie Six Thousand Years of human effort, human conquest: before us is the boundless Time with its yet uncreated and unconquered Continents and Eldorados, which we, even we, have to conquer, to create: and from the bosom of Eternity there shine for us celestial guiding stars' (*Works*, XXVIII, p. 43). From *On Heroes and Hero-Worship*:

> The latest generations of men will find new messages in Shakespeare, new elucidations of their own human being; 'new harmonies with the infinite structure of the Universe; concurrences with later ideas, affinities with the higher powers and senses of man.' . . . Such a man's works . . . grow up withal *un*consciously from the unknown deeps in him;—as the oaktree grows from the Earth's bosom, as the mountains and waters shape themselves; with a symmetry grounded on Nature's own laws, conformable to all Truth whatsoever. (*Works*, V, p. 108)

These few quotations suggest a far greater danger in not reading Carlyle's metaphoric message correctly than failing to appreciate his art—that is, the danger of failing to understand his message. LaValley, for instance, in his admirable study of Carlyle's 'modernity', does not grasp the ultimately optimistic note in Carlyle because he misses the 'emblematic' meaning. LaValley puts far too much weight on the editor's view of Teufelsdröckh as 'some incarnate Mephistopheles'; he completely misreads the Carlylean image and Teufelsdröckh's supernatural (really natural) approach towards 'this great terrestial and celestial Round, . . . where kings and beggars, and angels and demons, and stars and streetsweepings, were chaotically whirled'. To conclude from that that 'the fullness of meaning paradoxically seems to lead to meaninglessness' is to fail to grasp the coterie note and the 'true sphere-melody' of Carlyle's metaphoric manner.[2]

Even in his most pessimistic periods, Carlyle's 'message' seems more optimistic than he himself appears to be. In *Latter-Day Pamphlets*, often considered his most pessimistic work, the imagery seems, as Jules Siegel has stated, 'consistently negative'. 'One might say', continues Siegel, 'that Carlyle is describing a true social hell'; Carlyle's images, Siegel concludes, 'of darkness, aggression, and confusion, mud-pythons, dung heaps, beaver intellect, "spiritual Vampires and obscene Nightmares", and the "world-wide jungle of redtape", are attached to this central image of the Pig Philosophy' (*CPP*, pp. 167–8). Even in this work, however, filled as it is with images of chaos, filth and slime, Carlyle's 'prophetic vision', depicted by the now-familiar assertive image, overrides the pessimistic 'central image' of the *Pamphlets*: 'Wise obedience and wise command, I foresee that the regimenting of Pauper Banditti into Soldiers of Industry is but the beginning of the blessed process, which will extend to the topmost heights of our Society; and, in the course of generations, make us all once more a Governed Commonwealth, and *Civitas Dei*, if it please God!' (*Works*, xx, p. 166). If one remembers his tribute to his father: 'Looking towards a city that *had* foundations', one knows at once that this passage contains the heart of Carlyle's true feeling and serves to offset the negative imagery.

A better understanding and appreciation of Carlyle's assertive image would preclude the conclusion Siegel arrives at:

> Society, indeed the Victorian world, is the scene of a cosmic night battle. Democracy, on the one hand, is a reality and will not retreat, and the laws of nature, on the other hand, are inflexible and hierarchical, as Carlyle sees them. What we have is a confrontation out of which Carlyle, in the overview of the *Latter-Day Pamphlets*, is unable to imagine a resynthesis along the lines of *Sartor Resartus*, *Past and Present*, or *The French Revolution*. . . . Carlyle . . . feels himself led towards personal disillusionment and self-destruction. (*CPP*, p. 165)

This is far too extreme and misleading, for one must not be led astray by what Siegel calls the 'consistently negative' imagery of the *Pamphlets*; by this time, as I have said, Carlyle has come to expect the reader to recognise his 'positive' imagery. In contrast to the images of chaos, filth, slime, dungheaps, Carlyle consistently uses images of the Universe that one has come to expect: the everlasting luminaries, the sky, the eternal melodies, the eternal law. The imagery brings together his various ideas, by this time well known to those who are familiar with his other writings: the Bible, German idealism, his ideas from Newton and science, his Calvinistic concepts of work, duty, the Divine, and, of course, his sense of order, miracles and wonder. To talk of the impossibility of a 'resynthesis' is to ignore both the extensive, indeed pervasive, use of this image in the *Pamphlets*, as well as the depth of meaning it had for Carlyle personally.

The use in *Pamphlets* ranges from single words to whole paragraphs. In the first essay Carlyle refers to 'this divine Universe' and the need for an 'eye' to recognise it. He asks, later in the essay, 'How decipher, with best fidelity, the eternal regulation of the Universe; and read, from amid such confused embroilments of human clamour and folly, what the real Divine Message to us is? A divine message, or eternal regulation of the Universe, there verily is' (*Works*, xx, pp. 12, 17). In 'The New Downing Street' he refers to 'the blessed continents and delectable mountains', and he concludes that essay by praising Peel, who has 'a virtual England at his back, and an actual eternal sky above him' (*Works*, xx, pp. 168, 171). In 'Hudson's Statue' he becomes more 'technical':

> Will the law of gravitation 'abate' for you? Gravitation acts at the rate of sixteen feet per second, in spite of all prayers. Were it the crash of a Solar System, or the fall of a Yarmouth Herring, all one to gravitation. . . . You did not know that the Universe had *laws* of right and wrong; you fancied the Universe was an oblivious greedy blockhead, like one of yourselves. (*Works*, xx, p. 288)

In 'Stump-Orator' he is more cryptic: 'True, all human talent, especially all deep talent, is a talent to *do*, and is intrinsically of silent nature; inaudible, like the sphere Harmonies and Eternal Melodies, of which it is an incarnated fraction' (*Works*, xx, p. 185). In 'Hudson's Statue' he warns: 'What if Rhadamanthus doomed him rather, let us say, to ride in Express-trains, now hither, for twenty-five aeons, or to hang in Heaven as a Locomotive Constellation, and be a sign forever!' (*Works*, xx, p. 267).

That the Universe was both real and ideal to Carlyle rapidly becomes apparent to one who reads these essays; he thought of it as he thought of his native Ecclefechan. It was concrete, but also it was a reflection of one's own soul, which, in turn, determined one's Heaven. 'It is your own falsity', he states, 'that makes the Universe incredible. I affirm to you, this Universe, . . . is the express image and direct counterpart of the human souls, and their thoughts and activities, who dwell there'. He then falls back on an emblem:

> The first heroic soul sent down into this world, he, looking up into the sea of stars, around into the moaning forests and big oceans, into life and death, love and hate, and joy and sorrow, and the illimitable loud-thundering Loom of Time,—was struck dumb by it . . .; to him the 'open secret of his Universe' was no longer quite a secret, but he had caught a glimpse of it. (*Works*, xx, pp. 333–4)

Carlyle then concludes the essay, and the entire series of *Pamphlets*, with an 'optimistic' call, one not much different from the 'resynthesis' found in his other works:

> My friends, across these fogs of murky twaddle and philanthropism, in spite of sad decadent 'world-trees,' with their rookeries of foul creatures,—the silent stars, and all the eternal luminaries of the world, shine even now to him that has an eye. In this day as in all days, around and in every man, are voices from the gods, imperative to all, if obeyed by even none, which say audibly, 'Arise, thou son of Adam, son of Time; make this thing more divine; and that thing,—and thyself, of all things; and work, and sleep not; for the Night cometh, wherein no man can work!' He that has an ear may still hear. (*Works*, xx, p. 335)

'Under this brutal stagnancy there lies painfully imprisoned some tendency which could become heroic', Carlyle writes; he that has an ear can still hear the Carlylean metaphoric message, but he has to know what to listen for. The sensitive ear, the all-seeing eye, a pure religious temper and the heartfelt love of Nature, all these are necessary to bring one into true poetic relation with the spiritual and material world; they also help when one reads Carlyle's works.

The genuine Carlylean note is seen most clearly in the chapter 'Natural Supernaturalism' in *Sartor Resartus*, a note found in all of his writings. This climactic chapter is filled with 'natural imagery' taken from the heavens, earth and the universe, and it becomes the keys to grasping the Carlylean prophetic vision. In using the words 'wonder' and 'miracle', in emphasising the 'Spiritual Force' that lies behind the Laws of Nature and in expressing these ideas metaphorically and emblematically rather than straightforwardly; Carlyle himself demonstrates the close connection between his ideas and his way of expressing them. The Universe itself was the immense store for Carlyle. Carlyle's sense of wonder, too often ignored or simply forgotten, ultimately provides the basis for his ability to combine the supernatural and the natural, the spiritual and the real.

18

The Ulyssean Strain: The Projection of Self

'The older Carlyle got, the less he liked to speculate about aesthetics', writes Georg Tennyson; '. . . the pre-*Sartor* Carlyle is far from being a man without an aesthetic' (*SCR*, p. 88). True enough, given the preoccupation revealed in his *Journal*; for the rest, his post-*Sartor* writings can be categorised in various ways. Raymond Williams sees the 'larger part of Carlyle's writing' as 'the imaginative re-creation of men of noble power'. Saintsbury declares that although Carlyle's work 'is very great and [has] apparent variety', it

> will be found that history and her sister biography, even when his subjects bore an appearance of difference, always in reality engaged his attention. His three greatest books, containing more than half his work in bulk,—*The French Revolution*, the *Cromwell*, and the *Frederick*,—are all openly and avowedly historical. The *Schiller* and the *Sterling* are biographies; the *Sartor Resartus* a fantastic autobiography. Nearly all the Essays, even those which are not literary in subject—all the *Lectures on Heroes*, the greater part of *Past and Present*, *The Early Kings of Norway*, the *John Knox*, are more or less plainly and strictly historical or biographical. Even *Chartism*, the non-antique part of *Past and Present*, and the *Latter-Day Pamphlets*, deal with politics.[1]

There are, then, a number of approaches one could take to Carlyle: historiographer, biographer, journalist/essayist. One could even use Carlyle's own definition and view him as philosopher, one who could, in his own terms, use 'systematic discourse' rather than 'imaginative creation'. Saintsbury does, indeed, along with other critics, classify Carlyle as philosopher as well as historian. One could also use Carlyle's own terms and view his works as, ultimately, examples of one who failed to 'body forth' his insights into 'the Divine Idea of the World', as had Goethe, Schiller and other German writers. His work would remain the work of one who was able to convey or communicate the spirit of the age, but one who was unable 'emblematically' or figuratively to wed 'the unchanging essence of poetry to modern subject matter' (*SCR*, p. 90).

There is, however, one other way one can view Carlyle's influence and career and life. It is one thing to see a writer fail to live up to his own criteria; this is not an unusual phenomenon. One could simply say that Carlyle opted, in terms of two traditional functions of literature, for that which instructs rather than that which pleases. There would be nothing surprising about that. Tennyson, Arnold, Browning, Swinburne, all had that choice. In Carlyle's case, however, there were other reasons for the direction his writing ultimately took, not the least of which were his own personality and his early 'scientific' and empirical reading. His inability to blend Art and Religion, to merge these without 'hostility', is due in part to his awareness of Fact, an awareness that came to him early and never left him. In describing the influence of Carlyle on his age, Tillotson emphasises his own dismissal of what was 'cloudy'. One reason that Carlyle preferred to write history rather than fiction was that 'one has substantive stuff between one's fingers', not 'those slime and sea-sand ladders to the moon opinions'. 'It was true', Tillotson concludes, 'that he could be cloudy with the best of them, but also true that he had an abundance . . . of concrete soundness in him that did so much to help mid-century literature to its feet'. Even his injunction for the Poet to 'see', Tillotson reminds us, 'was used, first and foremost, in its straightforward sense, which applied to the bodily eyes, even if its secondary sense was almost as important' (Tillotson, pp. 85–6).

The point is a significant one; while praising Reason, Carlyle did not deny that man also had Understanding. One of the reasons for his disparagement of Coleridge was that too often Coleridge stayed 'cloudy'. As I have already suggested, one of the Coleridgean deficiencies was his fuzziness; Carlyle, with his sense of the concrete, of fact, missed that 'noble indignation at some injustice or depravity, rubbing elbows with us on this solid Earth'. I have, additionally, already indicated Carlyle's debt to Hume; he had been impressed by his essays, which Carlyle had found 'better than anything I have read these many days'. Carlyle had been impressed, too, with Hume's 'manner': 'the highest & most difficult effect of art—the appearance of its absence—appears throughout'.

As an 'enlightened' sceptic, Carlyle, keenly aware of the need for epistemological discriminations, did not dismiss completely the real. That there is a connection between his interest in 'science' and his belief in the 'real' is sometimes often forgotten. A significant entry in his *Journal* occurs at a crucial point in his career; he is being urged to apply for a professorship, but he wants to write. Writing, however, to him no longer means 'poetry', since 'true poetry', which is connected with the 'real', seems beyond him; 'natural' and 'magical' seems to be coming closer together:

> Dr. Irving advises immediate application for a certain Glasgow Astronomy Professorship. I shall hardly trouble myself with it. *Deeply* impressed with the transiency of Time; more and more careless about all that Time can give or take away. Could undertake to teach astronomy . . . by way of honest day-labour: not otherwise. . . . To *teach* any of the things I am interested in were for the present impossible; all is unfixed, nothing has as yet grown; at best is but growing. . . . Have long been almost idle; have long been out of free communion with myself. Must *suffer* more before I can begin thinking. Will try to write: but what? but when?

Then comes the clue to his real concern; he is beginning to realise that he is not, cannot be, 'true' poet: 'Daily and yearly the world Natural grows more of a world Magical to me: this is as it should be. Daily, too, I see that there is no true poetry but in *Reality*. Wilt *thou* ever be a Poetkin! *Schwerlich* [hardly]. No matter.—' (*CL*, VI, pp. 299–300).

The presence of the 'Real' and its relation to the magical always was of concern to Carlyle. In 'Signs of the Times' it is true that he argues in favour of the 'spiritual' and blames Hume for the present situation:

> The last class of our Scotch Metaphysicians had a dim notion that much of this was wrong; but they knew not how to right it. The school of Reid had also from the first taken a mechanical course, not seeing any other. The singular conclusions at which

> Hume, setting out from their admitted premises, was arriving, brought this school into being; they let loose Instinct, as an undiscriminating ban-dog, to guard them against these conclusions,—they tugged lustily at the logical chain by which Hume was so coldly towing them and the world into bottomless abysses of Atheism and Fatalism. (*Works*, XXVII, pp. 64–5)

However, Carlyle is pointing out the dangers of extremism; rather than absolutely condemning Hume, he is showing the dangers of the complete sceptic. As an enlightened sceptic, Carlyle sees the need for balance:

> To define the limits of these two departments of man's activity [the Dynamic and Mechanic], which work into one another, and by means of one another, so intricately and inseparably, were by its nature an impossible attempt. Their relative importance, even to the wisest mind, will vary in different times, according to the special wants and disposition of those times. Meanwhile, it seems clear enough that only in the right coordination of the two, and the vigorous forewarding of *both*, does our true line of action lie. Undue cultivation of the inward or Dynamical province leads to idle, visionary, impracticable courses, and, especially in rude eras, to Superstition and Fanaticism. . . . Undue cultivation of the outward, again, though less immediately prejudicial, . . . must, in the long run, by destroying Moral Force, . . . prove . . . pernicious. (*Works*, XXVII, p. 73)

It is important to keep in mind, too, that Carlyle not only wished to be an Artist; at one time he had also wished, after praising the *Principia* as a work of 'undecaying majesty', that he were an Astronomer. He had asked, also, when there would arise the man who would do for the science of mind what Newton had done for matter. Finally, there is that underlying 'rational' turn of mind of Carlyle's, cultivated to a large extent in the 'rational University' described in *Sartor*. 'To the author of the *Reminiscences*', as Campbell has reminded us, 'there is virtue in a man who retains a strong and unquestioning religious belief of a strongly authoritarian nature, yet simultaneously a questioning turn of mind which takes nothing for granted' (*CHC*, p. 6). In terms of his own 'creative aesthetics' Carlyle was too much a 'sceptic' to become the Artist he wished to be, the Artist he saw in Goethe. He was too aware of Fact to ascribe completely to the theory of the unconscious in practice as well as theory; he was too suspicious of Beauty. Instead of projecting that which comes from within rather than mirroring that which is outside—imaginative creation—Carlyle retained too vivid a sense of what had been lacking in Coleridge and the other Romantics: that noble indignation at some injustice or depravity, rubbing elbows with us on this solid earth. Bluntly put, Carlyle remained the Artisan rather than the Artist. To characterise him in this way is by no means to diminish his role as Sage; the difference between philosopher and poet was the means of presentation rather than what was being said, and Carlyle's sense of rage against hypocrisy, stupidity and blind bureaucracy remained with him until his death.

The chief result of his 'failure' as artist was that the 'prophetic' strain became more and more prominent in his writings, and the tendency to prophesy rather than poeticise resulted in his willingness to settle for 'manufactured' products instead of works of art. He also was more and more willing to resort to 'preaching' or just plain haranguing rather than attempting to communicate through writings that contained 'musical thought'. The result was such pieces as *Latter-Day Pamphlets* and *Shooting Niagara: and After?* Since he was not a journalist and had no regular column or journal through which he could comment on those subjects that interested him, he had to depend more and more on his own reputation as Sage or Prophet to hold the interest of his public. Again, the result was predictable; with the declining interest in his opinion and ideas, which had been taken up by contemporaries and disciples and spread in their own works and in different forms, Carlyle came to expect his own strong personality to attract and hold readers and, most disastrously, to impose a unity on his works.[2]

There is a deep irony in all this, one which Carlyle himself would perhaps appreciate. That the chief exponent of German Idealism, the leading transcendentalist in nineteenth-century Britain, would emerge finally as a practitioner of a method that would seem to be the opposite of all he advocated would probably amuse the author of *Sartor*, an admirer of Burns and Cervantes. One could find this subjective inclination running throughout Carlyle's own life and writing, however, and its appearance should come as no surprise. Sterling himself, the most sympathetic disciple of Carlyle, had, in discussing the form of *Sartor*, 'aligned Carlyle with the "subjective" masters of modern literature—and put him in the company of Rabelais and Montaigne, Sterne and Swift, Cervantes and Jeremy Taylor'. Sterling also, DeLaura writes, had noted that 'the bond of one's own personality could be used as aesthetic justification for one's writing' (DeLaura, p. 731).[3]

That Carlyle should come to trust finally the resources of his own character and the deepest foundations of his own beliefs also should not surprise anyone familiar with his life and personality. His admiration of his father rested in large part on genuine affection and love, part of which involved Carlyle's recognition of his individualism, an individualism bordering on stubbornness (*CHC*, p. 15). One need only read the tribute to his father to see the large role this played in their relationship. The fine line between self-help and inflexibility is indeed something to be aware of, and Campbell's description of Carlyle as the 'lonely individual that Carlyle increasingly became' from 1833 on is significant when one comes to evaluate his character and his increasing reliance on the projection of self in his writing (*CHC*, p. 16). There is a letter to his brother in 1821 that one can cite as a prime example of self-confidence, if not inflexibility: 'I know there is within me something *different* from the vulgar herd of mortals; I think it is something *superior*; and if once I had overpassed those bogs and brakes and quagmires, that lie between me and the free arena, I shall make some fellows stand to the right and left—or I mistake me greatly. Then what a thing it will be!' (*CL*, I, p. 327). The notes of wishing for success, confidence in self and loneliness are all struck in a letter to his mother on Christmas Day of that year:

> I must begin—*the book*. . . . I wish for the sake of all my friends, and of none more than you—tho' you care little for such things—that I could make this work famous & to be held in estimation. Alas! that the spirit is so willing, the flesh so weak! However what is *in me* I shall do; and the production must be as Providence will have it. In the mean time, I am slowly gaining ground here . . . I have a great deal more confidence in myself (which you will say I did not want already) than I had last year; and I find people generally disposed to treat me with

> more respect. I find no person whom I can *love* in Edin*r*: but many whom I can spend an hour or so talking with. . . . (*CL*, I, pp. 418–19)

His 'independence' is demonstrated fully in a letter to his brother in which he is discussing a projected essay on the Civil War, the Commonwealth of England:

> If I live with even moderate health, I purpose to do this; and if I can but finish it according to my own conception of what it should be, I shall feel much happier than if I had inherited much gold & silver. The Critics too may say of it either nothing or any thing, according to their own good pleasure; if it once please my own mighty *self*, I do not value them or their opinion a single rush. Long habit has inured me to live with a very limited & therefore a dearer circle of approvers: all I aim at is to convince my own conscience that I have not taken their approbation without some just claims to it. (*CL*, II, p. 94)

Certainly his wanting to satisfy mainly himself is borne out by his refusal to change *Sartor* to suit public taste. When Althaus suggests that Carlyle had, in fact, done so, Carlyle writes: 'Not a letter of it altered; except in the *last* and the *first* page, a word or two!' Clubbe also notes that 'Carlyle stresses that, in changing nothing in *Sartor* except on the first and last pages, he bent neither to public opinion nor to pressure from the magazine's publisher, James Fraser'. Clubbe adds: 'That he made no significant alterations in *Sartor* became a point of honor with him'.[4]

There is also Irving's curious but fascinating letter in answer to Carlyle's request for an appraisal of his nature. The entire letter is of great interest to one wanting to know what Carlyle was like at this time (1822), but one statement leaps out with great meaning to one interested in knowing more of Carlyle's 'independence' of spirit: 'There are things which you reverence, religion, liberty, domestic ties, trusty friendship, female love, and above all the independence of the soul' (*CL*, II, p. 63).

The identical notes are also struck in Carlyle's *Journal*, from which Froude quotes. His father's son, Carlyle records his determination to be independent and not concern himself with the opinions of others. A typical entry reads: 'One's ears are bewildered by the inane chatter of the people; one's heart is for hours and days overcast by the sad feeling: "There is none then, not one, that will believe in me!" ' Carlyle shrugs this off: 'Meanwhile, continue to believe in *thyself.* Let the chattering of innumerable gigmen pass by thee as what it is. Wait thou on the bounties of thy unseen Taskmaster, on the hests of thy inward *Daemon.* . . . Be not weak' (Froude, II, p. 345).

This was written in 1833 and reveals Carlyle's true feelings; he is waiting for the word from either Taskmaster or inward Daemon. 'The four months' experience of Edinburgh had convinced Carlyle that there at least could be no permanent home for him. If driven to leave his "castle on the moor," it must be for London—only London' (Froude, II, p. 346). The next year was to see the move to London and a new life for him and Jane. The move represents a watershed in Carlyle's life: for while he still was to record in letters, journals and other writings his doubts and desires, the London years were to be the start of the 'Carlylean' phase of his life and writing. 'At this moment I write only in *treble,* . . . of a set of feelings that longs to express itself in the voice of thunder. Be still! Be still!' He adds: 'In *all* times there is a word which, spoken to men, to the actual generation of men, would thrill their inmost soul. But the way to find that word? The way to speak it when found? *Opus est consulto* with a vengeance' (Froude, II, p. 354).

Some years earlier, in his essay on Voltaire, Carlyle had written words that revealed his own hopes and the vision of his own career:

> True, the object of the Poet is, and must be, to 'instruct by pleasing,' yet not by pleasing this man and that man; only by pleasing *man,* by speaking to the pure nature of man, can any real 'instruction,' in this sense, be conveyed. Vain does it seem to search for a judgment of this kind in the largest Cafe. . . . The deep, clear consciousness of one mind comes infinitely nearer it, than the loud outcry of a million that have no such consciousness; whose 'talk,' or whose 'babble,' but distracts the listener; and to most genuine Poets has, from of old, been in a great measure indifferent. For the multitude of voices is no authority; a thousand voices may not, strictly examined, amount to one vote. (*Works,* XXVI, pp. 421–2)

He concludes, sadly, regarding Voltaire: 'Fame seems a far too high, if not the highest object with him; nay, sometimes even popularity is clutched at: we see no heavenly polestar in this voyage of his; but only the guidance of a proverbially uncertain *wind*' (*Works*, XXVI, p. 422).

The irony is striking; one thinks of Carlyle's obsessive desire to become known: 'I know that there is within me something *different* from the vulgar herd of mortals; I think it something *superior*'. His driving ambition, his will to succeed, to make his mark, and his stubbornness (the only word one can use) all combined to force him on, of all things, a Voltairian voyage. He, too, while viewing the heavenly polestar, had for guidance an uncertain wind, the wind of self. One might speculate that the inward Daemon had triumphed, had whispered the direction he should take. We have in succession *Sartor Resartus*, nothing less than an autobiography, no matter what form Carlyle gave it; *The French Revolution*, a series of 'splendid impressions', as Traill characterises it; and *Chartism*, which Raymond Williams praises but then adds that 'after *Chartism*, the balance, or comparative balance, of Carlyle's first position is lost'; and, unthinkable to the early Carlyle of the Voltaire essay, a series of lectures on heroes and hero-worship. The irony, as I have stated, is striking; here was Carlyle preparing to speak to the very 'multitude of voices' he has so roundly condemned.

19

Prophetic Utterances

One of the fascinating features of this period in Carlyle's career is the emphasis he gives to speech; his letters to Emerson indicate that public speaking has now become an 'art': 'I found', he writes to Emerson, '. . . that extempore speaking . . . is an *art* [he then apparently realises the full implication of what he has said] or craft, and requires an apprenticeship'. He then tells Emerson he wants to go to America to speak, and DeLaura comments: 'Obviously, Carlyle does in some sense conceive of himself as a prophet, and "inspired," and he wishes to conquer a broad public on both sides of the Atlantic' (DeLaura, p. 713). Again, irony predominates; some years earlier Carlyle had, in fact, considered oratory in conjunction with art. In his *Journal* for 1831 he had followed his thoughts on Goethe's and Schiller's ideas on Art and Religion with his own comments on 'oral' teaching: 'What are the uses, what is the special province of *oral* teaching at present? Wherein superior to the written or *printed* mode, and when?—'. He had at that time dismissed that specific mode: 'For one thing, as I can see, London is fit for no higher *Art* than that of Oratory: they understand nothing of Art' (*2NB*, p. 212).

By 1840, however, his ideas had changed, and London was fit, if not for Oratory, then for Carlyle's prophetic speech; it was presumably also ready for Carlyle himself, since the 'ultimate hero of the *Heroes* lectures, as well as the source of their unity, is Thomas Carlyle: he is implicitly the chief character, and the work is nearly as autobiographical as Book II of *Sartor*' (DeLaura, p. 718). Carlyle's 'Art' had become, in fact, Carlyle himself. From that time on he would continue to write about the social and spiritual issues of his day, but there would be no longer any concern about Art's role. He had come to a point, 'where his fundamental doctrine and his personal quest for self-definition met' (DeLaura, p. 732). Campbell has put this idea in another way, one that is perhaps a bit more accurate in stressing the various implications of Carlyle's changing vision of himself, from Artist to Artisan, from Poet to Prophet. One need only substitute the appropriate words for 'religious' or at least extend its meaning far beyond the narrow limitations it has in Campbell's statement, which concludes an essay on that aspect of Carlyle's thought:

> He had been thrown upon his own resources by the disillusion with Edinburgh and its values, and the break with Ecclefechan: he *had* to believe in himself and the validity of his 'message.' . . . Certainly the self-awareness which sweeps over Teufelsdröckh . . . is one which implies a self-centered pitying . . . but self-responsible. (*CHC*, p. 17)

Campbell then astutely quotes the message that Carlyle insisted on telling, and that passage is most revealing; it indicates Carlyle's awareness that he was no longer interested in the way of telling the message (the Art), but only in getting it told; I have, however, kept the first line of the paragraph, a line Campbell omitted:

> Neither fear thou that this thy great message of the Natural *being* the Supernatural will wholly perish unuttered. One way or other it will and shall be uttered—write it down on paper any way; speak it from thee—so shall thy painful, destitute existence not have been in vain. (*CHC*, pp. 17–18; Froude, II, p. 345)

'This Journal entry', writes Campbell, 'echoes the semi-private *Reminiscences* and crystallises most clearly the nature of his "mission," as he recognised it in his mature years' (*CHC*, p. 18). It does indeed crystallise his mission, both the substance and the means of conveying it. No longer would Carlyle concern himself with Art in the old Greek sense, in which the whole Soul must be illuminated, made harmonious. Shakespeare had no religion, but his poetry; Carlyle now had his self and his prophetic utterances, which he would convey one way or another. Thus, in *Frederick* he can still say that 'all real *Poets*, to this hour, are Psalmists and Iliadists', but then he must add 'after their sort'. Then he qualifies even this: 'and have in them a divine impatience of lies, a divine incapacity of living among lies'. Likewise, he concludes, 'which is a corollary, that the highest Shakespeare producible is properly the fittest Historian producible' (*Works*, XII, p. 18). This sense of mission also explains why, even in *Heroes and Hero-Worship*, he can write that 'we want to get at . . . the *thought* the man had, if he had any: why should he twist it into jingle, if he *could* speak it out plainly?' (*Works*, v, p. 90). This willingness to utter the message (which Carlyle felt in his case was to be found in and shown through the self) one way or another lies behind the exhortation that seems so contrary to his early theories about art, but, in fact, turned out to be so prophetic: 'Be *men* before attempting to be writers!' (*CL*, III, p. 245). Finally, this view of the 'prophetic' Carlyle does much to make clear the tone and spirit of *Shooting Niagara: and After?* Overlooked in the criticism which focuses chiefly on his harsh comments on democracy is his discussion of what he designates as 'Art, Poetry, and the like'. Carlyle flatly states:

> Poetry? It is not pleasant singing that we want, but wise and earnest speaking:—'Art,' 'High Art,' etc. are very fine and ornamental, but only to persons sitting at their ease: to persons still wrestling with deadly chaos, and still fighting for dubious existence, they are a mockery rather. Our Artistos, well meditating, will perhaps discover that genuine 'Art' in all times is a higher synonym for God Almighty's Facts. . . . Let him think well of this! He will find that all real 'Art' is definable as Fact, or say as the disimprisoned 'Soul of Fact'; that any other kind of Art, Poetry or High Art is quite idle in comparison.

To gauge how far Carlyle has come in view of aesthetics or art, one need only read his comments on his one great literary hero, Shakespeare. Shakespeare is still his 'highest genius': 'Yes, of all the intellects of Mankind that have taken the speaking shape, I incline to think him the most divinely gifted; clear, all-piercing like the sunlight [the assertive image is still pervasive], lovingly melodious [Carlyle is still paying lip-service to this concept]; probably the noblest human Intellect in that kind'. Then he utters his 'message': 'And yet of Shakespeare too, it is not the Fiction that I admire, but the Fact' (*Works*, XXX, pp. 24–5, 26). Carlyle's conclusion is predictable, and a little sad:

> The Moral Sense, thank God, is a thing you never will 'account for'; that, if you could think of it, is the perennial Miracle of

> Man; in all times, visibly connecting poor transitory Man here on this bewildered Earth with his Maker, who is Eternal in the Heavens. . . . 'Two things,' says the memorable Kant, deepest and most logical of Metaphysical Thinkers [gone for the moment are Goethe and Schiller]; 'Two things strike me as dumb: the infinite Starry Heaven; and the Sense of Right and Wrong in Man.' (*Works*, xxx, pp. 28–9)

The Prophet has prevailed over the Artist.

The difference that one sees in the earlier and later Carlyle has been discussed by many critics, and many different theories have emerged. Usually the discussion focuses on when Carlyle became a Victorian and left off being a Romantic. In an early study Ernest Bernbaum put the time as 1841. Donald Stone places it in 1837, with the shift in interest from poetry to history.[1] DeLaura argues that as 'late as 1840 Carlyle still maintained a considerable complexity and "uncertainty" and a quasi-fictional set of "masks"' (DeLaura, p. 728). The truth seems to be, however, that to talk of Victorianism and Romanticism in this connection is beside the point; the change was, in fact, not a change in what he wrote about, but the way he wrote about it. He did not write history as history; he wrote history as a series of 'splendid impressions'. History was being written long before the Victorians existed. Carlyle, one could even say, became a Romantic at the very time he was supposed to become a Victorian, if one defines Romanticism as DeLaura does, as a 'personal quest for self-definition'. Therefore, he concludes, *Heroes* is 'a masterpiece of Romantic art' (DeLaura, p. 732). In fact, as I have argued, Carlyle's coming to depend on the presentation of self, this personal quest, is a sign of his desertion of his own definition of art, and a way of writing, and his assumption of his sage-like stance, Victorian by some standards, and just the opposite of Romantic self-definition. Labels become meaningless at some point.

A more fruitful and profitable approach might be one that seeks to account for this change in terms of Carlyle's own career and life. In a recent essay on Victorian autobiography Jonathan Loesberg puts forth various reasons for 'reliving' one's life and making a pattern of it, something Carlyle seemed to do most of the time through his writing. One can, as did Newman, do this without any duplicity and hypocrisy. There is, however, a thin line between Byronism and Goetheism. Loesberg writes:

> An autobiographer might then investigate himself not to justify his life but to understand it. He would escape the spectre of Bounderby, however, only to be confronted with a state of mind that many Victorian poets and social critics feared just as much: a morbid, debilitating overinvolvement with self. Carlyle's work-ethic and his concomitant insistence on self-forgetfulness were only the most extreme of Victorian reactions to an immobilizing self-consciousness. Even Mill noted . . . that Carlyle's principle of anti-self-consciousness was one of the discoveries which led him out of his mental crisis.

Loesberg, however, goes on to insist and demonstrate that the Victorians wrote autobiography 'because that form offered them the ability to elucidate [an interesting word in connection with Carlyle] a mediating position between those philosophies which claim that all knowledge is experiential and those which insist on the central importance of an intuitional knowledge of *a priori* truths about the world'. He cites Carlyle as one who effects this compromise in works such as *Sartor*, and he cites this work as an example of Carlyle as a Victorian 'whose gestures toward autobiography necessitated at least minimal compromise even as their extremist positions finally pushed them away from that form'.[2] One could say, in the light of Carlyle's consistent attempts to publish his self, that Loesberg does not go far enough. Carlyle did more than merely gesture towards autobiography; indeed, his entire canon can be seen as his attempt to show the dangers of extremism in either direction, and the consistent projection of self should be viewed not as self-justification so much as demonstration of his belief that the moral and ethical self were enough to combine experience and intuition and could serve as an example to others. The projection of self, in short, need not automatically be classified as Romantic or debilitating or morbid or immobilising. It could, when rightly presented and viewed, be seen as 'heroic', and this, evidently, was the way it was viewed by Froude and others. Carlyle was not so much justifying his life, they felt, as putting forth his experiences and belief in intuition as an example, for others, of the way to faith and fulfilment.

What Carlyle himself felt we will never be able to know with certainty. The final years were not days of fulfilment for him, certainly, although honours came from all places. Ironies also abound in his 'latter' days; there is a strange likeness for instance, between Carlyle and men not usually associated with Carlyle: Hume and Voltaire. Carlyle's words on Hume sound very much as though they could be, in fact, 'autobiographical':

> As to his scepticism, that is perfectly transcendental, working itself out to the very end. He starts with *Locke's Essay*, thinking, as was then generally thought, that logic is the only way to the truth. He began with this, and went on; in the end he exhibited to the world his conclusion, that there was nothing at all credible or demonstrable, the only thing certain to him being that he himself existed and sat there, and that there were some species of things in his own brain. (*Lectures*, p. 175)

How many passages are there in Carlyle's own writing that echo the thought of this one? Time and time again, as an enlightened sceptic or even a sceptical transcendentalist, Carlyle writes of others as being 'spectres' or 'ghosts', and of his being all alone in the world. Of the many passages in *Sartor* for instance there is one in the chapter on 'Natural Supernaturalism':

> Again, could anything be more miraculous than an authentic Ghost? The English Johnson longed, all his life, to see one; but could not, though he went to Cock Lane, and thence to the church-vaults, and tapped on coffins. Foolish Doctor! Did he never, with his mind's eye as well as with the body's, look round him into that full tide of human Life he so loved; did he never so much as look into Himself? The good Doctor was a Ghost, as actual and authentic as heart could wish; well-nigh a million of Ghosts were travelling the streets by his side. (*Works*, I, pp. 210–11)

There is also the letter to Jane, from which I have already quoted (p. 153), on his visit to her mother's grave:

> Nobody knew me. I sate two minutes in Thornhill Street, unsuspected by all men, a kind of ghost among men. The day was windless: the earth stood still: grey mist rested on the tops of the green hills, the vacant brown moors: silence as of eternity rested over the world. . . . I was as a spirit in the land of spirits, called land of the living. (Froude, III, p. 323)

The similarities are striking, and they may account for Carlyle's ambivalence towards Hume.

He is also ambivalent towards Voltaire; indeed, LaValley makes much of this ambivalence. 'Carlyle', he writes 'was also attracted by Voltaire's attack upon superstition, by his gaiety, clearness, and satiric wit, and even by his active skepticism'. Later he cites a quotation from *Frederick*: 'On the whole, be not too severe on poor Voltaire! He is very fidgety, noisy; something of a pickthank, of a wheedler; but above all, he is scorbutic, dyspeptick; hagridden, as soul seldom was; and (in his oblique way) *appeals* to Friedrich and to us,—not in vain' (LaValley, pp. 272, 273). Carlyle was in truth fascinated by Voltaire, and one can see, again, as in the case of Hume, certain similarities exist. Carlyle's essay on Voltaire, an early one, reveals his own ambivalence towards this man he called one of the 'two Original men' of the eighteenth century. In one passage he deplores his lack of *Werterism*, 'either in its good or bad sense':

> he never openly levies war against Heaven. . . . If he sees no unspeakable majesty in heaven and earth, neither does he see any unsufferable horror there. His view of the world is a cool, gently scornful, altogether prosaic one: his sublimest Apocalypse of nature lies in the microscope and telescope; the Earth is a place for producing corn; the Starry Heavens are admirable as a nautical timekeeper. (*Works*, XXVI, p. 427)

This last observation, we know by now, is a damning one in the terms of Carlyle's assertive image; a man who would view the heavens as unemblematically as that lacks something. However, Carlyle can later on recognise the fine qualities of this philosopher and poet:

> At the same time, let it not be forgotten, that amid all these blighting influences, Voltaire maintains a certain indestructible humanity of nature; a soul never deaf to the cry of wretchedness; never utterly blind to the light of truth, beauty, goodness. [At this time, of course, beauty and goodness carried heavily their Goethean connotations.] It is even, in some measure, poetically interesting to observe this fine contradiction in him: the heart acting without directions from the head, or perhaps against its

> directions; the man virtuous, as it were, in spite of himself. . . . Perhaps there are a few men, with such principles and such temptations as his were, that could have led such a life; few that could have done his work, and come through it with cleaner hands. If we call him the greatest of all *Persifleurs*, let us add that, morally speaking also, he is the best. (*Works*, XXVI, p. 436)

His conclusions concerning Voltaire reveal the closeness of the two writers. 'His task was not one of Affirmation', writes Carlyle, 'but of Denial; not a task of erecting and rearing up, which is slow and laborious, but of destroying and overturning, which in most cases is rapid and far easier' (*Works*, XXVI, p. 459). Since Carlyle is known today chiefly as a critic who delighted in tearing things down rather than building them up, one who kept calling for an apocalyptic change, these conclusions sound strange. It was David Masson, largely sympathetic to Carlyle, who reviewed *Latter-Day Pamphlets* as 'provocative of rage, hatred, and personal malevolence'.[3] It is Carlyle himself, in writing of the 'lean, tottering, lonely old man' that Voltaire had become, who praises him and feels 'drawn towards him by some tie of affection, of kindly sympathy' (*Works*, XXVI, p. 440). As I have suggested, there are some rather interesting bonds and similarities between these two apostles of reason, Hume and Voltaire, these sceptics and Thomas Carlyle. That Carlyle is a complex figure is not the question; rather, the various elements of thought and character and feeling that make up this complexity.

Are Carlyle's writings, then, autobiographical, a projection of self, or are they an attempt at justification or understanding? Is there not a third possibility, that they are Carlyle's 'artistic' way of presenting his thoughts and beliefs, his unique aesthetic? There is something almost arbitrary in the immediate equation of the projection of self with the Romantic ego. Carlyle himself believed in the starry heavens and the sense of right and wrong; he saw no discrepancy. Art in the old Greek sense was no longer possible, and one had to find new ways of expressing old thoughts. 'He *had* to believe in himself', states Campbell, 'and the validity of his message'. The result seems to be that to Carlyle these were one and the same. He had written in *Heroes*, speaking of perhaps his greatest English literary one, Shakespeare, that man's 'intellectual nature' and his 'moral nature' were not divisible; these divisions at bottom were but names. Unable to achieve the aesthetic vision of Goethe and Schiller, that which combined Art and Religion through Beauty and thus brought them together without hostility, Carlyle came to rely on the self, but not the Byronic self, the power man; instead, he saw his aesthetic in terms of the projection of the moral self. In this sense genuine Art became a synonym for God's Almighty Facts, and a Poet became a Man speaking to Men, a recorder of God's Facts. The most significant 'fact' of all, perhaps, was God's Universe, the emblem that came to have the greatest meaning for Carlyle. To see the heavens as a nautical time-piece, as did Voltaire, was a sign of corruption and aesthetic failure; to recognise them as a 'bodying forth' of the Laws of the Taskmaster Himself was a sign of integration, self-knowledge, and sympathy for one's fellow man. They revealed the seeing eye and loving heart.

Our ultimate judgement or evaluation of Carlyle, then, depends on our approach to both the man himself and his work. To ignore one or the other is to err badly, to misjudge the message or the presentation of that message. Labels, as I have said, are meaningless, for in the Carlylean sense the intellectual and moral nature are one and the same. The self as moral and aesthetic force seems to have been Carlyle's ultimate aim, the starry heavens and the sense of right and wrong. To say, as does Farrell, that Carlyle moved from an 'idealist vision of the artist' to 'his role as a social prophet' is to place the emphasis wrongly; it is true that Carlyle lost his idealist vision of the artist, but it was not a matter of replacement. In typical Carlylean fashion, he transformed his failure to achieve the idealist aesthetic into what he felt was the triumph of moral vision. The moralist became the artist, whose aesthetic lay in the moral self.

The 'autobiographical' basis of Carlyle's art, its appeal as well as its possible danger, was recognised early by Sterling. 'A reading of Sterling's review', DeLaura writes, 'suggests that it provided the germinal conception of the *Heroes* lectures—not simply the "doctrine" of heroes, . . . but the peculiarly personal intensity of its presentation. For Sterling saw . . . that Carlyle's art had a specially autobiographical basis'. An important quality in Carlyle, who was compared to Luther, was his 'religious awe of the Divine' (DeLaura, pp. 730–1). Whether, as DeLaura writes, this was a turning point in Carlyle's life is not so important in our context as the recognition of Carlyle's aesthetic. Froude reflects this recognition in his praise of Carlyle and his description of his influence on himself and others.

'Carlyle's voice', writes Froude in his well-known praise, 'was to the young generation of Englishmen like the sound of "ten thousand trumpets" in their ears. . . . In Carlyle's writings dogma and tradition had melted like a mist, and the awful central fact burnt clear once more in the midst of heaven'. Froude goes on to describe the basis of Carlyle's powers, the means of telling his message: 'Nor could anyone doubt Carlyle's power, or Carlyle's sincerity. . . . He was simply a man of high original genius . . . speaking out with his whole heart the convictions at which he had himself arrived in the disinterested search after truth. If we asked who he was, we heard that his character was like his teaching' (Froude, III, pp. 292–4). To Froude, as to Sterling and others, the basis of his art was his character, and he spoke with authority.

Carlyle's sympathy for the elder Voltaire becomes understandable in terms of his own frustration in his later years, a frustration as much artistic as personal. He could not get, had not succeeded in getting, his 'message' to the people, those who needed the word. He had always expressed difficulty in writing, but it was more than mere phraseology, as he had said; it was the way to say it. 'It is seldom or never the Phraseology, but always the Insight, that fails me, and retards me.' 'The whole thing I want to write seems lying in my mind; but I *cannot get my eye on it*.' One of his last statements is: 'I cannot get it explained, or enforced any more; and must leave it standing, for somebody that *has* still a *pen* and a *right hand*'. What was that *it*? As we have seen, that *it* included much; indeed one can still get a smile from any group by suggesting that the apostle of silence took thirty volumes to spread his message. However, the *it* was, as Froude and others have testified, the means of salvation for some. Others were influenced, some greatly, some less so. He left his mark not only on his own century but permanently; his message, the *it*, is still with us, although it may not take the form of the original. If he could not 'get it explained, or enforced' with the pen, he could, or attempted to, get it explained by the only way left: himself. His 'message', whether one agrees with it or not, is summarised in a few phrases: the worship of heroes, right makes might, leaders must lead, there is Divine Justice in this world, work is worship, faith in a transcendental God. One could say, simply, Carlyle believed in Duty, Suffering, Work, Truth and God. 'All of this', writes Georg Tennyson, 'may sound redolent of the pulpit and of course it was. Carlyle was a "prophet new inspired" with an ancient message' (*A Carlyle Reader*, p. xxviii).

We are left, then, with the man and the message, each depending on the other. There is, finally, no 'Art'; there is the prophet Carlyle. The message, ultimately, depends on the man; how one receives the message depends greatly on how one regards the man. W. E. Aytoun saw nothing of value in Carlyle's writings precisely because of Carlyle himself. He writes:

> It is natural to suppose that an individual who habitually deals in such wholesale denunciation, and whose avowed wish is to regenerate and reform society upon some entirely novel principle, must be a man of immense practical ability. The exposer of shams and quackeries should be, in his own person, very far indeed above suspicion of resembling those whom he describes, or tries to describe, in language more or less intelligible. If otherwise, he stands in imminent danger of being treated by the rest of the world as an impertinent and egregious imposter. Now, Mr. Thomas Carlyle is anything but a man of practical ability. . . . Can any living man point to a single practical passage in any of these volumes? If not, what is the real value of Mr. Carlyle's writing? What is Mr. Carlyle himself but a Phantasm of the species which he is pleased to denounce? (*Critical Heritage*, pp. 322–3)

Froude, on the other, and Sterling and many others found Carlyle the man equal to the message; he was a man speaking to men. 'His character was like his teaching', writes Froude. 'Carlyle', wrote Thoreau, 'to adopt his own classification, is himself a hero, as literary man. . . . As the laborer works, and soberly by the sweat of his brow earns bread for his body, so this man *works* anxiously and *sadly*, to get bread of life, and dispense it. We cannot do better than quote his own estimate of labor from *Sartor Resartus*' (*Critical Heritage*, pp. 288–9). The man is the message.

Emerson felt this too, and his reaction provides an insight into Carlyle and his influence. Interestingly enough, Emerson goes through a somewhat similar process to that Carlyle did; he is so impressed by a letter from Carlyle in which Carlyle talks of the speech of man to men that, as Porte tells us, Emerson 'redefines his own role and vocation'. 'Indeed', Porte states, 'Emerson could hardly help translating the "institution of preaching" into that of lecturing, or essay writing, or the literary vocation generally'. Porte gives as the 'source' of this Emersonian concept a letter from Carlyle:

> . . . that now at last we have lived to see all manner of Poetics and Rhetorics and Sermonics, and one may say generally all manner of *Pulpits* for addressing mankind from, as good as broken and abolished: alas, yes; if you have any earnest meaning, which demands to be not listened to, but *believed* and *done*, you cannot (at least I cannot) utter it *there*, but the sound sticks in my throat, as when a Solemnity were *felt* to have become a Mummery; and so one leaves the pasteboard coulisses, and three Unities, and Blair[']s Lectures, quite behind; and feels only that there is *nothing sacred*, then, but the *Speech of Man* to believing Men! *This*, come what will, was, is and forever must be *sacred*; and will one day doubtless anew environ itself with fit Modes, with Solemnities that are *not* Mummeries. (*CL*, VII, p. 265)[4]

'In reading such a passage', concludes Porte, 'one begins to understand just how crucial a role Carlyle played in helping Emerson to unchurch himself and to believe fully in the potentially sacramental nature and function of all writing'. One should add, of course, that Carlyle is thinking of writing that is understood to be the projection of self.

If the writing is the man, then the 'Emblem' is also the writer or man as well as the message. 'All language but that concerning *sensual* objects', Carlyle jotted down in his *Journal*, 'is or has been figurative. Prodigious influence of metaphors! Never saw into it till lately. A truly useful and philosophical work would be a good *Essay on Metaphors*. Some day I will write one!' (*2NB*, pp. 141–2). He did write the section on metaphors in *Sartor*, but the truth is that his 'philosophical work' on that subject is pervasive in all his writing. His metaphor, based on Fact, was the universe, that solemn temple, the skyey vault. 'All of Carlyle's conceptions, then', Georg Tennyson has observed, 'are infused with his conviction of the divine plan and harmony of the universe. . . . Because of his sense of the divine unity of the cosmos, Carlyle was extremely sensitive to the interrelations of things'. Tennyson then cites Carlyle's statement: 'It is a mathematic fact that the casting of this pebble from my hand alters the centre of gravity of the Universe' (*A Carlyle Reader*, p. xxxviii). As always, the mathematician and sceptic in Carlyle insisted on being heard.

It is significant that in attempting to provide a fitting eulogy for Carlyle, those who knew him best always fell back on his favourite metaphor or emblem. In his meditation on Carlyle Whitman wrote:

> In the fine cold night, unusually clear, (Feb. 5, '81) as I walk'd some open grounds adjacent to the condition of Carlyle, and his approaching—perhaps even then actual—death, filled me with thoughts eluding statement, and curiously blending with the scene. The planet Venus, an hour high in the west, with all her volume and lustre recover'd, (she had been shorn and languid for nearly a year,) including an additional sentiment I never noticed before—not merely voluptuous, Paphian, steeping, fascinating—now with calm commanding seriousness and hauteur—the Milo Venus now. Upward to the zenith, Jupiter, Saturn, and the moon past her quarter, trailing in procession, with the Pleiades following, and the constellation Taurus, and red Aldebaran. Not a cloud in heaven. Orion strode through the southeast, with his glittering belt—and a trifle below hung the sun of the night, Sirius. Every star dilated, more vitreous, nearer than usual. . . . To the northeast and north the Sickle, the Goat and kids, Cassiopea, Castor and Pollux, and the two Dippers. While through the whole of this silent indescribable show, inclosing and bathing my whole receptivity, ran the thought of Carlyle dying. (To soothe and spiritualize, and, as far as may be, solve the mysteries of death and genius, consider them under the stars at midnight.) (Stovall, pp. 252–3)

In his funeral sermon on Carlyle's death Arthur Stanley, groping for the fittest way to eulogise his dear friend, also fell back on this favourite Carlylean emblem, one taken from Carlyle's own *Journal*: 'Let us take one tender expression written three or four years ago', Stanley said, 'one plaintive yet manful thought.' He then quotes Carlyle:

> Three nights ago, stepping out after midnight, and looking up at the stars which were clear and numerous, it struck me with a strange, new kind of feeling—Hah! in a little while I shall have seen you also for the last time. God Almighty's own theatre of immensity—the infinite made palpable and visible to me—that also will be closed—flung to in my face—and I shall never behold that either anymore. The thought of *this* eternal deprivation . . . was sad and painful to me. And then a second feeling rose upon me. What if Omnipotence that has developed in me these pieties, these reverences, and infinite affections, should actually have said, Yes, poor mortal, such as you have gone so far *shall* be permitted to go *farther*? Hope, despair not!—God's will. God's will; not ours if it is unwise. (*Critical Heritage*, p. 520)

'And now that he has gone hence', asks Whitman, 'can it be that Thomas Carlyle, soon to chemically dissolve in ashes and by winds, remains an identity still? . . . does he yet exist, a definite, vital being, a spirit, an individual—perhaps now wafted in space among those stellar systems, . . . merely edge more limitless, far more suggestive systems?' (Stovall, p. 253). We know that Carlyle still 'exists' through his works, for his 'message' is still heard through his own books and the writings of others. Those qualities he stood for also help keep his memory alive, not the least of which is that stubbornness he inherited from his father. 'Human "obstinacy" grounded in real faith and insight', he wrote, 'is good, and the best.' In the *Reminiscences* he also speaks of his father, the last time he saw him. 'He was very kind, seemed prouder of me than ever. What he had never done the like of before, he said, on hearing me express something which he admired: "Man, it's surely a pity that thou should sit yonder with nothing but the Eye of Omniscience to see thee; and thou, with such a gift to speak"' (*Reminiscences*, pp. 32–3). Speak Carlyle did, and, in spite of his father's pity, there were many who listened. The son, however, always remained aware of 'the Eye of Omniscience'.

20

Tennyson's Idylic Vision

TENNYSON: OBLIQUE INSINUATIONS AND TELEMACHAN PERCEPTIONS

If at the end Carlyle rejected high Art for 'Fact', then Tennyson, one of the most gifted artists of his own day, also, but much earlier in his career, turned away from what he perceived to be useless 'Aestheticism' to the kind of writing that would convert man's perception of the world around him. The result of Tennyson's approach was indeed paradoxical: he became identified with his age (by the 1860s it seemed as if the whole nation was reading him, Tillotson, p. 287), but then he came to be regarded by some as 'the delicate Laureate of a cautious age; the shallow thought, the vacant compromise; the honeyed idyll, the complacent ode' (Nicolson, p. 304). Carlyle, as his various remarks on Tennyson's work and thought reveal, might have agreed with this assessment.

We are now in a position to take a more considered view of this eminent Victorian poet. In contrast to Nicolson, for instance, who simply dismisses the way the Victorian age 'reduced' and 'simplified' the meanings of such terms as 'truth', 'courage', 'wisdom' and 'duty', Tillotson states that Tennyson the poet was 'vulnerable because he chose to offer thinking on the problems of his time (as many poets do not), both in his own person and through fictitious personages; and his choice is an index of his sensitiveness to the claims of the Carlylean era' (p. 288). Tennyson's strategy of 'oblique insinuation', in short, deserves our attention precisely because it is through our understanding of it that we can come to know better both Tennyson's art and his 'solutions' to the problems of his time. Tennyson's poetry, and especially the idyls, takes up the topics of his own age and treats ideas that extend far beyond it with a subtlety and delicacy found in no other writer in his own century; and his idyls reveal more than any other genre his 'use' of literature as a 'method of converting man's perception of the world around him'.

Most critics agree that the idylic strain in Tennyson's poetry is the dominant one; there is nothing at all comparable in Carlyle's work, whose mode is rather one of 'confrontation' and 'challenge' than Tennyson's idylic 'oblique insinuation'. Earlier studies of the poet have failed to appreciate this particular Tennysonian 'strategy'. Baum, for instance, saw the idyls as 'Victorian' and therefore suspect:

> There was something genuine in Tennyson as in his contemporary readers which made this kind of thing attractive. Both he and they liked it. It was part of the sentimental *strain*, beginning before the accession of Victoria, which made Victorian hearts bleed easily and which he came to rely upon hereafter to satisfy his numerous following. A sincere insincerity made him falsely true.[1]

It is easy enough to dismiss Baum's remarks, and those of other recent criticism, as symptomatic of a 'modern' sensibility, but there seems to be something deeper than that in these responses to this most important genre in the Tennysonian canon. Part of it may be, as one perceptive writer on Tennyson has observed, the unwillingness or the inability to recognise a valid alternative to the Victorian 'wasteland'; if one is to grant validity to this strain, then one must be prepared to admit that there is, in fact, some substance to the 'Victorian' interest in hearth and home.[2] One begins to see Tennyson as something other than 'sincerely insincere' and his poems as something other than 'contrived'. One begins, above all, to grant Tennyson his artistic integrity as well as the sincerity of his belief.

TENNYSON'S IDYLIC VISION

When one speaks of Tennyson and 'Victorianism', then, one thinks primarily of his idylic vision, the vision most evident in his 'domestic' idyls but present in much of his other poetry. Culler, for instance, speaks of *The Princess* as containing the 'larger embodiment' of the idylic form.[3] The idylic 'strain', to use Baum's term, is represented in the major portion of Tennyson's poetry, and it contains more than any other aspect of his work the most artistic transmutations of the Carlylean message. Even Baum noted the importance of this strain:

> When the historical dramas and 'In Memoriam' and the numerous lyrical and occasional pieces are set aside, nearly all of what remains falls into the class which Tennyson thought of somehow as idyllic. These idyls, or idylls, not only comprise a very large portion of his poetic work, they contain most of his contributions to the history of Victorian England. As the self-chosen portrayer of his age Tennyson was an idylist. This was probably not deliberate but it turned out so. (Baum, p. 143)

If one disregards the condescending tone and takes exception to such statements as 'self-chosen portrayer' and 'probably not deliberate', then one is immediately made aware of the tremendous importance Tennyson attached to the idyl.

The poet's choice was significant. If Carlyle chose to emphasise Duty and obedience to God's Laws and Arnold chose to emphasise 'the best of what was thought and said in the world' and Huxley chose 'the habits of the scientific mind', then it can be said that Tennyson, concerned as were all these others with the quality of life, chose to call the attention of his readers to those human aspects and values of life that distinguish the truly civilised from the natural or bestial, that give life dignity and purpose. The family, as the last refuge of those human and 'humane' values, was Tennyson's answer; domestic morality and social morality were one and the same; one was dependent on the other. The family, the most important unit of culture or civilisation, was an artificial construct in the midst of a 'natural' Darwinian world, one that would revert back to brutality and savageness if those humane values it preserved were to disappear. 'Carlyle', Altick writes, 'had prescribed renewed spiritual faith as a cure for the social malaise.' Tennyson prescribed as his cure those 'domestic' values and 'humane' qualities found in the family; domestic morality and virtue, seen from the cosmic perspective, became the chief hope for the regeneration and salvation of human beings.[4]

As I have noted above, there is nothing in Carlyle's work parallel to this interest in Tennyson, an interest that was obviously heightened by the Sage's call for some 'cure' for the social malaise he found in England and elsewhere in his time:

> But it is in the marriage poems of the 1830s that Tennyson most obviously assumed a maturity in which the problems of existence were no longer distilled into the inactivity of mood and enchanted reverie. 'The Miller's Daughter' (1832) began a series of narrative-reflective poems in which 'holy human love' was viewed in increasingly pessimistic terms in its context of class barriers and financial restrictions. By the time of 'Locksley Hall' (1837–8) and 'Edwin Morris' (1839), the outlines of *Maud* (1855) and 'Aylmer's Field' (1863) had been mapped. . . . Finally, the poems themselves show how much more realistically and, in spite of their frequent humour, how seriously Tennyson now regarded his vocation. (Shaw, pp. 65–6)

It is to Tennyson's credit, then, that he made this connection between the domestic (familial) and the national; it was clearly a sign of his growing maturity as an artist. Carlyle's later writings, in contrast, were 'little more than [a] dying echo', and he ended his days complaining of matters in general and lamenting the inability of anyone to change anything. Like Ulysses, he thought more often of the happy isles than of his homeland. Perhaps one reason for this was his ignorance of the events of his day; certainly Tennyson's interest in the 'common things of life', particularly what Fredeman calls the 'love–marriage' nexus, was one shared by novelists of the period. Pitt makes an apt observation: 'It is foolish to laugh at Tennyson's concern with domestic relationships—they were at the forefront of the Victorian ethical tableau, they are the basis of a literary convention, and Tennyson uses the convention . . . as the medium of something else' (Pitt, pp. 136–7).

The 'larger meaning' or the 'something else' contains ideas of paramount importance to Tennyson and to the Victorians. Central to Tennyson's discovery of the 'essence of community' was the 'love–marriage' nexus, the home and the family. We know from the *Memoir* that the poet insisted that the stability and greatness of a nation depended upon the sacredness of home life and that he took 'true joy' in his 'family duties and affections' (*Memoir*, I, p. 189). The home and the family, then, become symbols for those positive values admired by the Victorians: love, devotion, loyalty, truth, co-operation, all the joys of human relationships.

They become 'something else', however, for in his idylic treatment of them Tennyson emphasised those implications of the 'larger meaning' beyond the merely domestic and local to the national and cosmic. There is, in fact, a close connection between the shift in his poetic stance relatively early in his career, one that can be characterised as 'antilyrical', and his 'deepening concern for social considerations'.[5] Contrary to Baum, Tennyson did deliberately make a choice; poetry, he felt, had to find new patterns or die. What specific role Carlyle played in influencing that decision is, of course, difficult to determine, but there is no doubt that Tennyson's poetry from the late 1830s and early 1840s becomes less 'lyrical' and more 'idylic', much more concerned with social issues and 'domestic' matters.

Sir Charles Tennyson has written that Tennyson turned to the idyls after the 'first rush of lyrical inspiration . . . had faded away and he was able to look at the world with more serenity and detachment'.[6] In commenting on the poems in the *Enoch Arden* volume, he wrote: 'Most significant was the consensus of feeling that Tennyson had at last brought his work into direct relation with the life of the time. . . . He had, it was felt, discovered at last that he must reach the hearts of his readers and that to do so he must be the poet of his own age' (*AT*, p. 353). Carlyle would have given much to be so designated, although he no doubt would have taken some comfort in knowing that he had had some influence on that work which spoke so directly to the hearts of those readers he had tried so hard to reach.

It becomes all the more interesting, then, to examine the way that Tennyson took the idylic strain, particularly in terms of the domestic emphasis he gave to it, and veered from the straight Carlylean line. Tennyson's independence, as I have stressed, must not be forgotten; he was always his own person and had his own ideas about his art and thought. There were also aspects of Carlyle's character that put him off, especially his arrogance and pride, those qualities that eventually led to the prophet's last years, bitter and withdrawn, in 'dissent from all the world' (*CAA* in *CPP*, p. 130). He clearly could never become a Carlylean disciple as others (such as Froude) did. Tennyson is Telemachan; Carlyle, Ulyssean. It was the turning inward that Tennyson refused to do, the quality that made the later Carlyle so unattractive to many of his former friends and disciples.

His poetry, instead, became 'public', concerned with national matters. His idylic strain is his attempt to counteract the Carlylean one; and his 'preoccupation' with domestic themes and subjects and with their religious, social and political 'extensions' can be viewed as his 'positive' solution in opposition to Carlyle's negative one. It is precisely in those idyls that depict the sacredness of marriage and home life that Tennyson is most explicit in this attempt, in taking up and demonstrating those universal values, in opposition to personal ones, that transcend distinction of sex, class, generations and even nations. While it is impossible to do a detailed and thorough summary of all of Tennyson's idylic poems, it is possible to examine a number of them, varying in 'idylic' degree in both subject and treatment, in order to trace in them Tennyson's superb handling of the genre (his strategy of oblique insinuation).

'It is perhaps difficult for readers brought up on the fashionable idea of woman as castrating female or Terrible Mother', writes Gerhard Joseph, 'to approach the angelic woman of Tennyson's poetry with absolute sympathy'.[7] It is not so much a matter of absolute sympathy, I think, as one of understanding the Tennysonian idea of the family and the place of the woman in that unit. It is misleading, for instance, to cite 'Isabel', one of Tennyson's early poems, as a portrait of what Tennyson thought was the 'perfect wife' (p. 184). For one thing, 'Isabel' *is* an early poem and shows signs of being an exercise. For another, it is more of a portrait in keeping with his early 'lady' poems than an idylic depiction of what he came to regard as the ideal wife and mother. Isabel, in spite of her virtues, seems formal and almost forbidding in her chasteness: 'Clear, without heat, undying, tended by/Pure vestal thoughts in translucent fane/Of her still spirit' (p. 183). Perhaps this is why Leigh Hunt was suspicious of the sincerity of the young Tennyson (p. 183), and perhaps this is why so many modern critics seem slightly embarrassed when talking about the poem.

One need only to turn to some of the idyls dealing with wives and mothers to see the difference in tone and sentiment; certainly chastity is not their primary virtue. Isabel may be the 'stately flower of female fortitude' (p. 184), but she is not one of Tennyson's most appealing women. One misses those qualities found in the 'ladies' of 'The Lord of Burleigh', 'Lucretius', 'Oenone', and 'Locksley Hall Sixty Years After', all of whom are loyal and true, to be sure, but are also aware of and assume their role as lover and wife. When the maiden of 'The Lord of Burleigh' (p. 603) discovers that her husband is indeed a lord, she 'shapes' her heart to all her duties and 'grows' a noble lady. She is also helped in this by her husband, who 'clasped her like a lover,/ And . . . cheered her heart with love' (p. 604). 'Locksley Hall Sixty Years After' depicts another loyal, virtuous and true wife, Edith now dead, 'Very woman of very woman, nurse of ailing body and mind./She that linked again the broken chain that bound me to my kind' (p. 1361). Edith's womanly charm and tenderness were balanced by her possessing 'the breadth of man', and she is also described as having been strong in will and rich in wisdom. Clearly responsible for the recovery of the narrator, Edith did indeed 'redeem' him, so that he is able, in spite of his ranting and raving against the ills of the world, to end his long rambling speech with the praise of love. He has been able to forgive those whom he hated, and, with the knowledge that 'man can half-control his doom' conclude: 'Love will conquer at the last' (p. 1369). Love, loyalty, wisdom, faithfulness, qualities not mentioned in 'Isabel', are predominant in 'The Lord of Burleigh' and 'Locksley Hall Sixty Years After'.

They also play a large part in three idyls usually not thought of as 'domestic', 'Oenone', (p. 384) 'The Death of Oenone' (p. 1427) and 'Lucretius' (p. 1206). Lucilia, the wife of Lucretius, may not be thought of immediately as an ideal wife, for, after all, jealous, petulant and wrathful, she does feed him the philtre that causes him to dream and ultimately kills him. She is, however, a faithful wife, one who is not willing to give in meekly to a rival. This is a point worth making, for Tennyson's 'saintly' women have too often overshadowed his active, passionate ones. Tennyson makes clear his own position at the end of the idyl. Hearing Lucretius fall, Lucilia runs in:

> Beat breast, tore hair, cried out upon herself
> As having failed in duty to him, shrieked
> That she but meant to win him back, fell on him,
> Clasped, kissed him, wailed.
>
> (p. 1217)

What she did was done to keep him, and the implication is clear that her grief is real and her loyalty undiminished. Her situation is, of course, similar to Oenone's, another one of Tennyson's 'active' women who have too often been dismissed without a fair hearing. While she is helpless in her attempts to 'redeem' Paris, she is not the passive, passionless heroine often associated with Tennyson's wives. In 'Oenone' (p. 384) she contrasts herself with Helen:

> Fairest—why fairest wife? am not I fair?
> My love hath told me so a thousand times.
> Me thinks I must be fair, for yesterday,
> When I past by, a wild and wanton pard,
> Eyed like the evening star, with playful tail
> Crouched fawning in the week. Most loving is she?
> Ah me, my mountain shepherd, that my arms
> Were wound about thee, and my hot lips prest
> Close, close to thine in that quick-falling dew
> Of fruitful kisses, thick as Autumn rains
> Flash in the pools of whirling Simois.
>
> (p. 395)

After reading these words, one may wonder at the foolishness of Paris. One is impressed with the spirit of Oenone, who exhibits the same hatred demonstrated by other 'domestic' heroines. 'I wish', Oenone declares, 'that somewhere is the ruined folds,/ Among the fragments tumbled from the glens,/Or the dry thickets, I could meet with her/The Abominable, that uninvited came/. . . And bred this change; that I might speak my mind,/ And tell her to her face how much I hate/Her presence, hated both of Gods and men' (p. 396). Her 'fiery thoughts' reach their height, however, when she thinks of herself as wife but not mother, and it is at this moment that she reaches some of Cassandra's 'vague prophetic power':

> I dimly see
> My far-off doubtful purpose, as a mother
> Conjectures of the features of her child
> Ere it is born: her child!—a shudder comes
> Across me: never child be born of me,
> Unblest, to vex me with his father's eyes!
>
> (p. 397)

Oenone's references to her fiery thoughts and her prophecy that she will not die alone, a foreshadowing of her death on

Paris's funeral pyre in 'The Death of Oenone' (p. 1427), contain not only the traditional imagery for love; they also help characterise her refusal to accept passively the loss of her redemptive role in marriage. Ricks points out that one of Tennyson's sources for the sequel, Quintus Smyraeus, had stressed the marriage bond between Oenone and Paris, and Tennyson surely was aware of this. Tennyson wanted the reader to see the irony in Paris's plea of Oenone to save him. 'Let me owe my life to thee', he tells Oenone. While he may be talking of his wound, Oenone (and the readers) would be aware that she might have 'redeemed' him in a much more profound way had he not broken the sacred bond of matrimony. Her awareness of his real guilt and her grief and frustration over her own loss are indicated by the accusation she flings at him: 'Adulterer,/Go back to thine adulteress and die!' (p. 1428). To see this merely as a 'domestic' event, without noting the larger implications of Tennyson's concern with woman's 'larger work' and her redemptive nature, is to undercut seriously the idylic vision of the poet. Her last vision is of what might have been; she has, in the Tennysonian scheme of marriage and family responsibility, been dead a long time, but she has never passively accepted it. Unlike the more successful domestic heroines, Oenone has fought, but lost. Not to recognise her valiant attempts, however, is to fail to see what Tennyson was about in his domestic idyls. Oenone remains one of his most attractive, albeit defeated, domestic heroines.

Tennyson is most explicit regarding the 'larger woman-world of wives and mothers' in a number of idyls that usually do not receive much attention. This neglect is partly understandable because of the subject matter of the idyls; the subject of leprosy, for instance, does not seem particularly apt for poetry, but Tennyson's treatment of the strong love of the leper's bride in 'Happy' (p. 1399) is tactfully done and strangely moving. There is no question of the wife's deep attachment to her diseased husband, but what is remarkable is the way that Tennyson makes us see the earlier physical sexual basis of their love without undercutting her spiritual faith. He accomplishes this by first reminding the reader of the earlier jealousy of the leper's bride, a jealousy based on a common situation in the idyls. The bride insists that she acted as she did only to make her husband jealous, and in a passage that Tennyson's wife and son made him take out of the printed version, we can see the depths of the feelings of the leper's bride and the lengths to which she would go to keep him:

And she, the wife, they told me she boasted she would make
  Your noble heart the villain vassal of her wanton smile.
I never glanced at her full bust but wished myself the snake
  That bit the harlot bosom of that heathen by the Nile.

(p. 1401)

She, too, as many of Tennyson's more appealing women, is associated with roses and fire imagery. When, at the end, her leper husband, her 'warrior of the Holy Cross and of the conquering sword', accepts her roses and kisses her, we become aware of her redemptive power. The marriage oath, the 'bond that linked [them] life to life', has indeed proven stronger than the leper plague that had come between them. In the light of her persuasiveness, her passionate pleas and moving arguments, it is difficult to see how the myth of Tennyson's passionless and helpless woman has become so widespread. There is no doubt that his 'emphasis of marriage, religion, and morality suggest that he may have thought of it as a contrast to the morbid necrophily of Swinburne's *The Leper*' (p. 1399), but the idyl is, in its situation, theme and general artistic manner, not radically different from other domestic idyls. He needed no Swinburne to nudge him into writing about women's larger work.

That larger work, with the concomitant human denominators, is shown more fully in those idyls treating in greater detail the role of women as mothers as well as wives and lovers. Perhaps 'Romney's Remorse' (p. 1417) is the most 'sentimental' of these, but there are some interesting idylic aspects to the poem that would make what might seem simply sentimental more deliberately exaggerated sentiment on the part of the poet to bring into sharper focus the quiet but impressive selflessness of the 'truest, kindliest, noblest-hearted wife/That ever wore a Christian marriage-ring' (p. 1419). What Tennyson does in the idyl is make his point through understatement, the muted melody and hushed imagery reflecting the quiet but firm strength of Mary Romney. Like Lucretius, Romney dreams, but with a difference. Like Browning's Andrea del Sarto, Romney thinks of the past and the part that his wife has played in it, and again, with a difference.

Mary's redemptive nature is made clear in the way that Romney himself contrasts her first with Lady Hamilton and then with painting, that 'harlot-like / Seduced me from you' (p. 1421). It is her presence that inspires him to paint again; it is her forgiveness that gives him hope at the end. Throughout the idyl it is her role as wife and mother that is stressed, and in his best idylic manner, that 'rich indirection' praised by Ricks, the poet describes this role. Romney's words are the words of a painter, one who knows the significance of detail; those qualities that Romney comes to appreciate in his wife—loyalty, duty, above all, love and self-sacrifice—are presented graphically and with much sentiment (but not sentimentally) as Romney describes his dream, a Madonna-like mother and child portrait:

> I dreamed last night of that clear summer noon.
> When seated on a rock, and foot to foot
> With your own shadow in the placid lake,
> You claspt our infant daughter, heart to heart.
> I had been among the hills, and brought you down
> A length of staghorn-moss, and this you twined
> About her cap. I see the picture yet,
> Mother and child. A sound from far away,
> No louder than a bee among the flowers,
> A fall of water lulled the noon asleep.
> You stilled it for the moment with a song
> Which often echoed in me, while I stood
> Before the great Madonna-masterpieces
> Of Ancient Art in Paris, or in Rome.
>
> (p. 1420)

Here is exaggerated sentiment, if you will, but exaggeration that comes from a depth of feeling. Everything is 'framed', domesticated rather than romanticised, brought into manageable proportions, enclosed within the circle of the family. In contrast to, say, Rossetti's 'Silent Noon', which is epiphanic in its celebration of 'the luminous silent stasis', Tennyson in 'Romney's Remorse' is more intent on celebrating those virtues that enable humans to triumph over those hostile forces about them.[8] In the centre of the pictures are mother and daughter, 'heart to heart', with all else 'stilled' by the song of the mother to the child. The visual and aural blend, but the emphasis is on the human figures clasping one another, the symbol of love and sacrifice that one sees time and again in the great Madonna masterpieces of ancient art. The knowledge that the daughter died, 'did not grow', makes the sentiment more poignant, but does not lessen its impact.

What Tennyson is doing, of course, is making the human important again, and he is doing this by making the figures in the portrait stand out, become the focal point. Carlyle, in his attempts to overcome the devastating effects of Darwinism, turned Nature into the garment of God. Tennyson makes Nature less 'religious', relegating it to the background, something that serves as a setting for the human action, but nothing more. The natural forces become 'stilled' and made acceptable. 'No louder than a bee among the flowers'; the song of Mary Romney becomes the dominant force, not only stilling the fall of water but becoming a vital influence on the way that her husband now looks at ancient masterpieces. Ancient art becomes meaningful in terms of the present mother-and-child relationship; and the meaning of art itself, for Romney at any rate, has changed because of all this. The 'white heather' of the child has caused him to see that Art is 'harlot-like'. No wonder, then, that the artist curses 'the master's apothegm,/That wife and child drag an Artist down!' (p. 1419). He at last has learned the value of 'the household fire on earth'; he now can truly recognise and praise 'how bright' she keeps her marriage-ring.

'Dora' (p. 641) and 'Sea Dreams' (p. 1095) also treat the marriage-nexus, and both again attempt to provide a context for the sacredness of home life. The family, was the 'cultural' institution that provided an important bulwark against the evils of commerce and nature. The point in 'Dora', for instance, is not that William dies, but that Dora succeeds in bringing about a reconcilement. Farmer Allan is able, in a moment of self-awareness, to admit his guilt. He can also, although broken with remorse, benefit from the love of his children: 'And all his love came back a hundredfold'. As in a number of idyls, we have an 'interior' scene, in which we are led to perceive the nature of farmer Allan's reconcilement and the causes of the change in him, the change from his 'inhuman' refusal to forgive to his confession of his love for his son: 'I loved him—my dear son./May God forgive me!' (p. 646). As the two women 'peep' into the house they see:

The boy set up betwixt his grandsire's knees,
Who thrust him in the hollows of his arms,
And clapt him on the hands and on the cheeks,
Like one that loved him: and the lad stretched out
And babbled for the golden seal, that hung
From Allan's watch, and sparkled by the fire.

(p. 645)

Here is, of course, the sacredness of the hearth once again, the sanctity of home and fireside. The variation of the Madonna portrait is repeated at the end of the idyl at the moment of farmer Allan's 'redemption', a redemption brought about by the two women and the child:

Then they clung about
The old man's neck, and kissed him many times.
And all the man was broken with remorse;
And all his love came back a hundredfold;
And for three hours he sobbed o'er William's child
Thinking of William.

So those four abode
Within one house together.

(p. 646)

These scenes in 'Dora' that bring out the sentiment and theme are developed through Tennyson's mediatorial approach to the idyl, the form that so disturbed Matthew Arnold and has puzzled many critics. It is the 'new pattern' he found for poetry. I have discussed elsewhere Tennyson's approach to the idyl in general and 'Dora' in particular, and Philip Drew has written of it in connection with 'Aylmer's Field'.[9] What must be kept in mind is that Tennyson was deliberately employing the mediatorial approach to stress the sentiment and pathos, so important to his idylic purpose, and was not so concerned as Arnold and other 'classical' critics about the 'construction' of the poem, about maintaining the story and action. What he had been seeking, and what this approach enabled him to do, was to bring thought and sentiment into the sphere of poetry and thus relate poetry to life.

'Sea Dreams' also portrays redemption, in this case redemption of a city clerk, who, at his wife's urging, is finally able to say that he forgives the man who has robbed him of his money and peace of mind. Tennyson 'paints' a family portrait.

> The woman half turned round from him she loved,
> Left him one hand, and reaching through the night
> Her other, found (for it was close beside)
> And half-embraced the basket cradle-head
> With one soft arm, which like the pliant bough
> That moving moves the nest and nestling, swayed
> The cradle, while she sang this baby song.
>
> (p. 1104)

The role of the wife is the most obvious, for it is she who is most active throughout the poem. Fulfilling her larger role, she refuses to let her husband fall, to become the victim of the age. In the end she is successful.

The idyl also demonstrates the way in which human values can overcome the pernicious influences of the time, the manner in which domestic morality influences social morality. It portrays the harmful effects of crass commercialism and religious hypocrisy on the human spirit, effects that were infecting heart and home. The 'wordy storm' of the preacher in 'Sea Dreams' reminds one of the sermon in 'Aylmer's Field', another idyl which reveals Tennyson's concern with the connection between domestic and social morality. In 'Sea Dreams', however, the emphasis remains on the effect of the times on the human spirit itself, and the poem becomes a study of the clerk's own battle with the Everlasting No, reminiscent of the Carlylean battle in *Sartor*.

> I stood like one that had received a blow:
> I found a hard friend in his loose accounts,
> A loose one in the hard grip of his hand,
> A curse in his God-bless-you: then my eyes
> Pursued him down the street, and far away,
> Among the honest shoulders of the crowd,
> Read rascal in the motions of his back,
> And scoundrel in the supple-sliding knee.
>
> (pp. 1100–1101)

Tennyson's fear of the brutalisation of man by the coldness of the age, the same fear felt by Carlyle, is heightened by the imagery of the passage, the contrast between the true and the false, the rascality of the scoundrel, a kind of Count Cagliostro, with his hardness, looseness, suppleness. While the dreams of the clerk only serve to persuade him of his gullibility, it is the song of the wife, with its stress on the innocence and simple faith of the child, and her own exaggerated morality that cause him to break out of his Centre of Indifference. His deep concern for her and the child results in his own renewal of spirit, symbolised by the picture of the family at peace.

In his later years Tennyson seemed intrigued and fascinated by the terrible strength of maternal love, one facet, of course, of the 'larger woman-world / Of wives and mothers' (p. 1396). In both 'The Grandmother' (p. 1106) and 'Rizpah' (p. 1245), two idyls that celebrate the bond between mother and child, the sentiment is indeed exaggerated, with more care given to stimulate the reader's emotions rather than to develop character. The Grandmother, though she appears 'hard and cold' to Annie, remembers very well the death of the first 'that ever I bare', who was dead before he was born; and she knows that Willy, her eldest-born, has gone only into the next room, into which she too will go in a minute. Hers indeed is 'a time of peace', and in the light of her full and satisfying life, there 'is Grace to be had' (p. 1109). 'The Grandmother' '*quite* upset' Carlyle. '[Carlyle] kept saying, "Poor old body, poor old body. And Alfred wrote that: well, I didn't know it"' (*Memoir*, II, p. 241).

In 'Rizpah' the exaggeration of sentiment borders on the grotesque; however, Tennyson is careful to stress the rightness of the old woman's cause. She is neither Dickensian nor Brontean; instead, the focus remains on her love for her son and the need to redeem him. He is 'flesh of her flesh' and 'bone of her bone'; *they* are not his mother. 'You have never borne a child—you are just as hard as stone' (p. 1249). She is certain that he will not go to Hell, for the Lord 'has looked into my care,/And he means me I'm sure to be happy with Willy' (p. 1249). As with the Victorian artist, Tennyson is intent in the idyls on appealing to sentiment. It is no wonder that in a trial edition of the poem the title *The Mother* was added, preceding *Rizpah,* and there was an introductory note, the end of which was: 'She is here represented on her deathbed with a lady visitor' (p. 1246). The response was expected to be as much visual and emotional as intellectual, and Tennyson made certain that it was.

Perhaps the poem that should, instead of 'Isabel', be cited as Tennyson's most successful tribute to wives and mothers is 'Demeter and Persephone' (p. 1373). Hallam Tennyson tells us that it was written at his request, because he knew that his father considered Demeter 'one of the most beautiful types of womanhood'. The idyl's effectiveness comes primarily from the fact that although the poet does bring in other matters, such as the coming of Christianity, he never lets us lose sight of Demeter as mother, as one whose 'childless cry,/A cry that rang through Hades, Earth, and Heaven!' (p. 1375) was able to thwart Fate itself and 'redeem' her child. Her deep distress over Persephone's absence, her envy of human wives, even 'nested birds' and 'the cubbed lioness', her grief for man through her grief for her child—'the jungle rooted in his shattered hearth'—all of this depicted by Tennyson in his finest poetic manner, makes clear those qualities that he felt went into the making of 'perfect' womanhood. Most movingly depicted is her profound sense of loss; the sentiment in this case seems not exaggerated at all because of the enormity of the punishment and the overwhelmingly touching response of the mother. She is, after all, 'Earth—Goddess', cursing the 'Gods of Heaven', and her child has been banished, has been doomed to be the Bride of Darkness 'for ever and for evermore' (p. 1377).

The poet's success in conveying the sentiment comes from the kind of exaggeration, then, that would still seem to carry its own logic. These are gods and goddesses, but they display human traits, and Demeter herself indicates her great concern for the closeness to humans. She, as we have already seen, envied human wives and gave 'Thy breast to ailing infants in the night,/And set the mother waking in amaze/To find her sick one whole' (p. 1375). The identification with humans goes further, for when Persephone returns:

> Queen of the dead no more—my child! Thine eyes
> Again were human-godlike, and the Sun
> Burst from a swimming fleece of winter gray,
> And robed thee in his day from head to feet—
> 'Mother!' and I was folded in thine arms.
>
> (p. 1374)

Thus the sentiment is kept in bounds, made believable as well as affective by the blurring of the human-godlike. These are not the same gods and goddesses one finds in 'The Lotos-Eaters', 'careless of mankind'. Demeter knows the mother's childless cry and the worship which is love.

It is, finally, the firm control of the poetry itself that makes the exaggerated sentiment just that rather than the sentimentality of which Tennyson has been accused. It is the imagery and the language that convince the readers of the rightness of their emotional response. Demeter is, indeed, more sinned against than sinning, and both the nature of her grief and the manner by which she redeems her child are perfectly expressed by the poet's 'vaguely suggestive' imagery, his perfect blending of mood and landscape, his use of the rich tradition. Demeter's grief touches everything and all, as it should, since she is, after all, Earth-Goddess:

> My quick tears killed the flowers, my ravings hushed
> The bird, and lost in utter grief I failed
> To send my life through olive-yard and vine
> And golden grain, my gift to helpless man.
> Rain-rotten died the wheat, the barley spears
> Were hollow-husked, and leaf fell, and the sun,
> Pale at my grief, drew down before his time
> Sickening, and Aetna kept her winter snow.
>
> (p. 1377)

There is just the right note to all this, and the same effect is achieved in lyrics like 'Tears, Idle Tears' and 'Now Sleeps the Crimson Petal', the perfect blending of rage, sorrow, despair, the 'ultimate oxymoronic' thrust. Tears 'kill' the flower; ravings 'hush' the bird; she fails 'to send' her life through that which is her 'gift' to man, who is 'helpless' because of her 'utter grief' at the loss of her child, who is now the Bride of Darkness.

The poet's control is just as much in evidence as he depicts the change that occurs in Demeter when she once again sees her child. The opening image of the 'climate-changing' bird that flies all night and 'falls' on the threshold captures perfectly the initial realisation of Demeter that her child is, indeed, coming to her; the following images—the 'sudden nightingale' flashing into song, a gleam 'as of the moon'—depicts the growing emotional as well as intellectual response of Demeter: 'Persephone/Queen of the dead no more—my child!' (p. 1374). With the word *child* we are brought into complete identification with Demeter's strong maternal feeling, and Tennyson presents the embrace of mother and child in the climactic sun image: 'and the Sun/Burst from a swimming fleece of winter gray,/And robed thee in his day from head to feet—/"Mother!" and I was folded in thine arms' (p. 1374). With truth might Demeter say: 'But when before have Gods or men beheld/The Life that has descended re-arise,/And lighted from above him by the Sun?' (p. 1375). It is her love that has accomplished this transformation from Earth–Goddess and Bride of the Dead to mother and child.

The structure of the idyl is worth noting. In some ways Tennyson has given the climax at the very beginning, with the emergence of Persephone and the reunion of mother and child. The rest seems almost anticlimactic, especially the quiet ending, with its Keatsian overtones of autumn (p. 1378). Ricks insists that 'Christian love and resurrection are the frame' for Demeter and Persephone, but one could argue with that. It is not Christian love that brings the child back but mother love, and the Tennysonian 'frame' seems as much Swinburnian as Christian.[10] What is idylic about the ending and provides the climactic effect is the Tennysonian emphasis on the control of time and nature by Demeter and, through her, by humans. If man is to assert his morality and resist becoming 'Darwinised', one with nature and heedless of time and ethics, then he must be able to 'play' with time, to control it.

This becomes one of Tennyson's idylic themes, and one reason why the ending of 'Demeter and Persephone' is important and truly prophetic. In contrast to the time when she was deep in sorrow, when she failed to send her gift to men and the sun itself, pale at her grief, sickened, and Aetna kept her winter snow, in contrast to this time, we return to a time not so much of 'mists and mellow fruitfulness' as one of discipline and self-control:

> Once more the reaper in the gleam of dawn
> Will see me by the landmark far away,
> Blessing his field, or seated in the dusk
> Of even, by the lonely threshing-floor,
> Rejoicing in the harvest and the grange.
>
> (p. 1378)

The emphasis here is on the regularity of time and the quiet joy that comes from the 'harvest hymns of Earth' and the 'worship which is Love'. The emphasis is also on resurrection and redemption, on spring as well as autumn. While there are clearly Christian echoes and meanings, Tennyson still stresses the 'harvest hymns of Earth'. Earth is that to which Persephone returns; it is there that humans dwell. In the future they may become Carlylean 'heroes', may make themselves 'as God'; for now they must learn to live by those virtues that make life more than merely bearable. Unlike the isolated Carlyle or the stoical Arnold, Tennyson in his idylic vision sees the future as something other than mere survival; humans can control time, even Nature, and through Love gain that peace and joy symbolised in the reunion of Demeter and Persephone, mother and child.

The idyls examined up to this point illustrate clearly, then, that to make a distinction between the bard of public sentiments and the poet of private sensibilities is not only untenable but misleading. Tennyson's finest poetic moments are often found in his idyls and nowhere is this claim better illustrated than in his longer efforts: 'Enoch Arden', 'Aylmer's Field', *Maud, The Princess* and *Idylls of the King*. The last three have not often been considered under that rubric, although recently Dwight Culler has in fact suggested that they might be. The other two—'Enoch Arden' and 'Aylmer's Field'—have, but not often in the context which I have provided for Tennyson's idyls. They are, in fact, often dismissed as 'interruptions in Tennyson's career' instead of being seen as some of his finest poems. They are often dismissed for the very qualities that Tennyson found most desirable to gain his idylic effects: simplicity, 'single-mindedness', the 'narrowing of emotion and focus', the very artistic effects he felt necessary to emphasise those ethical and moral human denominators that separate humans from non-humans. To appreciate Tennyson's subtlety and art, it is from this view that these longer idyls should be approached.

21

'Aylmer's Field'

Certainly one should note in 'Aylmer's Field' the poet's emphasis throughout on the spectre of Darwinism and the value associated with the hearth and the family. From the very beginning we are told of the fragility of our 'frames', and throughout the idyl the contrast is made between the bestial and the human. The introduction of Sir Aylmer makes clear his connection to non-human, material things; we see him only in terms of his 'capacious hall', the 'hundred shields', his 'blazing wyvern'. From the beginning he is also directly associated with the bestial, with the hunt and killing. In this respect he is somewhat reminiscent of the narrator in *Maud*. Sir Aylmer and a neighbour talk of 'the latest fox—where started—killed'; they go on:

> and did Sir Aylmer know
> That great pock-pitten fellow had been caught?
> Then made his pleasure echo, hand to hand,
> And rolling as it were the substance of it
> Between his palms a moment up and down—
> 'The birds were warm, the birds were warm upon him;
> We have him now:'
>
> (p. 1167)

At one of the climactic moments of the idyl, when he and his wife warn Leolin to stay away from Edith, we find Tennyson's description in the same vein: 'Him glaring, by his own stale devil spurred,/And, like a beast hard-ridden, breathing hard' (p. 1168). And again:

> 'Boy, should I find you by my doors again,
> My men shall lash you from them like a dog;
> Hence!' with a sudden execration drove
> The footstool from before him, and arose;
> So, stammering 'scoundrel' out of teeth that ground

As in a dreadful dream, while Leolin still
Retreated half-aghast, the fierce old man
Followed, and under his own lintel stood
Storming with lifted hands, a hoary face
Meet for the reverence of the hearth, but now,
Beneath a pale and unimpassioned moon,
Vext with unworthy madness, and deformed.

(p. 1169)

Right up to the very end the bestial association of Sir Aylmer is emphasised. As he leaves the church before the sermon itself is ended he reels, 'as a footsore ox in crowded ways/Stumbling across the market to his death,/Unpitied' (p. 1182). Indeed, at the very end of the poem nature and the animals have completely taken over. It is as though the poet is intoning over the death of Sir Aylmer not only ashes to ashes, dust to dust, but beast to beast. He has gone back to his 'natural' element:

Then the great Hall was wholly broken down,
And the broad woodland parcelled into farms;
And where the two contrived their daughter's good,
Lies the hawk's cast, the mole had made his run,
The hedgehog underneath the plantain bores,
The rabbit fondles his own harmless face,
The slow-worm creeps, and the thin weasel there
Follows the mouse, and all is open field.

(p. 1183)

There is something strikingly unpleasant about the description here. Ricks quotes as a parallel Isaiah 13: 20–22 (p. 1183), and certainly the 'houses full of doleful creatures' is a fitting parallel to the Tennysonian passage. There is something still more sinister about the whole passage, however, and Tennyson is obviously attempting to demonstrate by the creatures he chooses the particularly insidious effect of Aylmerism and its far-reaching implications. There is not, in this description, the pleasant effect one has from a poem like 'Tintern Abbey', in which the soothing influence of the natural scene is paramount; instead, there are those 'doleful creatures' and their deceitful, treacherous ways: the hedgehog 'bores', the rabbit 'fondles', the slow-worm 'creeps'. While, as Kincaid says, there is some irony in the final passage—'the two contrived their daughter's good'—there is very much more than irony.[1] The tone, rather, is more one of despair, and the thematic thrust lies in the direction of grim prophecy, for this is what happens when humans ignore those basic virtues that begin with the family and affect nations and determine, ultimately, the survival of the race itself.

It is no accident that in 'Aylmer's Field' the hearth and home play such an important role. At the end the great Hall is 'wholly broken down'. The theme of the sermon is 'your house is left unto you desolate'. Part of the blame for the desolation of the house lies directly on Aylmer's wife, who has neither understood nor assumed her full responsibilities. She is, we learn, 'a faded beauty of the Baths/Insipid as the Queen upon a card;/Her all of thought and bearing hardly more/Than his own shadow in a sickly sun' (p. 1161). She does nothing but cool 'her false cheek with a featherfan' as Sir Aylmer berates Leolin for thinking seriously of Edith, and she 'flow[s] in shallower acrimonies' when Edith is forbidden to see him any more: 'Never one kindly smile, one kindly word' (p. 1175). She has, certainly in idylic terms, abandoned her true role, and it is no wonder that she is unable to bear the sermon, the words of which reveal to her the 'sense of meanness in her unresisting life'. Like those doleful creatures of the concluding passage, she has lived much of her life underground and in darkness, 'creeping' and 'burrowing', refusing to take on those duties and responsibilities rightfully hers as wife and mother.

Her responsibility is at least as great as Sir Aylmer's himself, perhaps in some ways greater, since her 'domestic' role is such an important one. Unlike her daughter, she never visits 'the labourer's homes/A frequent haunt of Edith'; Tennyson's description of these huts is especially significant, since it stresses the importance of the hearth and is done in that vaguely suggestive style that blends mood and landscape so well:

> At random scattered, each nest in bloom.
> Her art, her hand, her counsel all had wrought
> About them: here was one that, summer-blanched,
> Was parcel-bearded with the traveller's joy
> In Autumn, parcel ivy-clad; and here
> The warm-blue breathings of a hidden hearth

Broke from a bower of vine and honeysuckle:
One looked all rosetree, and another wore
A close-set robe of jasmine sown with stars:
This had a rosy sea of gillyflowers
About it; this, a milky-way on earth,
Like visions in the Northern dreamer's heavens,
A lily-avenue climbing to the doors;
One, almost to the martin-haunted eaves
A summer burial deep in hollyhocks;
Each, its own charm; and Edith's everywhere.

(p. 1165)

Contrast these huts to the emptiness of the manor house, desolate, the burden of the sermon's message. Tennyson's insistence on having Edith's mother assume full responsibility for the failure of her hearth and home is best illustrated, perhaps, in the scene, already referred to, in which Leolin is denounced and she does nothing to prevent it; however, there is no denying the force of the 'hut' passage in depicting her as having abandoned her redemptive role. She has clearly failed as a wife and mother.

The extent of her failure may also be seen when she is compared to other heroines of Tennyson's domestic idyls, particularly those who are 'active', and to Edith herself. Certainly Edith reveals a determination never shown by her mother. As the lovers part, a 'perilous meeting', she 'In agony, . . . promised that no force,/Persuasion, no, nor death could alter her'. That this is no hysterical rambling is proved by her own steadfastness, even to her death, 'crying upon the name of Leolin' (p. 1175). Her mother—'Listless in all despondence'—stands in marked contrast. She stands, too, in marked contrast to the determined 'redemptive' women, as well as to those Tennysonian 'ladies' who actively, sometimes violently, fight for their lovers in such poems as 'The Sisters' [We are two daughters of one race], 'The Bandit's Death' and 'The Flight'. One might object that this is placing too heavy a burden on one whose protests and attempts at change would have no effect on the 'country God', long made 'stubborn' through pride and prejudice, but that is not the point at all. The women of Tennyson's idyls do have a large part to play, and the measure of their success is how well they succeed as wives and mothers.

Theirs really, we must remember, is the task of redeeming human civilisation.

'Aylmer's Field' illustrates still further Tennyson's technical approach to the idyl, especially the way he employed the mediatorial form to stress the sentiment and pathos of situation and theme. As he does in 'Dora' and so many other idyls, in 'Aylmer's Field' Tennyson is clearly neglecting what Arnold called the 'construction' of a poem to expand those sections dealing with the sentiment and theme. He willingly sacrifices the 'story' to concentrate on those elements so important to his idylic purpose. He feels no artistic compunction about stopping the 'action' of the idyl to dwell on the pathos and sentiment, since the mediatorial approach, after all, stresses the 'emotive and referential' and seeks to bring fact and value into some kind of meaningful relation. 'Aylmer's Field', then, is typical in its idylic pattern; Tennyson expands those sections directly contributing to theme and sentiment, such as the moments between the lovers, those showing the selfish pride and arrogance of Aylmer and, of course, the sermon itself. These passages, seemingly disruptive and digressive to modern critics, are intrinsic to the idylic mode; the mediatorial approach, in its attempt to relate life and poetry, is the prosodic key to Tennyson's idylic vision.

22

'Enoch Arden'

The 'idylic vision' also informs our understanding of 'Enoch Arden', a poem whose central purpose has often been misunderstood and characters unfairly judged. In speaking of Philip Ray, for instance, Kincaid grudgingly notes some of his virtues: 'there is a Philip Ray, a character whose victory ought certainly to be a subject for irony, as he has nothing but the opposite of heroic qualities: extreme reticence, prudence, weakness, and the kind of morbid tenacity one associates with creeping plants. But he is, I suppose, made a hero' (Kincaid, p. 230). Even if one disregards the tone of this criticism, there is something astonishing about the denial of prudence, say, as a virtue. What exactly are 'heroic' qualities in the modern mode? Is reticence really a vice or unheroic?

The problem becomes much more serious, of course, when the contextual basis of the poem is disregarded and the idylic vision ignored. What Kincaid calls a 'wild misreading' of the idyl, for instance, is really neither all that 'wild' nor a 'misreading' (Kincaid, p. 230). He talks about the completion of a pattern, which need not disturb us, but he does suggest the possibility of the 'defeat of Enoch by the very money he sought' (p. 230). This defeat is by no means as impossible as Kincaid imagines, and one can have this defeat without necessarily having Enoch become 'the image of the archetypal ironic victim'. One can have complexity without having 'a pattern', and one can have sentiment and even domestic tragedy without necessarily 'turning the shock of irony into . . . mild and comfortable sensationalism' (p. 231).

Kincaid is correct, then, in some details, but in his seeking always a specific pattern of irony or comedy he fails to note the poet's larger 'idylic' achievement. Because of his failure, he underrates Tennyson's triumph in the genre. Ray is, in fact, a heroic character, one redeemed by Annie. Enoch is a lost character, one whom Annie tries but fails to save. Not to see these relationships is to ignore the complexity of the idyl. Enoch is wrong to go off on his voyage, just as Ulysses is, and nothing he says or does makes it right. His reason is to go 'As oft as needed—returning rich, / Become the master of a larger craft, / With fuller profits lead an easier life' (p. 1133). These are hardly convincing reasons, and Annie indicates her concern. In fact, for the first time since their marriage, she 'fought against his will', not with 'brawling opposition', but with 'many a tear, / Many a sad kiss by day by night renewed / (Sure that all evil would come out of it) / Besought him, supplicating, if he cared / For her or his dear children, not to go' (p. 1133).

She is right, of course, but she cannot convince him, and he selfishly goes. Douglas C. Fricke comments on the ambivalence of Enoch's desires, and he correctly characterises Enoch as 'strong-willed, possessive and fearful of poverty', one who 'in his pursuit of economic independence . . . seems to become almost blind to love'.[1] His blindness is such that even Annie cannot save him. The result is his 'death' on the island, the death which is finally and ironically acknowledged by the 'costly funeral' at the end of the idyl. Fricke correctly comments on the last two lines as being 'multi-levelled' in their irony. It is, indeed, a 'costly' funeral, and the 'little port / Had seldom seen a costlier' one. Enoch never does achieve 'a new life' (Fricke, p. 111) because he has betrayed his wife and family; he cannot be redeemed, even by Annie, who has tried desperately but in vain to save him.

The Darwinian context is important, for in 'Enoch Arden' Tennyson makes the same contrast he often stressed in much of his poetry between 'death' on an island paradise and 'life' in civilisation (p. 697). In 'Locksley Hall' in fact, he had rejected those 'knots of Paradise' for 'fifty years of Europe'. The implied commendation of 'civilisation' is found, also, in such poems as 'The Lotos-Eaters' and in such idyls as 'The Wreck' and 'Aylmer's Field', in which he condemns that 'land of hops and poppy-mingled corn. / Little about it stirring save a brook! / A sleepy land' (p. 1161). When Enoch is stranded in his 'Eden of all plenteousness', that place of 'eternal summer', we know that he has lost all contact with the human element and is himself no longer 'human' (p. 1145). 'Downward from his mountain gorge / Stept the long-hair long-bearded solitary, / Brown, looking hardly human, strangely clad, / Muttering and mumbling, idiotlike it seemed / With inarticulate rage, and making signs / They knew not what'. He never can return to the land of the living; he must perish. We can gauge precisely his state of his gradual loss of all human (and humane) contact:

> but what he fain had seen
> He could not see, the kindly human face,
> Nor even hear a kindly voice, but heard
> The myriad shriek of wheeling ocean-fowl,
> The league long roller thundering on the reef,
> The moving whisper of huge trees that branched
> And blossomed in the zenith, or the sweep
> Of some precipitous rivulet to the wave,
> As down the shore he ranged, or all day long
> Set often in the seaward-gazing gorge,
> A shipwrecked sailor, waiting for a sail
>
> (p. 1144)

That the 'human' part of Enoch is gone is made abundantly clear by the concluding lines of this passage, lines that show how 'dwarfed' Enoch has become by those natural elements about him and suggest once again Tennyson's skill in blending mood and landscape:

> No sail from day to day, but every day
> The sunrise broken into scarlet shafts
> Among the palms and ferns and precipices;
> The blaze upon the waters to the east;
> The blaze upon his island overhead;
> The blaze upon the waters to the west;
> Then the great stars that globed themselves in Heaven,
> The hollower-bellowing ocean, and again
> The scarlet shafts of sunrise—but no sail.
>
> (p. 1144)

Enoch is in hell, and it is with Enoch's 'death' in mind that one comes to understand and appreciate fully Annie's redemption of Philip. Philip's 'heroic' qualities are Telemachan: 'domestic' or 'idylic' ones. He is, as Kincaid states, reticent and prudent, qualities which Enoch clearly lacked. He is also unselfish, loyal, kind, generous, willing to make sacrifices for Annie and the children. These are qualities civilisation needs in order to resist nature, qualities nurtured in family life. Unlike Enoch, particularly, Philip is not strong-willed and possessive. There is not the ambivalence regarding Philip that there is about Enoch, and this is artistically as it should be. It is Philip, after all, who will become associated with hearth and home. He is the 'civilised' rather than the 'natural' person, and it is Annie who helps him become so. At the end of the idyl it is Philip we (along with Enoch, looking in) see 'on the right hand of the hearth':

> Stout, rosy, with his babe across his knees;
> And o'er her second father stoopt a girl,
> A later but a loftier Annie Lee,
> Fair-haired and tall, and from her lifted hand
> Dangled a length of ribbon and a ring
> To tempt the babe, who reared his creasy arms,
> Caught at and ever missed it, and they laughed;

Annie, of course, is on the other side of the hearth:

> glancing often toward her babe,
> But turning now and then to speak with him,
> Her son, who stood beside her tall and strong,
> And saying that which pleased him, for he smiled.
>
> (p. 1148)

Consider the marked contrast of Philip and Annie with Sir and Lady Aylmer, who are also seen on either side of their hearth. In the 'desolate' Aylmer household are found bitterness, selfishness, greed, pride; in the Ray household are warmth, love, joy. We can now fully appreciate Tennyson's idylic vision. Enoch is associated with poverty, it is true, but also with death and sorrow, with selfishness and self-will and possessiveness. Enoch had his own kind of Aylmerism. Enoch's last view of his family, just before his voyage, is a sad one; he casts his strong arms 'about his drooping wife' and leaves his children, two 'wonder-stricken', the third 'sickly', who is sleeping after 'a night of feverous wakefulness'. In contrast to Enoch, again, Philip's relations with his family are joyful and richly satisfying. Because, unlike Enoch, Philip has refused to impose blindly his will on Annie and because he has openly responded to her, she is able to save him. He knows, as does the Prince and the narrator of *Maud*, that women must be treated as equals before they can do their 'larger work'. 'Philip's true heart, which hungered for her peace', ultimately prevails; Annie, as she has not been able to do with Enoch, can now enter the 'larger woman-world of wives and mothers':

> but when her child was born,
> Then her new child was as herself renewed,
> Then the new mother came about her heart,
> Then her good Philip was her all-in-all,
> And that mysterious instinct wholly died.
>
> (p. 1142)

The difference in Philip and Enoch may be seen, then, through the different places with which they are finally identified: Enoch with the lush island of death, Philip with the life-giving home in which the family resides. Enoch is a lost soul and is identified as such in terms of the way that he is dwarfed by those elements of nature that finally overwhelm him. When he leaves he tells Annie to keep a 'clean hearth and a clear fire' for him; instead, he is forced to live on the island which, paradoxically, seems to have no limit. He remains alone, haunted by memories of the past, but ever mindful of his own frailty and insignificance. Some of this fear has already been suggested by passages quoted above in which he waits for a sail. The sense of his own 'smallness' is best seen, perhaps, in the following passage:

> The mountain wooded to the peak, the lawns
> And winding glades high up like ways to Heaven,
> The slender coco's drooping crown of plumes,
> The lightning flash of insect and bird,
> The lustre of the long convolvuluses
> That coiled around the stately stems, and ran
> Even to the limit of the land, the glows
> And glories of the broad belt of the world,
> All these he saw.
>
> (pp. 1143–4)

Everywhere for Enoch there is nothing that he can control or grasp; all is winding up to heaven or running to the limit of the land; he is Ulyssean, conscious always of the limitless expanses of space and, of course, time.

Philip and Annie, on the other hand, are seen always in 'confined' spaces and are always associated with domestic activities. Unlike Enoch, who can only wait for his rescue while 'The sunny and rainy seasons came and went/Year after year', Philip and Annie are seen at specific times, on specific occasions, in familiar places. On the occasion of the child's burial Philip speaks to Annie in her own home. Annie and Philip talk of years in specific numbers. Philip can, in fact, wait, for he knows there is an end; a year is not so long. The merry sound of the wedding bells is far different from the sound of the breaking waves on Enoch's isle, the hollower-bellowing ocean, the human as opposed to the natural. The hearth-scene that we witness at the end is the culmination of all, for the family around the hearth symbolises the way by which humans come to control the natural, especially time and space.

Again, contrast this scene with that in 'Aylmer's Field' when the two Powers of the House stand on either side of the hearth and berate Leolin. They betray their trust in their way as much as Enoch did his, and the indication of their betrayal is the way by which they too, like Enoch, are eventually overcome by time. Unlike Philip and Annie, Sir and Lady Aylmer are members of a 'vanished race', for once they lose their civilised values they can no longer govern time, space or themselves. This is why Averill in his sermon links them with those who were overcome by the flood, 'Which rolling o'er the palaces of the proud,/When since had flood, fire, earthquake, thunder, wrought/Such waste and havock' (p. 1177). In Tennyson's idylic vision one is either defeated by nature or one controls it and all it contains, and the triumph of the family becomes the triumph of human civilisation itself.

23

Maud

In *Maud, The Princess* and *Idylls of the King* we see the culmination of Tennyson's idylic art. In each, Tennyson has managed to blend idylic elements, contextual and artistic, and thus provide the most effective examples of the genre. More than any of the idyls they are 'challengingly Tennysonian', reflecting both the tremendous care and time he devoted to the genre and the special Tennysonian approach to sentiment and love, qualities at the heart of the idyl. They translate old motifs into modern terms and bring the 'common' things of life within the sphere of poetry; in fact, they were condemned by some critics for being too concerned with 'contemporary' subjects. All three also exhibit the 'new pattern' Tennyson established in the idylic mode. Again, all, especially *The Princess,* received harsh words from the critics because of the 'mixed' nature of the poetry. Indeed, much ink has been spilt over the mixture of different kinds of poetry in these poems—*The Princess* is sub-titled a 'medley'—but they simply reflect the special nature of the genre itself, its tendency to 'break its bounds', its principal artistic device being 'digression'. All of this puzzled Arnold, who could not understand the way that Tennyson was working to blend narrative and lyric into an idylic whole and who saw only a lack of 'careful construction'. The 'medley-like' characteristic of *The Princess* would not have disturbed or even surprised anyone who had read Tennyson's poetry carefully, particularly since the idyls had comprised such a 'very large portion of his poetic work' and, further, contained 'most of his contribution to the history of Victorian England' (Baum, p. 175).

What *Maud* and *The Princess* particularly demonstrate, however, and what the critics, from Tennyson's own time up to the present, have always recognised and praised, is his own special kind of 'love poetry', particularly his 'love-landscapes', the perfect fusion of mood and landscape. In both are found the culmination of this 'rich indirection in natural description' by which Tennyson is able to convey those 'domestic' situations that are the basis of each poem. Whether this love ends in 'tragedy', as in *Maud,* or in joy and happiness, as in *The Princess*, Tennyson's delineation of it, from inception to end, is always artistically sure and impressive. One need not, I think, dwell on this point, for the poetry is its own best evidence. The rich lyric treasures of *Maud* all attest the poet's perfect artistry in this respect. In *The Princess* one thinks not only of the added songs but those blank-verse lyrics that were always included in the idyl. Buckley cites particularly 'Now Sleeps the Crimson Petal', 'Come Down, O Maid' and 'Tears, Idle Tears', and all three certainly illustrate that rich indirection in natural description by which the poet was able to convey to deepest feelings and emotions (Buckley, *Tennyson*, p. 105). All three, occurring as they do at crucial times in the idyl, serve not only to convey substantive meaning but also, through the poet's exquisite blend of mood and landscape, portray tellingly and convincingly Tennyson's domestic vision.

The substantive powers displayed in these idyls are as impressive as the artistic ones, and, of course, the Carlylean influence is evident. Tennyson, however, provides his own 'solutions'. In speaking of *The Princess*, Killham talks of 'variations upon a fundamentally similar situation' and of how 'certain elements' of this fundamentally similar situation are 'assembled'. He mentions such specific elements as Tennyson's dissatisfaction with modern life, a neurotic or unbalanced hero, women obliged to decide between love and interest and an absorption in the discoveries of science, all 'fitted to a story of a young man's risks in dangerous meetings with a woman'.[1] While this is accurate enough, Killham and other critics have failed to note other more profound 'elements' found in the idyls. I refer specifically to the Darwinian threat, the cosmic dwarfing of man and the consequent exaggerated sentiment and morality to offset this dwarfing in the attempt to show man's self-esteem and his 'control' of space and time and, finally, the way that the 'natural' must be offset by the 'civilised', especially in terms of the family and its beneficial influences.

In an illuminating essay on the function of the imagery in *Maud* Killham has shown, although he does not use the term, the extent of the Darwinian threat as revealed in Tennyson's images of animals. The hero of the poem, Killham tells us, see men 'in general to be no better than the vilest animals'; and he also points out that the English are represented in terms of a rat, serpents and various other animals, and men are represented by the bull, the fly, the lean and hungry wolf, the raven, the drone, the venomous worm, the bird of prey and, shades of 'Aylmer's Field', the titmouse.[2] The Darwinian threat is also the basis of Tennyson's depiction of war, both the war of battles and the undeclared commercial and social war in his own country. The unifying thread is the one of unchecked competition, the survival of the fittest, the elimination of the weak by the strong. At the heart of Tennyson's condemnation of his own country and the abuses of his 'civilised' countrymen is his recognition that they have let their 'natural' selves triumph; hence, there is no distinction to be made between the Darwinian natural struggle and the battles fought on the battlefields of commerce or war:

VI

> Why do they prate of the blessings of Peace? We have made
> them a curse,
> Pickpockets, each hand lusting for all that is not its own;
> And lust of gain, in the spirit of Cain, is it better or worse
> Than the heart of the citizen hissing in war on his hearthstone?

VII

> But these are the days of advance, the works of the men of
> mind,
> When who but a fool would have faith in a tradesman's ware
> or his word?
> Is it peace or war? Civil war, as I think, and that of a kind
> The viler, as underhand, not openly bearing the sword.

(pp. 1041–2)

After citing these abuses—the trampled wife, the poor hovelled and hustled together like swine, the babe killed by the Mammonite mother for the burial fee—Tennyson can conclude:

> Is it peace or war? better, war! Loud war by land and by sea,
> War with a thousand battles, and shaking a hundred thrones.

The cosmic dwarfing of man is also a significant concern in *Maud*. Killham quotes the unCarlylean lines that indicate the poet's awareness of that 'sad astrology' that 'teaches that even the stars are tyrants':

> Innumerable, pitiless, passionless eyes,
> Cold fires, yet with power to burn and brand
> His nothingness into man.
>
> (p. 1068)

Earlier in the poem the hero had talked of the 'many a million of ages' that have gone into the making of man (p. 1050) and the many suns and the wide world, our own planet being just one (p. 1051). The 'nothingness of man' is what he feels, and it is that feeling which the love of and for Maud dispels. It is significant, for instance, that just after he has commented on the 'tyrant' stars in the sky, those 'passionless eyes' and 'cold fires', he is able to defy them because of his newly realised love for Maud. No longer do they concern him; he has learned how to govern them, or at least he has come to realise that they no longer can brand him with a 'nothingness'. Love has shown him that he is something more than a beast; he has feelings and human qualities:

> V
>
> But now shine on, and what care I,
> Who in this stormy gulf have found a pearl
> The countercharm of space and hollow sky,
> And do accept my madness, and would die
> To save from some slight shame one simple girl.
>
> (p. 1068)

Buckler has commented on how this issue of war in *Maud* is really 'incidental'. It is a poem not about war, but 'a poem about the search of a morbidly self-conscious man for an alternative to burying himself in himself'.[3] It is about more than that, too, but certainly Buckler is right in emphasising Tennyson's stress on the way that the hero escapes the Centre of Indifference and accepts his Everlasting Yea. He has come to reject the crushing oppression of space and time and accept his own humanity and humanness. The 'pure and holy' love has not so much raised his nature as enabled him to arrive at the full realisation of it. Thus, after the temporary setback in the Brittany episode, he can still see the stars as friendly rather than threatening forces. In fact, he can see hope in the sky:

My mood is changed, for it fell at a time of year
When the face of night is fair on the dewy downs,
And the shining daffodil dies, and the Charioteer
And starry Gemini hang like glorious crowns
Over Orion's grave low down in the west,
That like a silent lightning under the stars
She seemed to divide in a dream from a band of the blest,
And spoke of a hope for the world in the coming wars—
'And in that hope, dear soul, let trouble have rest,
Knowing I tarry for thee,' and pointed to Mars
As he glowed like a ruddy shield on the Lion's breast.

(pp. 1090–91)

Whether one agrees with the sentiment or not, the point is that the poet has shown the triumph of the hero over his previous, shell-like self, his Prufrockian personality. His humanness enables him to conclude:

And myself have awaked, as it seems to the better mind;
It is better to fight for the good than to rail at the ill;
I have felt with my native land, I am one with my kind,
I embrace the purpose of God, and the doom assigned.

(p. 1093)

As these lines indicate, the issue of war really is incidental. What is to the point is the hero's final acceptance of his oneness with his kind. Indeed, one vital concept in *Maud*, that has up to now not been given due consideration is the close connection that Tennyson establishes, through the hero of course, between the plight of the family and the nation. From the very beginning of the poem we are shown how the familial difficulties of the hero are reflected in the nation itself. The poem starts with the lament by the hero over the family that was destroyed by the villainy of Maud's father. His own father and mother are dead, and he remembers not only the mangled and crushed body of his father but also the 'shrill-edged shriek of a mother divide the shuddering night' (p. 1941). The spirit of the land is that found in each family:

> Pickpockets, each hand lusting for all that is not its own;
> And lust of gain, in the spirit of Cain, is it better or worse
> Than the heart of the citizen hissing in war on his own
> hearthstone?
>
> (pp. 1041–2)

The desecration of the hearthstone is everywhere; the poet insists that the family is the unit on which the nation and the world are built. The corruption of one leads to the corruption and destruction of the other. Everywhere the hero turns there is evidence that the family unit has disintegrated. The 'filthy by-lane rings to the yell of the trampled wife'; a 'Mammonite mother kills her babe for a burial fee'. When he first thinks of Maud, the hero sees her in this context; he flees from her and from the 'cruel madness' of love because she is 'unmeet for a wife':

> Your mother is mute in her grave as her image in marble
> above;
> Your father is ever in London, you wander about at your
> will;
> You have but fed on the roses and lain in the lilies of life.
>
> (p. 1052)

It is, however, Maud's 'mute' mother and the hero's own mother who bring about the change in his attitude towards Maud, from first seeing her as unmeet for a wife, neither 'courtly nor kind' (p. 1053), to one for whom he would die 'to save from some slight shame'. His first favourable thoughts of Maud are in conjunction with his own family, for he remembers her as a child, the 'delight of the village', with her 'sweet purse-mouth when my father dangled the grapes' and, more importantly, 'the beloved of my mother' (p. 1045). The more favourable his response to Maud, the more he is reminded of his mother, of perhaps it is the other way around. As he speculates on the motivation for Maud's smile and tender tone—perhaps it comes out of her 'pitying womanhood'—he thinks immediately of his own mother, 'gentle and good', whose love for and devotion to his father serve as reminders of the 'regenerative values of love'. We are also told that it is Maud's dying mother who had told her of the compact between the fathers, and it is for her sake that Maud wants to be reconciled to the man that her father had wronged (p. 1056). It is not from her father that Maud gets her sweetness and grace; it is from her mother. The hero's logic may not be accurate, but given the circumstances it is understandable:

Scarcely, now, would I call him a cheat;
For then, perhaps, as a child of deceit,
She might by a true descent be untrue;
And Maud is as true as Maud is sweet;
Though I fancy her sweetness only due
To the sweeter blood by the other side;
Her mother has been a thing complete,
However she came to be so allied.
And fair without, faithful within,
Maud to him is nothing akin:
Some peculiar mystic grace
Made her only the child of her mother,
And heaped the whole inherited sin
On the huge scapegoat of the race,
All, all upon the brother.

(p. 1063)

When his love for Maud reaches its zenith, he realises that he has experienced 'an atonement' of some kind, one that he is anxious to preserve. Again most naturally Maud and his mother become combined in his thoughts:

O when did a morning shine
So rich in atonement as this
For my dark-dawning youth,
Darkened watching a mother decline
And that dead man at her heart and mine:
For who was left to watch her but I?
Yet so did I let my freshness die.

III

I trust that I did not talk
To gentle Maud in our walk
(For often in lonely wanderings
I have cursed him even to lifeless things)
But I trust that I did not talk
Not touch on her father's sin:
I am sure I did but speak
Of my mother's faded cheek
When it slowly grew so thin,
That I felt she was slowly dying.
And Maud too, Maud was moved
To speak of the mother she loved
As one scarce forlorn,
Dying abroad and it seems apart
From him who had ceased to share her heart,
And ever mourning over the feud,
The household Fury sprinkled with blood
By which our houses are torn.

(pp. 1071–71)

These lines contain the substantive and thematic concerns of *Maud*: the hero's past hatred, his 'atonement' through Maud and his consistent view of her as one with his mother and her mother. They also contain the Tennysonian idylic vision. There is no doubt, for instance, that the hero is 'raised to a pure and holy love which elevates his whole nature, . . . driven into madness by the loss of her whom he has loved, and, when he has at length passed through the fiery furnace, . . . giving himself up to work for the good of mankind' (p. 1039). The hero does indeed realise his debt to Maud: 'As long as my life endures/I feel I shall owe you a debt,/That I never can hope to pay' (p. 1073). She has enabled him to escape from his 'shell', to think of others. When he states that he is, in fact, willing to die for her, he is reflecting this change. More importantly, however, he states that he does not want to die but, instead, 'live a life of truest breath,/And teach true life to fight with mortal wrongs' (p. 1069). This is a resolution that the earlier hero would not have been able to hold or utter. When he is in Brittany, he thinks not of himself, but of Maud; and it is a sign of his sanity that he does think only of her, for no longer is he buried within himself. His recovery becomes evident when he is able to make what is one of his (and the poet's) most important statements:

> I swear to you, lawful and lawless war
> Are scarcely even akin.
>
> (p. 1090)

He has come a long way from the narrator at the beginning, the one whose first words are 'I hate', the one who could utter: 'I have neither hope nor trust;/May make her heart as a millstone, set up a face as a flint,/Cheat and be cheated, and die' (p. 1042). No longer will he 'bury myself in myself, and the Devil may pipe to his own' (p. 1046). Now he can 'fight for the good' rather than 'rail at the ill'; because of Maud, who has recalled him to his humanness and those qualities associated with it, he has become one with his kind.

These last points bring into focus the specific nature of Tennyson's idylic purpose. The hero's identification with others, his awareness of his own humanness, are the first steps to his own (and the reader's) recognition of those values associated with a common humanity. These values go 'well beyond personal relationships'; they reach 'that social and moral order that encompasses the lives of man' (Fredeman, pp. 379, 381). Ultimately, of course, they influence the family, the nation and the world. The hero, then, with his concern for Maud, his family and her family, becomes increasingly 'domicentric' rather than egocentric, and to overlook or ignore his domicentricity is to misjudge Tennyson's purpose in *Maud*. The hero's feelings for Maud are those of a lover, of course, but they always must be seen in terms of Tennyson's idylic vision; Maud becomes 'meet' for a wife and a mother just because the hero comes to see her in those same qualities and virtues he saw in his own mother and in Maud's mother, those qualities and virtues that reflect the values that Tennyson saw as universal, the 'humanising denominators' on which the future of the human race depends. This is why Maud, in what is perhaps the most moving section of the poem, is identified not only with her own and the hero's mother but with Eve, our first Mother, as well:

There is none like her, none
. . . .
Dark cedar, though thy limbs have here increased,
Upon a pastoral slope as fair,
And looking to the South, and fed
With honeyed rain and delicate air,
And haunted by the starry head
Of her whose gentle will has changed my fate,
And made my life a perfumed altar-flame;
And over whom thy darkness must have spread
With such delight as theirs of old, thy great
Forefathers of the thornless garden, there
Shadowing the snow-limbed Eve from whom she came.

(pp. 1067–8)

Through his newly gained awareness the hero is able to overcome his own madness, to embrace the doom assigned. He, like Hamlet, who had his own family problems, has come to know that 'the readiness is all'. In its outward and upward movement from the personal to the family to the nation, the poem illustrates perfectly Tennyson's idylic vision, his argument for 'a concept of order that moves along an ascending hierarchical ladder from personal security, through familial stability, to a higher order in the state and in the cosmos' (Fredeman, p. 376). It is particularly significant, for instance, that in one of his earlier drafts Tennyson had tried to relate the war to the love for Maud:

Let it go or stay, so I walk henceforth resigned
By the light of a love not lost, with a purer mind
And rejoice in my native land, and am one with my kind.

(p. 1092)

Buckler is partially right, then; the issue of war is incidental in *Maud*, and the poem is not a poem about war. Yet, the war is to some extent all-important, for it helps to show the quintessential idylic Tennyson—and thus the quintessential Victorian poet—who can see the basis of national and world order in the personal and the domestic. *Maud* may be a poem about two people in love, but it is also a poem about what people must be; it may be a poem about the regenerative power of love, but it is also a poem about how that regenerative power reflects those values associated with a common humanity. It may be a poem about one man's embracing the purpose of God, but it is also a poem that illustrates those qualities that enable one to become one with one's kind and, ultimately, will enable the human race to triumph over those forces, internal and external, that would combine to destroy it. 'Not die;' says the hero, 'but live a life of truest breath, / And teach true life to fight with mortal wrongs'.

24

The Princess

Maud and *The Princess* have much in common. The two families in each have betrothed the children, and there has been some obstacle to the fulfilment of that pact. The man in each case—or the hero—pursues the heroine and has to fight her brother. The heroine's father in each poem seems particularly obnoxious, but the mothers are saintly. The hero in each poem suffers because of his love for the heroine, and their suffering takes essentially the same form. The hero of *Maud* has what seems to be a nervous breakdown and is temporarily mad, or seems to be. His delusions of not being buried deep enough would seem to indicate a certain kind of disorientation, although he makes particularly acute observations during this period. His stay in the madhouse indicates, at the least, an inability to cope with the world. The hero of *The Princess* suffers essentially the same fate. His weird seizures are evident from the beginning, but certainly his stay in the 'hospital' is very similar to that of the hero of *Maud* in the madhouse. The hero in *Maud* cried:

> Always I long to creep
> Into some still cavern deep,
> There to weep, and weep, and weep
> My whole soul out to thee.

And he goes on:

> And my bones are shaken with pain,
> For into a shallow grave they are thrust,
> Only a yard beneath the street,
> And the hoofs of the horses beat, beat,
> The hoofs of the horses beat,
> Beat into my scalp and my brain.
>
> (pp. 1086–7)

Compare these with the words of the Prince:

> And twilight dawned; and morn by morn the lark
> Shot up and shrilled in flickering gyres, but I
> Lay silent in the muffled cage of life:
> And twilight gloomed; and broader-grown the bowers
> Drew the great night into themselves, and Heaven,
> Star after star, arose and fell; but I,
> Deeper than those weird doubts could reach me, lay
> Quite sundered from the moving Universe,
> Nor knew what eye was on me, nor the hand
> That nursed me, more than infants in their sleep.
>
> (p. 830)

Both he and the hero of *Maud* experience what the Prince calls 'some mystic middle state', a condition in which, until they both wake to higher aims through the purifying experience of love, in the words of the Prince: 'Seeing I saw not, hearing not I heard' (p. 818). Both must, then, break out from this 'muffled cage of life'.

One other striking similarity between both poems is the emphasis given to the mothers. I have already indicated, in the discussion of *Maud*, the great influence of the mothers on both Maud and the hero. The hero's mother, gentle and good, provides for him the example of what love can do; it is her love and devotion that illustrate the regenerative values of love. Maud, we remember, gets all her sweetness and grace from her mother. In *The Princess* we find the same emphasis. 'The mother makes us most', says the Prince. The influence of the mothers is everywhere in *The Princess*, as in *Maud*, and that influence is most apparent at key points. Certainly there is no question as to the Prince's mother, 'mild as any saint, / Half-canonised by all that looked on her' (p. 751). At the end of the poem, at the moment when the Prince is declaring how he and his Princess will 'type' the crowning race of humankind, he again pays tribute to his mother, through whom he came to love woman:

> No Angel, but a dearer being, all dipt
> In Angel instincts, breathing Paradise,
> Interpreter between the Gods and men,
> . . . .

Happy he
With such a mother! faith in womankind
Beats with his blood, and trust in all things high
Comes easy to him, and though he trip and fall
He shall not blind his soul with clay

(p. 840)

The Princess, too, like Maud, and like the Prince, is her mother's child. When she finds the wounded Prince, and his father holds up the painting and the tress which had hung round his neck, she remembers the day when her mother, the 'good Queen', showered the tress with kisses, 'ere the days of Lady Blanche'. It is at this moment that she begins to change; there is now some self-awareness and, consciously or not, some recognition of passion as well as iron will:

Till understanding all the foolish work
Of fancy, and the bitter close of all,
Her iron will was broken in her mind;
Her noble heart was molten in her breast.

(p. 821)

She thinks of her mother again, or is reminded of her by her father, as he tries to persuade her to forgive Lady Psyche:

Whence drew you this steel temper? not from me,
Not from your mother, now a saint with saints,
She said you had a heart—I heard her say it—
'Our Ida has a heart'—just ere she died.

(p. 824)

Ida does, of course, forgive Psyche, and as she opens up the college to become a hospital, once more she invokes her mother's memory:

'Fling our doors wide! all, all, not one, but all,
Not only he, but by my mother's soul,
Whatever man lies wounded, friend or foe,
Shall enter if he will.'

(p. 827)

The similarities are there, then, because both reflect their generic characteristics. More important, however, are the differences, for they demonstrate more forcefully than anything else the reasons for Tennyson's great success with the genre in *The Princess*. Basically, the differences are those of emphasis; they reflect subtly but clearly the poet's thematic concerns, and they demonstrate, too, what he was able to do when not writing under certain pressures brought about by specific contemporary events or issues. *Maud*, with all its virtues, is marred by Tennyson's parochial interest in current events and his lifelong concern over Rosa Baring. *The Princess* is marred by neither.

One of the difficulties with *Maud* is Tennyson's apparent conviction that war is a solution to the ills of the world, at least of the nation. Somehow, he seems to be saying, perhaps partly as a result of his reading in Carlyle, somehow might seems to make right and all should 'hail once more to the banner of battle unrolled'. 'God's just wrath', accomplished through men, of course, 'shall be wreaked on a giant liar' (p. 1092). The spectre of Darwinism clearly is involved here, for war is but the ultimate result of the survival of the fittest; and in *Maud* the identification of competition and battle seems to be complete. It is only through fighting for the good, with the emphasis on the fighting, that man can overcome the terrible effects of this 'lawless war' that characterises the life of man, the peace that is no peace.

This complete identification of Darwinism with battle and the concomitant cosmic dwarfing of man, so prominent in terms of the universe itself in *Maud*, are not so apparent in *The Princess*. There is, of course, the concern with time, about which I shall say more below, but there is nowhere in *The Princess* the bleak despair evident in the words of the hero in *Maud*, as he looks up at the stars and laments the 'sad astrology':

> the boundless plan
> That makes you tyrants in your iron skies,
> Innumerable, pitiless, passionless eyes,
> Cold fires, yet with power to burn and brand
> His nothingness into man.
>
> (p. 1068)

In *The Princess* Tennyson's depiction of the hero is different in terms of his attitude towards war and battle, and the difference is a profound one. It is as though the Prince can see beyond the immediate and forecast what happens when one lives by the sword, even though his cause seems to be righteous. In many ways it is the Prince's father, rather than the Prince, who most resembles the hero of *Maud*; he, who 'cared not for the affection of the house', is always ready to seek war as a solution, always chewing his 'thrice-turned cud of wrath' (p. 853). The Prince on the other hand, represents good sense and moderation; unlike his father and unlike the hero of *Maud*, he can see no good coming from war:

> 'Not war, if possible,
> O king,' I said, 'lest from the abuse of war,
> The desecrated shrine, the trampled year,
> The smouldering homestead, and the household flower
> Torn from the lintel—all the common wrong—
> . . . .
> More soluble is this knot,
> By gentleness than war.
> . . . .
> rather, Sire, than this
> I would the old God of war himself were dead,
> Forgotten, rusting on his iron hills,
> Rotting on some wild shore with ribs of wreck,
> Or like an old-world mammoth bulked in ice,
> Not to be molten out.'
>
> (p. 805)

We remember that at one of the climactic moments of the poem Ida's noble heart was molten in her breast. Gama tells the Prince that he talks 'almost like Ida' (p. 807), and he is right, of course. The difference between the heroes of these two poems in their attitudes towards the solution of the Darwinian predicament, the lawless war in which man seemed to be engaged, is a sign of Tennyson's subtle but significant distinction between those who have knowledge and those who have wisdom. Tempered by his experience and illness, the hero of *Maud* has not yet reached the point where he can say, as does the Prince, that gentleness rather than force is the right way. Unlike the Prince, the hero of *Maud* still cannot fully distinguish between chivalric notions and practical solutions. Tennyson provides a valuable clue in this respect when he has him praise the 'chivalrous battle-song' that Maud 'warbled alone in her joy!' (pp. 1059–60). It is true that the song helps connect his love for Maud with his belief in the efficacy of war as therapeutic, but the fact remains that he still has not reached the point where he can see Maud as 'true woman' and gentleness as better than war. It is for this reason, too, that Tennyson has him say at this point: 'And ah for a man to arise in me/That the man I am may cease to be!' The Prince is that man.

The differences between the heroes demonstrate one aspect of Tennyson's theme in the poems; there are other differences that are also important, for they illustrate other concerns of Tennyson, one being the question of his epistemological position. If the Prince does come to know, *how* does he come to do so? How does he learn to distinguish between the illusory and the real? In addition, what does *The Princess* reveal about the other important contextual elements of the genre of the domestic idyl: the family and the civilisation or culture in which the family exists? How does Tennyson resolve the problem that really forms the central action of *The Princess*—that is, the conflict set up by the opposing forces on the woman. On the one hand she must redeem the man she loves through her unquestioning devotion and loyalty; on the other she must remain independent, intellectually and emotionally, so that she does not become completely absorbed into his life and the unit which is so important for the preservation of the race itself—the family.

There has been much said about the 'weird seizures' of the Prince; in fact, as Ricks tells us, this revision has been often deplored (p. 742). Whether or not one agrees with Wallace that these seizures are meant to show that 'it was not the glamour of [the Prince's] physical or moral brilliance that won his lady from her isolation' (p. 742), the fact remains that the seizures come at very crucial times in the poem and they serve to indicate Tennyson's real progress from romanticist to realist. They serve to show the hero's progress from 'selfishness' to a concern with other human beings and to his ultimate belief in the 'statelier Eden', which includes, not incidentally, 'true marriage'. Buckley states that the Prince's 'weird seizures' may 'prove to be a blessing' rather than a curse (Buckley, *Tennyson*, p. 100); they are indeed a blessing, for they are a sign of his eventual recognition of the true from the false, of the real Ida from the false Ida, of the real society and culture from the false, of the real purpose of life itself. They represent the Prince's ultimate grasp of reality and enable him, finally, to utter those words that convince Ida that he loves her as she is, not the woman in 'the crust of iron moods' that 'masked' her from 'men's reverence'. They also are a sign that he comes to know himself, something that the hero of *Maud* has not yet fully done at the end of the poem.

That the Prince does not know himself at the beginning of the poem is obvious enough. He is given to romanticising, wearing her picture by his heart and 'one dark tress'. 'And all around them both', he tells us, 'Sweet thoughts would swarm as bees about their queen' (p. 752). His actions, in fact, remind one of the pre-Juliet Romeo. When the council breaks up, the Prince, in the most accepted Romantic manner:

> rose and past
> Through the wild woods that hung about the town;
> Found a still place, and plucked her likeness out;
> Laid it on flowers, and watched it lying bathed
> In the green gleam of dewy-tasselled trees:
>
> (pp. 753–4)

His plan to dress as a woman is another obvious clue to his immaturity and romanticism; it is true, of course, that the disguise is necessary for the entrance to the college, but there is still a sense of 'saucy boyhood' about the whole escapade. Tennyson even gives a romantic lilt and tone to the poetry: 'mounted our good steeds,/And boldly ventured on our liberties' (p. 757). In these early passages the poetic vocabulary is indicative of the character: 'sweet', 'wild', 'green-gleam', 'boldly' and 'liberties'. This same picture of the Prince is conveyed in still another way when the three come before Ida for the first time. When the Princess asks Cyril if they know the Prince, he replies:

> The climax of his age! as though there were
> One rose in all the world, your Highness that,
> He worships your ideal.

She replies: 'We scarcely thought in our own hall to hear/This barren verbiage, current among men,/Light coin, the tinsel clink of compliment/. . . Your language proves you still the child' (p. 760).

It is with his first 'seizure' that the Prince begins to know himself as well as the 'real' Ida. Up to that time he has simply thought of her as someone to whom he has been 'pre-contracted', and he has worshipped that ideal. Now, in the midst of the seizure, he, for the first time, feels his heart 'beat thick with passion and with awe'; he begins to have doubts if 'that strange Poet–Princess with her grand/Imaginations might at all be won' (p. 780). His second seizure comes when he is thrust out of the gates and lasts but a short time. At this point the Prince is able to 'shake off' all doubts and 'ghostly shadowings'; his sense of reality has become stronger and he can now distinguish shadow from substance. With the third seizure comes full recognition of his 'real' self as well as Ida's. This long 'dream' (which also includes his illness) is very much like the experience Dorothea has in *Middlemarch* during that long night in which she finally decides she will marry Will Ladislaw. The Prince, too, experiences a 'rebirth' or perhaps a birth of his real self, and it is only then that he can escape his own 'muffled cage of life' and truly unite with Ida. It is only after his own false self has been exorcised that he can succeed in helping her get rid of her own.

The epistemological search for self—the real 'I'—in *The Princess* is seen to be, in Tennysonian terms, a search that encompasses not only knowing one's true self but also in learning of one's place in the 'human' world—that is, one's relationship to others. In addition to finding his real self—one with passions and feelings that go beyond the superficially romantic—the Prince discovers what is real in terms of human relationships; that is, those 'emotional ties which link men one to another' (Fredeman, p. 382). These, of course, lie at the heart of his idylic vision, and that is why *The Princess* is more than just a pretty tale. It is important that the Prince finds out what the real Ida is like because there is much more at stake than the dissolution of a pre-contract made by two petty kings. In the idyl the stakes are much higher; the love–nexus marriage, which is at the very centre of Tennyson's idylic vision, links man 'not only within the individual relationship but to his kind'. Further, the personal relationships in that nexus have implications that go far beyond; they have a bearing on 'that social and moral order that encompasses the lives of men' (Fredeman, pp. 376, 381). No wonder that the Prince is so intent on 'pursuing' the Princess and in trying to find out who the real Ida is, for the success of his quest means his own salvation and, ultimately, 'a miraculous participation in the development of man' (Killham, *The Princess*, p. 264).

One reason for *The Princess*'s being Tennyson's most successful domestic idyl is that in it he has taken up and, in his terms, successfully 'solved' one of his most perplexing problems: In what way can there be a resolution to the situation in which woman seems to have opposing roles? On the one hand she is expected to play a dominant role as lover and redeemer, emotionally and intellectually alive and assertive. It is this aspect of which Killham writes of Tennyson's conviction that 'a worthwhile love could only be achieved in the modern age by a degree of courageous independence on the part of woman' (*The Princess*, p. 192). On the other hand, she is expected to perform her proper function as wife and mother, serving her husband and family with love and devotion. In *The Princess* Ida successfully fulfils the role, and it is precisely because she succeeds that *The Princess* is Tennyson's most typical Victorian poem.

Ida must be regarded as one of Tennyson's greatest 'domestic' heroines—some named, some unnamed—with those specific qualities he most admired: courage, integrity, sexuality, loyalty, devotion, determination, intellect. That Tennyson wanted her to possess these we know, for, as Shannon tells us, he made certain in his revisions that she would be portrayed this way. Shannon points out that in the first edition the Princess might be seen as merely the dupe and tool of Lady Blanche and Lady Psyche. In the third, however, she 'becomes a dynamic figure, assuming leadership'. In that edition, the Princess's objects are immeasurably higher: 'She is motivated by a desire for service to humanity and a hope for a lasting name based on sure foundations of worth'.[1]

It is the qualities that inspire her aims that the Prince is able to see in Ida. Just as his weird seizures enable him to know himself, they also help him to know the real Ida, the woman rather than the Princess and Pedant. Even before he has his first seizure, we can see that the Prince, who woos Ida as a 'human' rather than as a man (p. 796), understands Ida's chief difficulty, her inability to break through the role she has assumed:

> My princess, O my princess! true she errs,
> But in her own grand way; being herself

Three times more noble than three score of men,
She sees herself in every woman else,
And so she wears her error like a crown
To blind the truth and me.

(p. 776)

She cannot 'blind the truth' and deceive the Prince forever, and gradually he is able to see the true woman. During his first seizure he is able to distinguish the 'hollow show' of Ida from the real one (p. 778). She is not that seemingly cruel Head, her back against a pillar, her foot on one of the tame leopards. All things are and are not, and the Prince is able to see that.

The Princess still retains her 'iron will/That axelike edge unturnable' (p. 765), but inexorably the Prince breaks through it. During his second seizure he again distinguishes the things that are and are not. The Princess, he knows, spoke but in wrath, not as she really felt. Her eight daughters of the plough are but a 'monstrous woman-guard'. It is significant, I think, that the real Lilia is brought into the poem just at this point, for the 'real' Princess, one suspects, would be much like the real Lilia. She is there to remind us of what the true woman is like. The words of Lilia's song are important, too, but I will say more of these later.

The Prince's third 'weird affliction' comes just before the battle, and here again the real from the false Ida is recognised by him. Significantly, he sees her at first as both saint and cruel lady, 'highest among the statues, statuelike' (p. 816). All these 'statuelike' images are the false ones, of course, the real one seen in the clue provided by her wanting, through all this, to keep Psyche's baby near her, a detail that does not escape the Prince. At the first opportunity he had to speak with her, we remember, he had reminded her of that which every woman counts her due: love, children, happiness (p. 779). This third seizure, combined with his long illness, during which he lies 'silent in the muffled cage of life' (p. 830), brings about the resolution both of his attempt to know the real Ida and their strange courtship. At the magic moment her 'falser self', which the Prince has been able to recognise all the while, 'slipt from her like a robe': and she is 'left' as 'woman' (p. 834). We must not forget that Ida's transformation, or perhaps discovery of her true self is the better term, involves her passionate response to the Prince's request that she but 'fulfil yourself'. 'If you be that Ida whom I knew', he tells her, 'I ask you nothing' (p. 833). Her response is unabashedly passionate and wholehearted, much like the response of the heroines of other domestic idyls:

She turned; she paused;
She stooped; and out of langour leapt a cry;
Leapt fiery Passion from the brinks of death;
And I believed that in the living world
My spirit closed with Ida's at the lips;
Till back I fell, and from mine arms she rose
Glowing all over noble shame.

(pp. 833–4)

It is at this moment in the poem that two of Tennyson's most moving lyrics appear, 'Now Sleeps the Crimson Petal' and 'Come Down, O Maid', both of which sum up the emotional as well as the intellectual union of the two. At the conclusion, after he has been able to convince her that he sees her goals as she does and will work with her to accomplish them, he can tell her, truthfully, that he has always been able to see her as she really was, as 'true woman', through 'the crust of iron moods/That masked thee from men's reverence' (p. 840). 'You cannot love me', Ida had told the Prince, thinking of herself as she was in her crust of iron moods. 'Nay, but thee', he replies, and in that 'thee' lies his recognition of the real heroine of Tennyson's domestic idyls, the heroine who, though she will rise or sink together with him, will always retain her own identity, her own being. This diversity, in fact, is the basis of their love, for it is the Prince who insists of that 'distinctive womanhood' as he utters the crucial lines:

For woman is not undevelopt man,
But diverse: could we make her as the man,
Sweet Love were slain: his dearest bond is this,
Not like to like, but like in difference.

(p. 838)

One of the 'differences' is, of course, the role of the woman in the family, as wife and mother. Towards the very end of his passionate and moving appeal to Ida, the Prince calls her, 'My bride,/My wife, my life', and these are most explicit endearments. He has always seen her as bride, but more importantly he has never lost sight of her as wife. We know that Tennyson added the songs between the sections to emphasise the child's role, but the significance of hearth and family are never lost sight of in the development of the poem. Indeed, some might argue that Tennyson was too obvious in presenting this aspect. The first lines of the poem celebrate 'the people', more specifically Sir Walter Vivian's 'tenants, wife and child' (p. 743). When the tale proper begins, we know that the Prince's father will be found wanting for he 'cared not for the affection of the house' (p. 751). By the time we reach the first song, 'As through the land at eve we went', with its lament over the dead child, we are fully aware of the crucial nature of familial relationship as well as the persuasiveness of its responsibilities. Ricks very aptly points out in a note to the first song the pertinency of two other lines from 'The Miller's Daughter': 'Although the loss had brought us pain,/ That loss but made us love the more' (p. 382). The sentiment expresses perfectly Tennyson's feelings about the special meaning one must place on the unique unit, the family.

References to family and hearth permeate the poem. As Lady Psyche concludes her lecture and begins to prophesy, she 'dilates' on the future: 'Everywhere/Two heads in council, two beside the hearth' (p. 764). When Florian and Lady Psyche get their first opportunity to chat together, 'betwixt them blossomed up/From out a common vein of memory/Sweet household talk, and phrases of the hearth' (p. 767). We are able to learn much about Blanche and Melissa from just the few lines the latter says about her family: 'I never knew my father, but she says/(God help her) she was wedded to a fool' (p. 775). We also learn much about Cyril from his simple act of taking Psyche's child:

> And held her round the knees against his waist,
> And blew the swollen cheek of a trumpeter,
> While Psyche watched them, smiling, and the child
> Pushed her flat hand against his face and laughed.
>
> (p. 769)

After Ida closes the college, she says that she will 'scatter all our maids/Till happier times each to her proper hearth' (p. 826). Not only do child, family and hearth figure prominently in the songs that were added in the third edition, as the poet himself indicated, but they are also central to some of the blank-verse lyrics that were in the poem in its first publication, the most important one, of course, being 'Come down, O maid', with its eloquent plea:

> So waste not thou; but come; for all the vales
> Await thee; azure pillars of the hearth
> Arise to thee; the children call, and I
> Thy shepherd pipe, and sweet is every sound.
>
> (p. 836)

Love is found by the 'happy threshold' states another line in the 'Sweet Idyl' that, it must be remembered, Ida, not the Prince, reads.[2]

All of these more general references to family and child and hearth are reflections of those that apply directly to the relationship between Ida and the Prince. It is through these that Tennyson indicates from the very beginning that *The Princess* is concerned with more than the telling of an 'airy romance' and that the wooing of Ida by the Prince is more than simply another version of his earlier romantic poems. The Prince has said to Ida: bride, wife, life. Their courtship is no game; it is the means by which civilisation survives. We can recognise, then, because of Tennyson's 'domestic' approach in *The Princess*, that Ida's 'rejection' of the hearth and family and children in her first serious conversation with the Prince reveals a flaw in her character, but one that fortunately, is only part of that superficial nature seen through from the very beginning by the Prince. She keeps comparing children to other things and always rejects the children:

> we like them well:
> But children die; and let me tell you, girl,
> Howe'er you babble, great deeds cannot die;
> They with the sun and moon renew their light
> For ever, blessing those that look on them.
> Children—that men may pluck them from our hearts,
> Kill us with pity, break us with ourselves.
>
> (p. 780)

This is hardly an auspicious beginning for a courtship that will lead to a 'statelier Eden', and the Princess herself senses this: 'No doubt we seem a kind of monster to you', she tells the Prince, and he himself, at this point wonders if she, with her 'grand imaginations', might at all be won.

It is not too long afterwards, however, where the real turning point in their relationship occurs, and this is the moment when Ida, the 'real' Ida, refutes her earlier logic by assuming the responsibility of the 'lily-shining' child. She dismisses Lady Blanche, but significantly refuses to let her have the child: 'We dismiss you: go./For this lost lamb (she pointed to the child)/ Our mind is changed; we take it to ourself' (pp. 794–5). From this time on we know that Ida is true woman and human; she is no longer a 'monster'. Shortly after the Prince is expelled from the college and suffers his second weird seizure, but, significantly, the song that follows, 'Thy voice is heard through rolling drums', contains the lines that reveal the future happiness of both: 'A moment, while the trumpet blow,/He sees his brood about thy knee;/the next, like a fire he meets the foe,/And strikes him dead for thine and thee' (p. 801). Thereafter follow many specific references to Ida and the child. In the message to Arac, her brother, in which she asks that he not take the Prince's life, since he risked it for her own, she adds in the postscript:

> indeed I think
> Our chiefest comfort is the little child
> Of one unworthy mother; which she left:
> She shall not have it back: the child shall grow
> To prize the authentic mother of her mind.
> I took it for an hour in mine own bed
> This morning: there the tender orphan hands
> Felt at my heart, and seemed to charm from thence
> The wrath I nursed against the world: farewell.
>
> (p. 814)

This is, indeed, an Ida different from the one who prized good deeds over children. As the Prince fights he sees Ida watching, but Ida with Psyche's baby beside her. When Ida opens up the college to the wounded and speaks to all, she has the 'babe yet in her arms'. Again, as she walks on the field:

Through open field into the lists they wound
Timorously; and as the leader of the herd
That holds a stately fretwork to the Sun,
And followed up by a hundred airy does,
Steps with a tender foot, light as on air,
The lovely, lordly creature floated on
To where her wounded brethren lay; there stayed;
Knelt on one knee,—the child on one,—and prest
Their hands, and called them dear deliverers,
And happy warriors, and immortal names.

(p. 820)

It is the 'adoption' of Psyche's child that reveals the true Ida, but even more revealing of the true woman in her is her willingness to give the child back to its rightful mother, for in this act lies the clue to those virtuous qualities that are part of her genuine nature. The 'monster' is finally destroyed, the 'true woman' revealed. By this act Ida discloses that there is no longer iron in her blood; instead, there is 'a genial warmth'. Her very human qualities—those human denominators that are the distinctive mark of man—are again seen in conjunction with children. In lines reminiscent of Tennyson's moving plea in *In Memoriam*: 'And like a man in wrath the heart/Stood up and answered 'I have felt.'/No, like a child in doubt and fear:/But that blind clamour made me wise' (p. 974), the Princess asks Psyche to forgive her:

'Come hither.
O Psyche,' she cried out, 'embrace me, come,
Quick while I melt; make reconcilement sure
With one that cannot keep her mind an hour:
Come to the hollow heart they slander so!
Kiss and be friends, like children being chid!
I seems no more: *I* want forgiveness too.'

(p. 826)

It is meaningful, I think, that the only other time Ida speaks of her 'I' so emphatically is when she speaks in wrath of her unwillingness ever to wed the Prince: '*I* wed with thee! *I* bound my precontract/

Your bride, your bondslave! not though all the gold/That veins the world were packed to make your crown/And every spoken tongue should lord you' (p. 800). These are strong words, indeed, but the 'I' in this case is obviously the old, monstrous, inhuman Ida. The 'I' who wants forgiveness from Psyche, who loves her in spite of her transgression, the 'I' who now wants to nurse the Prince, is the 'I' whom the Prince has always seen. 'Everything was changed' is the final line in Part VI, and this is followed by the song that describes Ida's transformation but also provides a strong clue as to the 'evolutionary' aspect of the work:

> Ask me no more: thy fate and mine are sealed;
> I strove against the stream and all in vain:
> Let the great river take me to the main:
> No more, dear love, for at a touch I yield:
> Ask me no more.
>
> (p. 829)

One of the reasons for *The Princess*'s being a domestic idyl and something more is the extra dimension given to it by the poet's making the love–marriage nexus more than the simple coming together of two people. Buckley states that in the poem 'the human reality is somehow to be equated with wedded love' (*Tennyson*, p. 104), and it is true, as we have seen, that Ida does become less monstrous and more human (and humane) as she comes closer and closer to her final union with the Prince. There is, however, Tennyson seems to be suggesting, something more than human in the final coming together of the two, something 'cosmic' in nature. This stress would be in keeping with one of the consistent ideas found in the contextual elements of the idyl—that is, man's attempt to oppose the cosmic dwarfing caused by the threat of Darwinism. In *The Princess* Tennyson has his hero and heroine emphasise the potential of the human race, and that potential is found in the evolutionary aspects of man, man as a developing animal, capable of becoming 'the crowning race of human kind' (Killham, *The Princess*, p. 261). Throughout the poem much is made of man's development and evolutionary fulfilment rather than his smallness and weakness. There is also the emphasis on the need for recognising that man and woman cannot be separate in this development, that either sex 'alone is half itself'.

There is, finally, the stress on marriage as symbol of both sexual 'parity' and the 'crowning race'. 'The theory that evolution might fulfil the dream of "a grand crowning race,"' he writes, 'gave particular importance to marriage and the family. . . . It is in consequence of this, I suggest, that a marriage concludes *In Memoriam;* in marriage we come closest to participating in the cosmic purpose, though we must continuously seek to "type" the qualities we desire to make permanent in man' (*The Princess,* p. 263). He makes the same point about the ending of *The Princess,* 'where', he says, 'the love of the Prince and Princess is shown to be no inferior cast from a heavenly mould, but humanity's means of entering a paradise that never was' (*The Princess,* p. 264).

Certainly it is true that Tennyson means for us to see in the love of Ida and the Prince a 'miraculous participation in the development of man'. In the course of their courtship one is made aware not only of their own 'typing' of future humans, but also of the way that they, unlike the characters in *Maud,* constantly negate the terrifying aspects of space and time. The reader is made aware of man's past, but he is also alerted to the hope that he has in the future. One perceives the 'evolutionary' thread running throughout *The Princess.* The first lecture the three interlopers hear is that of Lady Psyche's on the nebular theory, 'This world was once a fluid haze of light' (p. 762). The Prince and Ida, in their first outing, gaze at the 'bones of some vast bulk that lived and roared / Before man was', and the Princess philosophises: 'As these rude bones to us, are we to her / That will be' (p. 781). They spend the rest of the day, along with the other students, 'Hammering and clinking, chattering, stony names / Of shale and hornblende, rag and trap and tuff, / Amygdaloid and trachyte, Till the Sun / Grew broader toward his death and fell' (p. 783). The Princess is always aware of time. 'Six thousand years of fear have made you that / From which I would redeem you', she tells her students; they will no longer be the 'laughing stocks of time' (p. 799). In her message to Arac, before the battle, she tells him that he and his friends will be:

> The sole men to be mingled with our cause,
> The sole men we shall prize in the after-time,
> Your very armour hallowed, and your statutes
> Reared, sung to, when, this gad-fly brushed aside,
> We plant a solid foot into the Time,

And mould a generation strong to move
With claim on claim from right to right, till she
Whose name is yoked with children's, know herself.

(pp. 813–14)

The contrast between the attitude towards time in *The Princess* and in *Maud* is readily apparent, I think, and it is indicative of the more 'optimistic' approach of the former. There is, however, one interesting point about the Princess's declarations about 'development' that is particularly revealing. Until her 'transformation' she is always talking of *woman's* development rather than *human* development. When she talks of when 'We plant a solid foot into the Time,/And mould a generation strong to move', she is referring to women, of course. It is the Prince who articulates for the first time the concept of both man and woman—human beings—together working towards cosmic development. It is the Prince, in short, who helps Ida come to know herself not only emotionally but intellectually as well; it is he who is able to articulate what she has always believed but has, because of her mask, never been able to state. He does not change her; he simply articulates her ideas and longings. His statements at the climactic moment of his wooing, shortly after she has declared herself still loth to yield to one 'That wholly scorned to help their equal rights/Against the sons of men' (p. 837), are only the culmination of what he has all along felt and thought.

At the very beginning of their 'education' the Prince declares to his fellows, 'Why, Sirs, they do all this as well as we' (p. 770). He tells Ida that he did break her precinct, not 'a scorner' of her sex, but 'venerator', that he was 'zealous it should be/All that it might be'. He adds what Ida must learn: 'hear me, for I bear,/Though man, yet human, whatsoe'er your wrongs'. A short time later he says: 'yours, yours, not mine—but half/Without you; with you, whole' (pp. 796, 797). It is no surprise, then, or it should not come as one, when he responds as he does to her statement that she is 'loth' to yield herself to one who scorns to help their equal rights. It remains only for him to put into words that which she herself has 'learnt in little time' during his illness. When she tells him that she now realises that she had 'sought far less for truth than power/In knowledge', he replies that it is as humans they must come together, not as 'either sex alone'. 'You talk almost like Ida', Gama had told him earlier; at this moment he and she can and do speak the same language. His concern, as hers, is with the cause of human justice and service to humanity, and she gradually comes to realise, as he is speaking, that she has indeed been wrong to try to separate woman's cause from man's. No longer 'a Queen of farce' (p. 837), she can now see the justice of his remarks and, perhaps even more importantly, she can now understand that the motivation for them comes from love of her rather than self-aggrandisement. He is, she knows now, perhaps realises for the first time, sincere in his offer to her: 'Henceforth thou hast a helper, me, that know/The woman's cause is man's: they rise or sing/Together, dwarfed or godlike, bond or free' (pp. 837–8).

Once her 'falser' self has slipped off, she can see that those ideas which the Prince is espousing are, indeed, those she has always held. In his 'wooing' of her, a wooing that is in many ways as strange as that of Anne by Richard III, the Prince is able to win her acceptance because he speaks not only of those causes for which she has long fought but he also places them in a perspective which has eluded her up to now.[3] His remarks on the diversity of the sexes and on the common goal of both reflect the 'idylic' view and serve to resolve for Ida the dilemma by which she has been bound. She can now see that the role of woman as bride or 'redeemer', whose sexual love exerts an 'enobling spiritual power' upon her lover, and as wife and mother, whose presence in the family is a civilising and crucial influence for both the present and future, is indeed dependent on her 'distinctive' womanhood. Certainly the Prince's words concerning her role as 'redeemer' are convincing as well as moving:

> For she that out of Lethe scales with man
> The shining steps of Nature, shares with man
> His nights, his days, moves with him to one goal,
> Stays all the fair young planet in her hands—
> If she be small, slight-natured, miserable,
> How shall men grow?
>
> (p. 838)

How shall men grow indeed? She has the power to help him grow; far from being 'dwarfed', she has the whole world in her hands.

Her role as wife and mother is, of course, equally important, and the Prince emphasises this role by stressing both the 'civilising' and the cosmic nature of true marriage. It is at this moment that Ida is able to identify her own hopes and aspirations with those cited by the Prince, for while she has always been concerned with the future, she has constantly worked for betterment in the present as well, the here and now. The Prince's hopes for the crowning race of humankind become convincing to Ida only after he puts them in the context of the present. When she protests, 'I fear/they will not', he replies:

'Dear, but let us type them now
In our own lives, and this proud watchword rest
Of equal; seeing either sex alone
Is half itself, and in true marriage lies
No equal, nor unequal: each fulfils
Defect in each, and always thought in thought,
Purpose in purpose, will in will, they grow,
The single pure and perfect animal,
The two-celled heart beating, with one full stroke,
Life.'

(p. 839)

Ida's only response to these words, which obviously have touched her deeply, is 'what woman taught you this?' It is no longer a protest on her part, however, only a sense of wonder that he should speak the words that she herself, the woman within the crust of iron moods, has tried to say. Tennyson's choice of language here, is most revealing, for it conveys the urgency of his own convictions. The statelier Eden, the chaste and calm great bridals, will come; it is the present which must be paid attention to, the present which involves woman and man and children, the family with all the idylic implications the term carries.

Tennyson's tribute to his mother follows this passage celebrating 'true marriage'. In this description are found those qualities that are found in the true woman, man's redeemer and the perfect wife and mother. There is the stress on her bringing an 'enobling spiritual power' to her lover, the reflection of her being the instrument for 'conveying God's love to men' (Killham, *The Princess*, p. 81). There is the emphasis on her role as wife and mother, 'full of tender wants' and 'learned in gracious household ways'. There is, too, the careful delineation of her as human rather than angelic' 'Not perfect, nay, . . ./No Angel, but a dearer being, all dipt/In Angel instincts, breathing paradise,/ Interpreter between the Gods and men' (p. 840). One must not forget, too, that when Ida protests that the mother seems 'a mockery' to her own self, the Prince insists, implicitly, that she is very much the same 'true woman'. She will have the same 'Redemptive' role as his bride and play an important part as 'wife' and 'life'.

All this, of course, is not to deny the ultimate spiritual and cosmic significance of the union of two people; in spite of her specific concerns with raising the status of women, Ida has always been, as Shannon writes, 'motivated by a desire for service to humanity and a hope for a lasting name based on sure foundations of worth' (Shannon, p. 136). By his talk of true marriage, the Prince has struck a chord in her own nature and thought, for he has insisted always on something beyond the immediate. Here again, however, he reflects her own desire, for his stress is always on the development of man, the crowning race of 'human-kind'. His 'statelier Eden' has not the abstract nature of a dreamer but the more solid one of civilisation that reflects those qualities found in the family, virtue, love, co-operation, loyalty, justice. Tennyson, always the artist, conveys them indirectly (obliquely) rather than directly, in the moving lyric, 'Come down, O Maid', which was part of the poem from the beginning. In this piece, which Tennyson considered one of his 'most successful works' (p. 835), Tennyson invokes the qualities associated with family and hearth, the peace and calm of the 'happy threshold', the 'sweet call' of the children, the domestic bliss of the idylic family.

Carlyle's reaction to *The Princess* is instructive, for it helps put into perspective the distance between these two. In his *Journal* (9 February 1848) Carlyle, who had told Espinasse that *The Princess* had 'everything but common-sense' (Espinasse, pp. 213–14), recorded: 'His "Princess" a gorgeous piece of writing, but to me new melancholy proof of the futility of what they call "Art." Alas! Alfred too, I fear will prove one of the *sacrificed*, and in very deed it is a pity' (Froude, III, p. 422). *Maud*, also, did not appeal in any way to Carlyle; he characterised it to FitzGerald as a 'cobweb', and took a walk instead of consenting to listen to Tennyson's reading of the poem (Sanders, p. 212). It is evident that Carlyle had very little sympathy for or understanding of Tennyson's later variations of his idylic vision; he had reacted favourably to 'Dora', which had reminded him of the *Book of Ruth*; *Maud* and *The Princess* evidently lacked the pulse of a real man's heart or the music of a genuine singer's heart. Alfred had come to value 'Art' over humanity, and to the later Carlyle that was the greatest sin of all. Tennyson had become a lost soul.

25

The Idylic Vision of *Idylls of The King*

Carlyle's despair over Alfred is also evident in his dismissal of the one work that is often regarded as Tennyson's greatest; I have already cited his comments on the *Idylls*, and it is obvious that his dislike of that poem is based on his moral aesthetics. To Carlyle, Tennyson in the *Idylls* was again simply 'spinning rhymes' and talking of 'Art'; Alfred had forgotten that the times demanded not mere aestheticisms but poetry that dealt with truth, the truth that Carlyle had seen in some of Tennyson's earlier idyls. He had failed to image the age.[1]

We now know enough about Carlyle's views on art to see how it was possible for him to fail completely in assessing Tennyson's own art and purpose in the *Idylls*; indeed, in spite of the poet's own attempts to distinguish 'idyll' from 'idyl', the fact remains that the *Idylls* are simply idyls writ large. The themes are those found in his various poems that contain his idylic vision or are labelled idyls. I need not go into detail concerning this matter, for much has been written on precisely that point.[2] One might say with much justification that the 'domestic' aspect of the poem controls all; in 'Guinevere' Arthur, in recounting his past to Guinevere, stresses both her 'sin' and his obligations as husband and ruler in the light of that sin:

> For thou has spoilt the purpose of my life.
> Bear with me for the last time while I show,
> Even for thy sake, the sin which thou has sinned.
>
> . . . .
>
> For think not, though thou wouldst not love thy lord,
> The lord has wholly lost his love for thee.
> I am not made of so slight elements.
> Yet must I leave thee, woman, to thy shame.
> I hold that man the worst of public foes
> Who either for his own or children's sake,

> To save his blood from scandal, lets the wife
> Whom he knows false, abide and rule the house:
> . . . .
> Better the King's waste hearth and aching heart
> Than thou reseated in thy place of light,
> The mockery of my people, and their bane.
>
> (pp. 1736–8)

In 'The Holy Grail' Arthur emphasises his rightful place as ruler and husband:

> And some among you held, that if the King
> Had seen the sight he would have sworn the vow:
> Not easily, seeing that the King must guard
> That which he rules, and is but as the hind
> To whom a space of land is given to plow.
> Who may not wander from the allotted field
> Before his work be done.
>
> (p. 1687)

One must not forget, too, that Tennyson himself found the *Idylls*, if his son is to be trusted in this instance, gave a fuller, if not a truer, picture of an 'ideal Arthur' than *In Memoriam* (pp. 1463–4).

Without oversimplifying, then, one can see that the idylic vision controls the *Idylls*, and it is the 'generic impulse' that provides both unity and meaning to the work.[3] Carlyle was unable to sense either, for Tennyson's oblique instructions and Telemachan perceptions evaded his narrow aesthetic view. He was looking for Fact, not subtlety, not obliqueness. Even so, however, it is surprising that even he, as much as he tended to skim those works he was commenting on, failed to grasp some of the obvious artistic means and thematic statements that Tennyson so clearly provided. While he might not understand fully Tennyson's narrative variations, including flashbacks, story within story, and indirect narrators or reflectors, surely he could not overlook the more (direct) oblique insinuations found throughout the poem:

> And Arthur, passing thence to battle, felt
> Travail, and throes and agonies of the life,
> Desiring to be joined with Guinevere;

And thinking as he rode, 'Her father said
That there between the man and beast they die.
Shall I not lift her from this land of beasts
Up to my throne, and side by side with me?
What happiness to reign a lonely king, . . .
                                        for saving I be joined
To her that is the fairest under heaven,
I seem as nothing in the mighty world,
And cannot will my will, nor work my work
Wholly, nor make myself in mine own realm
Victor and lord. But were I joined with her,
Then might we live together as one life,
And reigning with one will in everything
Have power on this dark land to lighten it,
And power on this dead world to make it live.'

(p. 1472)

Or:

But when a rumour rose about the Queen,
Touching her guilty love for Lancelot,
Though yet there lived no proof, nor yet was heard
The world's loud whisper breaking into storm,
Not less Geraint believed it; and there fell
A horror on him, lest his gentle wife,
Through that great tenderness for Guinevere,
Had suffered, or should suffer any taint
In nature, . . .

(pp. 1526–7)

Or:

                                        I am yours,
Not Arthur's, as ye know, save by the bond.

(p. 1625)

And finally:

Mine is the shame, for I was wife, and thou
Unwedded: . . .

(p. 1728)

The generic impulse, then, provides the unity of the whole and the thematic integrity, and one wonders at Carlyle's misunderstanding. Perhaps, however, just as Tillotson saw only rhetoric rather than the assertive image, so Carlyle mistook 'vacancy' and elaborate execution for Tennyson's art. The idylic vision, however, is clearly there, and one must not be thrown off the track, as Carlyle and other readers evidently have been, by those elaborate ways that Tennyson, evidently attempting to impose epic qualities to the work, occasionally added trumpets and bugles. I have deliberately limited the quotations above to the 'early' *Idylls* to illustrate Tennyson's unwavering aim from the beginning to give his work this vision, and all his later statements about his meaning in the *Idylls* being 'spiritual' and Arthur's representing 'the Ideal Soul of Man' may be seen as his attempts to provide answers to irksome reviewers or inquisitive, albeit well-meaning, friends. *Idylls of the King* is Tennyson's most ambitious attempt to provide 'solutions' for the problems of his age. From an examination of the four idylls published in 1859, the four idylls that serve as the core for the rest of the elaborately executed poem, it is clear that Tennyson saw clearly that the 'domestic' solution was the only one; it would set the example for the nation and, indeed, the world. It is the work that represents, as one writer has put it, the 'voice of the laureate'.[4]

In June 1859, 40 000 copies of *Idylls of the King* were published, and 10 000 copies were sold within the week. The idylls in that volume were 'Enid', 'Vivien', 'Elaine' and 'Guinevere'. My concern here is not the various revisions, additions and changes in order of these in subsequent editions of the *Idylls* but, instead, to focus on their generic impulse, the idylic vision contained in them. One could impose any number of patterns on these four, but Tennyson's purposes seem clear enough. Enid is obviously meant to contrast with Vivien; Elaine with Guinevere. They all fit into the category of 'women' poems or 'lady' poems Tennyson was fond of writing, and they follow naturally such longer idylic pieces as *Maud* and *The Princess*. One can also impose other patterns on the four idylls. While Enid is a contrast to Vivien, she can also be contrasted with Guinevere; while Elaine is obviously meant to be a foil for Guinevere, she can also be played off against Vivien. There are still other possibilities. For instance, Elaine is as much a pursuer as is Vivien, and her 'revenge' on Lancelot is in some ways as effective as is Vivien's imprisonment of Merlin. Vivien and Guinevere, while obviously meant to show that the possibility of 'redemption' is always present, also demonstrate how much alike they really are; they both have the same view of Arthur's 'fault' or 'flaw'. Guinevere sees him as 'all fault who hath no fault at all:/For who loves me must have a touch of earth;/The low sun makes the colour:'; and Vivien condemns him as the King who blinds himself and the entire Table Round through his 'innocence'. Merlin, in defending Arthur, signals the similarity of the two women:

> O selfless man and stainless gentleman,
> Who wouldst against thine own eye-witness fain
> Have all men true and leal, all women pure;
> How, in the mouths of base interpreters, . . .
> Is thy white blamelessness accounted blame!
>
> (p. 1616)

Rather than simply citing these variations of the idylic vision, one can instead note Tennyson's art in portraying these four women. They all not only deal with the relationship of men and women, either in actual marriage or not, but, more importantly, they all have a direct bearing on Arthur as King and as human being. Every one has some connection to the relationship of the King and Queen. All the women demonstrate in different ways Guinevere's acceptance of her responsibility. In replying to Lancelot's statement: 'Mine be the shame; mine was the sin', Guinevere counters: 'Mine is the shame, for I was the wife'. Each in her own way also illustrates the truth of the idylic vision: 'My house hath been my doom' (p. 1746). 'Upon the sacredness of home life he would maintain that the stability and greatness of a nation largely depend'.

In the 1859 publication and in the final ordering of the *Idylls* 'Guinevere' serves as the climactic idyl(l). Gladstone in the *Quarterly Review* praised it effusively:

> No one . . . can read this poem without feeling, when it ends, that what may be termed the pangs of vacancy—of that void in heart and mind for want of its continuance of which we are conscious when some noble strain of music ceases, when some great work of Raphael passes from the view, . . . or when some transcendent character upon the page of history disappears, and the withdrawal of it is like the withdrawal of the vital air.[5]

Even at this early date Tennyson stressed the importance of this idyl(l), for it conveys better than any other his idylic vision. As poet laureate he realised his special responsibility, and 'Guinevere' was meant to emphasise the 'domestic' solution.

Gladstone's praise of 'Guinevere' was typical of the reaction of most readers of the *Idylls*. The reasons are, perhaps, not so readily apparent, but the character of Guinevere herself must be one consideration. She is Tennyson's supreme achievement in the genre, at once heroic and base, attractive and repulsive. While she is a blend of the characteristics of the other women (Enid, Vivien and Elaine) she brings to her 'role' all the qualities that Tennyson saw as necessary if the words of the Prince in *The Princess* were to come true: 'this proud watchword rest/Of equal; seeing either sex alone/Is half itself, and in true marriage lies/ Nor equal, nor unequal: each fulfils/Defect in each' (p. 839). Indeed, the saving grace of Guinevere is her insistence on assuming responsibility for her deed and her recognition that Arthur is speaking at the end not as an individual but as a 'human' type. One is again reminded of the Prince's answer to the Princess, who has difficulty in conceiving of the 'statelier Eden': 'I feel they will not'. 'But let us type them now', replies the Prince, 'In our own lives' (p. 839).

Guinevere, who has already told Lancelot that the blame and responsibility for their adulterous act is hers, has the vision to sense that Arthur's 'forgiveness' of her is not, as some critics have insisted, the act of a pompous prig who has failed to note any wrongdoing in his realm because of his foolish pride. She has the wisdom to understand, ultimately, that Arthur, far from being a 'moral child without the craft to rule' (p. 1625), is exactly what others, especially Lancelot, know him to be: 'a King who honours his own word,/As if were his God's' (p. 1625). That is why at the last interview she not only believes Arthur but assents in every way to his final words; it is not so much that she experiences any radical change as that she is able finally to subdue those Vivien-like qualities and let emerge fully those found in Enid, Elaine, and the other 'idylic' heroines in Tennyson, the saviours of man and society itself. Guinevere emerges in her idyl(l) not as a grovelling 'sinner' but, rather, in true idylic fashion, as 'redeemer', an excellent example of the poet's belief in 'woman's high, redemptive destiny', a destiny closely joined to that of the race itself. Guinevere is Tennyson's fullest portrait of woman as redeemer, a tragic heroine who achieves, in idylic terms, her own and mankind's redemption. Her final speech concerning her relationship with Lancelot, her lover, and Arthur, her husband, conveys her newly-won insight:

> Let the world be; that is but of the world.
> . . . .
> And blessed be the King, who hath forgiven
> My wickedness to him, and left me hope
> That in mine own heart I can live down sin
> And be his mate hereafter in the heavens
> Before high God. . . .
> To whom my false voluptuous pride, that took
> Full easily all impressions from below,
> Would not look up, or half-despised the height
> To which I would not or I could not climb—
> I thought I could not breathe in that fine air
> That pure severity of perfect light—
> I yearned for warmth and colour which I found
> In Lancelot—now I see thee what thou art,
> Thou art the highest and most human too,
> Not Lancelot, nor another. . . .
> Ah, my God,
> What might I not have made of thy fair world,
> Had I but loved thy highest creature here?
> It was my duty to have loved the highest:
> It surely was my profit had I known:
> It would have been my pleasure had I seen.
> We needs must love the highest when we see it,
> Not Lancelot, nor another.
>
> (pp. 1740–1)

In this remarkable passage Tennyson manages to bring together all those conflicting passions portrayed in this complex character; even Morris fails to do as well in his own version of the story. Although attracted by the senses of touch and sight (warmth and colour) to Lancelot, she at last comes to recognise that duty and love, an interesting Carlylean touch, are higher. She also arrives at that wisdom (made so much of in *In Memoriam*) that sees love as the way to future bliss: 'Now I see what thou art,/Thou art the highest and most human too'.

There is a symbiotic relationship between *The Princess* and 'Guinevere,', one that enables us to see the idylic vision in its ideal form. *The Princess* shows us Tennysonian woman as 'stately Pine/Set in a cataract on an island-crag,/When storm is on the heights'; 'Guinevere' reveals Tennysonian woman as dreamer, one whose memory, from old habit, keeps 'slipping back upon the golden days'. In contrast to the Princess, whose 'falser self' finally 'slipt off her like a robe,/And left her woman', Guinevere must slip into a nun's habit to rid herself from the 'old habit of mind':

> In which she saw him first, when Lancelot came,
> Reputed the best knight and goodliest man,
> Ambassador, to lead her to his lord
> Arthur, and led her forth, and far ahead
> Of his, and her retinue moving, they,
> Rapt in sweet talk or lively, all on love
> And sport and tilts and pleasure, (for the time
> Was maytime, and as yet no sin was dreamed,)
> Rode under groves that looked a paradise
> Of blossom, over sheets of hyacinth
> That seemed the heavens upbreaking through the earth.
>
> (pp. 1734–5)

Both women come to see, finally, that evasion is impossible, no matter what form it takes. The Prince's words and Arthur's farewell make the same point: 'The woman's cause is man's: they rise or sink/Together, dwarfed or goldlike, bond or free'. To see this as simply 'Tennysonian' or 'Victorian' is to miss the generic impulse, the guiding theme of Tennyson's idylic poetry. Behind the Prince's final words and Arthur's parting to Guinevere lie the poet laureate's strong belief in domestic love and his profound trust in 'human' values, social order, a purposeful existence. To see in *Idylls of the King* the clearest statement of Tennyson's profound belief in the connection between the 'sacredness of home life' and the 'greatness of a nation' is to understand his claim as the spokesman for his time, the revered public poet. It is no wonder that Gladstone, who himself understood so well the thought and feeling of his countrymen, could conclude his review of the *Idylls* with what would seem on the surface embarrasingly fulsome praise but in truth only reflected accurately their true response to his poems.

> Of it [*Idylls of the King*] we will say without fear, what we would not dare say of any other recent work; that of itself it raises the character and hopes of the age and the country which have produced it, and that its author, by his own single strength, has made a sensible addition to the permanent wealth of mankind. (*Critical Heritage*, p. 266)

Telemachus, indeed, had done his work, and we know how Ulysses, that 'gray spirit yearning in desire', responded.

Epilogue

How does one conclude a study of two such complex figures, whose relationship so accurately reflects the age in which they lived and whose writings helped create that age? Sanders implies that from a study of the two, particularly from a study of the 'full impact of Carlyle's mind on Tennyson's poetry', one could gain a richer and deeper understanding of the age. Among those areas that would yield results, he suggests, would be the

> protest against all kinds of shams and a holding up of veracity and sincerity as high ideals; with a literary art making extensive use of materials handed down by the past but also vitally interested in contemporaneous economic, social, political, and religious problems; . . . with a persistent protest against materialism and a fresh interpretation of the Christian religion; with the protection of individualism against mass pressures and many kinds of conformity. (*CFS*, p. 224)

My 'study' of the two figures has not followed that 'line'—that is, I have not tried to show the 'full impact' of Carlyle's mind on Tennyson's work. What I have attempted to do is to indicate the way that each came to have certain ideas and how they both came to express those ideas in their writings, both necessarily contending with the major problems of their age. I have tried to demonstrate that Carlyle's influence was so great that no one in his age could escape it, and that the more interesting 'study' is that which indicates how the 'younger' writer absorbed some of that influence but resisted much of it.

The key to understanding both writers and their time lies in their complex relationship, personal and ideological. The personal might be gauged from a letter written by the Carlyle of the 1870s, the Carlyle who regarded *The Princess* as 'melancholy proof' of the futility of 'Art' and *Maud* as a 'cobweb'. He wrote to his brother and described Tennyson in these terms: 'Good-natured, almost kind; but rather dull to me! He looks healthy yet, and hopeful; a stout man of 60,—with only one deep wrinkle, *crow* wrinkle, just under the cheek bones.—I was lucky enough (for my then mood, lucky) to find nobody; nothing required but a *card*'. Three years later: 'Tennyson was distinctly rather wearisome; nothing coming from him that did not smack of utter indolence, what one might almost call torpid sleepiness and stupor' (*CFS*, p. 218). One sees plainly that Carlyle has given up on his friend; his words are as cutting as any that he can use in terms of one's moral nature, which to him is all important.

For the ideological relationship, there remain a number of outstanding differences that reflect Carlyle's personal estimate of his younger contemporary. Tennyson's 'indolence' and 'stupor' account for his work, which is cobwebby, lacks common sense. For Carlyle, who had over the years developed an aesthetic based chiefly on morality, anything that smacked of indolence was suspect. In terms of religious, political and social problems, it is evident that he was really better at pointing them out than helping solve them. His keen analyses of the dangers of dependence on the mechanical, the commercial, the material and the 'theological' affected every sensitive soul in the period; however, his message clearly was, in the final analysis, far too abstract and personal to be of help to any but the most 'Carlylean' in spirit and thought. His social solution became another version of drill and force under a strong leader, and his religious remedy became a version of his personal belief that as long as one suffered in silence and did one's duty, one would be rewarded, somehow and somewhere, perhaps in the City of God, by the understanding but stern Taskmaster who had provided for man those Divine Laws he must attempt always to obey. Art for Carlyle became a variation of that moral code; the best artists, the greatest ones (Goethe, Shakespeare, Burns [almost]), were those who had overcome suffering and had shown in their work the relationship of life to God.

For Tennyson Carlyle's message, inspiring in many ways, impressively true in some ways, was far too abstract, subjective and 'destructive'. Influenced not so much by specific ideas but by 'the general quality of his response to mid-nineteenth-century life', Tennyson responded to the Carlylean call for action; Carlyle seemed to the younger poet, as to so many others, 'the spokesman for qualities increasingly called into question in an age of material progress and advancing disbelief' (Goldberg, pp. 3–4). Unable and unwilling to be a disciple, far too independent, Tennyson absorbed much of the 'general quality' of the Prophet's message but provided his own 'solutions', solutions much more in tune with his own beliefs and, as it happened, with those of his era. He turned the Carlylean hero into a Christian leader; he showed that the hope for the nation lay not in a disciplined work force but in the family unit that could provide those values, those humanising denominators, that bridge distinction of sex, class, generations and nations; and he placed his faith not on a stern Taskmaster but on a loving, caring God deeply concerned about His creation, man. Rather than an apocalyptic event that would suddenly change all things for the better, Tennyson found the answer in 'That God, which ever lives and loves,/One God, one law, one element,/And one far-off divine event,/To which the whole creation moves'.

One is tempted to do what some critics have in fact done and disparage the contribution of Carlyle, especially in the light of his later years, sunk in utter isolation, in 'dissent from all the world'. A number of pictures come immediately to mind in this respect. There is, of course, Whistler's portrait, 'Arrangement in Grey and Black No. 2'; one critic has described it as showing 'a profoundly sad and tired man, the expression vacant and melancholy in the extreme'.[1] One is reminded of Carlyle's own words condemning 'introspection' as 'a constant rehearsing the same paltry drama before the same beggarly audience'. Many would see the later Carlyle in this way.[2] Cate also has his own Ruskinian 'portrait' of Carlyle. He quotes Ruskin in *Praeterita*:

> There was this grand original difference between the two [Carlyle and Scott] . . . [Scott's] story-telling and singing were all in the joyful admiration of [the] past . . .; while Carlyle's mind, fixed anxiously on the future, . . . saw and felt from his earliest childhood nothing but the faultfulness and gloom of the Present.

Then Cate concludes:

> Ruskin also admitted that Carlyle was often melancholy and irritable and, while he did not dislike Carlyle for this, he did find that all the more personal works of Carlyle published after 1881 had 'vexed' and 'partly angered' him with their 'me miserum'—never seeming to feel the extreme ill manners of his perpetual whine.[3]

One remembers, too, the figures in Tennyson's 'Ulysses', a poem Carlyle greatly admired. In his complimentary letter on the 1842 *Poems* Carlyle quoted from 'Ulysses', and there is much matter for speculation in the light of his comments. There is Achilles, whom Ulysses thinks of meeting in the 'Happy Isles'. Is Carlyle thinking of that Achilles in Shakespeare's *Troilus,* sulking in his tent, refusing to do battle? Ulysses in that drama tells Agamemnon: 'The great Achilles, whom opinion crowns/This sinow and the forehand of our host,/Having his ear full of this airy frame,/ Grows dainty of his worth, and in his tent/Lies mocking our designs' (I. iii. 142–6). There is Ulysses himself, the Dantean Ulysses of Tennyson's poem, leaving the task of subduing the 'rugged people' to 'the useful and the good' to his son Telemachus. There is much here to suggest that this poem could very well serve as an emblem of the roles of these two Victorian figures, Tennyson advocating adoration of the household gods, observance of common duties and slow prudence; Carlyle, a 'gray spirit yearning in desire', 'made weak by time and fate', urging one more 'work of noble note', but desperately aware of impending death and the need for rest.

However, these views are terribly misleading, for they tend to diminish the valuable contribution of Carlyle. To point out the different path that Tennyson took, and to indicate his contribution to his age, should in no way detract from the vital and, indeed, crucial influence that Carlyle had on Tennyson and on a whole generation of Victorian writers. We know that Tennyson himself was troubled by the picture of Carlyle presented in Froude; he preferred to remember the Carlyle who was at his best 'rollicking' at the Ashburton house, where Carlyle and Lady Ashburton were the life of the party (*CFS*, p. 233). If Tennyson was, in fact, able to 'compromise', and through that compromise arrive at those views that served to comfort and console his readers and contemporaries, what can be said of one who refused to 'compromise' where he saw no way to do so? Is there not some glory to be ascribed to one unable to come to terms with the values and ideas of his generation, who keeps pointing out its faults and insists on urging it to higher aspiration and different goals? To emphasise the potential rather than the actual, to keep reminding man that he is 'A Soul, a Spirit, and divine Apparition' is not, after all, such a terrible thing. Nor can we, or should we, forget what attracted Tennyson and all the others to Carlyle: 'A man and writer of exceptional vision and force whose works contend manfully with the perplexities and mysteries of the human condition' (*A Carlyle Reader*, p. xxxviii). Perhaps the most appropriate words to describe these two eminent Victorians are those spoken by Ulysses himself, for they do justice to the contribution of both to the times in which they lived and the mark they made on that time. 'He works his work', says Ulysses, 'I mine'. What more can one ask of any human being? Carlyle, we know, did not, and Tennyson would not.

Notes and References

PROLOGUE

1. William E. Buckler, *The Victorian Imagination* (New York: New York University Press, 1980).

PART ONE: FOUNDATIONS

1 Carlyle: The Scottish Dimension

1. Matthew P. McDiarmid, 'Carlyle on the Intuitive Nature of Poetical Thinking', in Drescher, p. 125. See also Carlisle Moore, 'Carlyle and Goethe as Scientist', in *CHC*, pp. 21–34; and Daiches, in Drescher, pp. 374–5.

2 New Intellectual Forces: Hume and Newton

1. Constance Maund, *Hume's Theory of Knowledge* (London: Macmillan, 1937), pp. 4–8.
2. Thomas Carlyle, *Lectures on the History of Literature*, ed. J. R. Greene (London: Ellis & Elvey, 1892), p. 171—hereafter cited as *Lectures.*
3. Richard H. Popkin, *The History of Scepticism, from Erasmus to Descartes* (New York: Harper Torchbook, 1964), p. 132.
4. See, however, Carlyle's unfavourable comments on Gibbon in *CL*, I, 115.
5. Jane Rendall, *The Origins of the Scottish Enlightenment* (New York: St. Martin's Press, 1978), p. 19.
6. David Hume, *The Natural History of Religion*, ed. by A. Wayne Colver (Oxford: Clarendon Press, 1976), p. 25; Masson speaks of Carlyle's 'fervid Natural Theism', p. 88.
7. George Elder Davie, *The Democratic Intellect: Scotland and Her Universities in the Nineteenth Century* (Edinburgh: Edinburgh University Press, 1961), esp. Part II.
8. *Last Words of Thomas Carlyle* (London: Longmans, Green, 1892), pp. 30–1—hereafter cited as *LW*.
9. Carl L. Becker, *The Heavenly City of the Eighteenth-Century Philosophers* (New Haven: Yale University Press, 1932), p. 62. 'Mathematics', Campbell writes, 'as taught by Leslie, was part of the university system which comprehended the universe, and by a series of philosophical studies; mathematics was one of the means of studying the universe, and the relationship of its parts, described by the Edinburgh philosopher Sir William Hamilton as "the transition study

from the concrete to the abstract, from the science of matter to the science of mind." ' For Carlyle, of course, this too must have been 'illuminative', as he later described his reading in Gibbon. Campbell adds: 'Carlyle at this time was not merely becoming a mathematician, he was studying all available subjects, and in his ferocious reading on the subject soon found himself studying Newton till long past midnight. . . . This came to be one of the most important aspects of his life' (Campbell, pp. 18, 20).

10. Perhaps the best summary of this aspect has been provided by Carlisle Moore, one of the more perceptive critics writing on Carlyle and mathematics. One reason for Carlyle's fascination with Newton, Moore has written, was his cultural inheritance:

> In early nineteenth-century England Isaac Newton was revered as the founder of the new Truth—a Truth which was needed to strengthen the weakening faiths of orthodox religion. He was the genius who had geometrized space, who had brought mathematics into the area of intellectual discourse, and had 'explained' the phenomena of the heavens and the earth by a single mathematical law. His discoveries were taken as having re-established the idea of design and were regarded as counters to eighteenth-century scepticism, for they were implicitly neither anti-Christian nor anti-Trinitarian, but brought mathematics, physics and astronomy together in a triumphant demonstration of cosmic order which pointed to God as creator of all things. (Carlisle Moore, 'Carlyle: Mathematics and "Mathesis" ' in *CPP*, p. 63)

11. *Sir Isaac Newton's Mathematical Principles of Natural Philosophy and Philosophy and His System of the World*, tr. into English by Andrew Motte in 1729. The translations revised, and supplied with an historical and explanatory appendix, by Florian Gajori (Berkeley, California: University of California Press, 1934), p. 544—hereafter cited as *Principia*. Carl Becker has given us one philosopher's view of Newton's influence: 'To describe the phenomena of nature, to explain their causes . . . and to inquire into the whole constitution of the universe, is the business of natural philosophy. . . . But natural philosophy is subservient to purposes of a higher kind, and is chiefly to be valued as it lays a sure foundation for natural religion and moral philosophy; by leading us, in a satisfactory manner, to the knowledge of the Author and Governor of the Universe' (p. 62).

12. One must not forget, also, that Newton was not as 'tainted' as Hume: there was never the heretical stamp on him that had been placed on Hume. A historian of science has written:

> Newton's physics . . . was far less materialistic and concrete than is commonly supposed and than Becker believed. Becker's strongly empiricist interpretation of the work of Galileo and Newton would hardly satisfy a modern historian of science. . . . Newton's physics was highly abstract, a true mathematical physics, dealing with idealized bodies moving in a wholly idealized time and space. Indeed, for his cautious use of the word 'attraction' to describe the

mysterious force exerted between all bodies in the universe, Newton was accused of departing from the solid ground of Cartesian materialism and introducing ideas that were neither clear nor precise. He was even charged with introducing mysterious entities in a manner shockingly reminiscent of the Scholastics. . . . What was new, as a result of the Scientific Revolution was that these uniformities were seen to be *mathematical* in character.

Henry Guerlac, 'Newton's Changing Reputation in the Eighteenth Century' in *Carl Becker's Heavenly City Revisited*, ed. Raymond O. Rockwood (Ithaca, NY: Cornell University Press, 1958), pp. 16–18.

13. A. J. Snow, *Matter & Gravity in Newton's Physical Philosophy* (London: Oxford University Press, 1928), pp. 162–4.
14. Sir Isaac Newton, *Opticks*, reprinted from the 4th edn with a Foreword by Prof. Albert Einstein and an Introduction by Prof. E. T. Whittaker (London: G. Bell & Sons, 1931), pp. 401–2.
15. Campbell, for instance, talks of Carlyle's 'mechanical search for connections', a search that could lead one to the 'sort of nadir to which Tuefelsdröckh's semi-fictitious university has sunk in Sartor'. 'It could also lead', Campbell writes, 'to a habit of mind which Carlyle was himself to satirize in a cancelled passage of *Wotton Reinfred*', that habit being one that emphasised logic and theories without end and no practice. All this, states Campbell, was to 'Lead him into the new ground of German literature and thought which was to open a "new heaven and new earth" to him'. Even Campbell, however, pulls back just a bit, maintaining that 'it [science and mathematics] sustained him through a difficult period when his grasp of Ecclefechan Christianity was wavering, and his restless mind needed the stimulus of some challenging subject. The Scottish schools of mathematics and natural philosophy provided this: more, they allowed him to earn a living tutoring in these fields till his tutorship in the Buller family from 1822 onwards and later his German studies brought him some adequate income' (p. 13). While correct in these observations, Campbell does not give enough recognition to the real significance of Carlyle's interest, his obsession, with these subjects, focused largely on physics and Newton; they were more than a substitution until the adequate income developed. They were means to an end, that end being a 'final' position in which he could rest. To speak, then, of a 'severe reaction' to these studies when he read Goethe, Kant, Fichte, Novalis is to ignore the evidence.

   In the same way Carlisle Moore 'misreads' Carlyle's statements in his letters. It is true that Carlyle wrote to his friend Allen in 1820 to tell him that he was not surprised that he had 'quitted science', since, Carlyle added, the 'thing designated by that name now-a-days in Britain is little else than a dry bread-roll of facts'. He added: 'I have even nearly lost all relish for Mathematics, which some years ago I reckoned the loftiest pursuit of the human intellect' (*CL*, I, p. 252). Some months later he wrote again to tell Allen that he had become 'nearly tired of what is called natural science, mathematics, and the ordinary systems of philosophy'. He adds, however, and significantly so, that this had not 'prevented me from coasting all summer on the borders of German or Italian literature: and in winter it was my purpose to spread out "sailboard vans" and to explore the secrets of those vast seas' (*CL*, I, pp. 272–3). All these comments are typical of Carlyle. By this time he had begun his reading of German and glimpsed the new heaven and earth before him. He also seemed to have behind him the unhappy years of trying to find a career, the one problem that had really bothered him for a long time. The summer at Mainhill had been a wonderful period for him; he had read what he wanted, had taken long walks, had had long chats with his mother and in general recovered from what had been a period of anxiety. No wonder mathematics looked as it did and literature seemed to promise much more. He was still to go through hard times, but in some respects he had rejected much. It is still misleading, however, to imply that for some reason Carlyle had gained little from mathematics and his study of Newton because he had 'reached his limit as a mathematical thinker' (*CPP*, pp. 81–2). To say this seriously is to limit the rewards Carlyle had gained from both, to make too much of the fact that Carlyle had not 'ever wholly mastered' the *Principia*. The truth is that Carlyle read Newton as he was to read, and was reading, Goethe, Fichte, Novalis, and the German literature he did read. He took from them what he needed, just as he took from the *Principia* what he needed. In this respect it was far from a 'reaction' when he turned from Newton to Goethe, from the *Principia* to *Faust*. Of course he urged Jane to read literature and no mathematics. Just as he turned from one subject to another, from one career to another, Carlyle turned from science to literature, but it was not a 'rejection' of the former. It was another logical step, and he took is eagerly. Of course, as Moore concludes, Carlyle became increasingly ambivalent concerning the sciences; he had done so in regard to Hume, to some aspects of his early religious training. He may have rejected mathematics as being 'unphilosophical', but from Newton at least he had retained some very important philosophical ideas, especially those that applied to the universe, God's cosmos. (Ian Campbell, 'Carlyle's Religion: The Scottish Background' in *CHC*, pp. 12–13; see also p. 8, where Campbell calls the study of mathematics and natural philosophy a 'substitute' for the certainties of life he had known in Ecclefechan.)

3 The Stupendous Whole: Newton and Carlylean Belief

1. John Cunningham, *The Church History of Scotland*, 2 vols (Edinburgh: Adam & Charles Black, 1859), II, 589; see also A. L. Drummond and James Bulloch, *The Church in Victorian Scotland 1843–1874* (Edinburgh: The Saint Andrew Press, 1975), pp. 179, 180, 183.
2. *The Interpreter's Bible*, 12 vols (New York, Abingdon Press, 1955), IV, 12, 16.

3. An eminent theologian has recently written: 'It was important for Newton's theoretic system of the world that time and space should constitute an isotropic, necessary and unchanging frame of reference for the orderly reduction of all bodies in motion to patterns which were amenable to mathematico-mechanical calculation and to formulation in immutable laws'. He did this, states Torrance, 'by relating time and space not only to the eternity and infinity of God but to his immutability and impassibility. . . . Time and space thus identified with the unchanging presence and reality of God constituted an independent cause or inertial system in the whole geometrico-causal structure of Newtonian physics and mechanics'. Thomas F. Torrance, *Christian Theology and Scientific Culture* (New York: Oxford University Press, 1981), pp. 18–19.
4. See M. Timko, 'Carlyle, Sterling, and the Scavenger age', *Studies in Scottish Literature*, 20 (1986), pp. 11–33.

5 Prophetic Utterance: Nature, Human History, Divine Justice and the Universe

1. See Ian Campbell, 'Carlyle's Religion: The Scottish Background' in *CHC*, pp. 3–20; A. A. Ikeler, *Puritan Temper and Transcendental Faith* (Columbus: Ohio State UP, 1972); and Fred Kaplan, *Thomas Carlyle: A Biography* (Cornell University Press, 1983), esp. pp. 357–60.
2. Sir Charles Gavan Duffy, *Conversations with Carlyle* (London: Sampson Low, Marston, 1892), pp. 92–3; my italics.

6 The Carlylean Dilemma: the Riddle of Destiny

1. Louis Cazamian, *Carlyle*, translated by E. K. Brown (Archon Books, 1966; originally published 1932), pp. 106, 151.
2. In essence Carlyle is guilty of what George Orwell describes in his essay 'Politics and the English Language'. 'It is clear', Orwell writes, 'that the decline of a language must ultimately have political and economic causes'. Perhaps 'decline' is not the best word, but there is no doubt of Carlyle's using terms to suit his purpose. The Orwell essay is in *A Collection of Essays* (New York: Harcourt Brace Jovanovich, 1946), pp. 156–71.
3. For an excellent treatment of Carlyle's interest in Novalis and 'Nature' see Laurence Poston, 'Millites and Millienniums: The Context of Carlyle's "Signs of the Times" ', *VS*, 26 (1983), pp. 381–406.

7 Tennyson: Ulyssean Influences and Telemachan Modulations

1. *Tennyson and His Friends*, ed. Hallam, Lord Tennyson (London: Macmillan, 1911), p. 131—hereafter cited as *THF*.

2. *The Correspondence of Emerson and Carlyle*, ed. Joseph Slater (New York: Columbia University Press, 1964), p. 363; some of the spelling in the letters has been silently regularised.
3. See the accounts in *Memoir*, I, p. 225; and Elisabeth L. Cary, *Tennyson: His Homes, His Friends, and His Work* (New York: G. P. Putnam's Sons, 1898), pp. 77–8.
4. *The Letters of Alfred, Lord Tennyson*, ed. Cecil Y. Lang and Edgar F. Shannon, Jr., vol. I (1821–50) (Cambridge, Mass.: Harvard University Press, 1981), p. 281; hereafter referred to as *Lang*.
5. M. Shaw, 'Tennyson and His Public 1827–1859', in *Tennyson*, p. 62.

8 The Individual and Society

1. Murray Baumgarten, *Carlyle and His Era* (Santa Cruz: Dean E. McHenry Library, 1975), p. 21.
2. For what the term 'Ulyssean' has meant to various readers over the years, see Ricks, pp. 560–1, and J. Pettigrew, *Victorian Poetry*, 1 (1963), pp. 27–45.

9 The Religious Question

1. Carl Dawson, *Victorian Noon: English Literature in 1850* (Baltimore: Johns Hopkins Press, 1979), p. 8.
2. E. D. H. Johnson, '*In Memoriam*: The Way of the Poet', *Victorian Poetry*, 2 (1958), p. 145.
3. Valerie Pitt, *Tennyson Laureate* (London: Barrie & Rockliff, 1962), p. 192.
4. David J. DeLaura, 'Carlyle and Arnold: The Religious Issue', in *CPP*, p. 135—hereafter cited as *CAA*.
5. Carlisle Moore, '*Sartor Resartus* and the Problem of Carlyle's Conversion', *Publications of the Modern Language Association*, 70 (1955), pp. 662–81.

10 Darwin, Nature and Man

1. Walter Houghton, *The Victorian Frame of Mind* (New Haven: Yale University Press, 1957), p. 67.
2. By 'Darwinism' is meant the whole movement of thought that sees man as a 'natural' object, the product of evolution, and not as a 'special' being. See Peter Caws, *Science and the Theory of Value* (New York: Random House, 1967), p. 19. See also Milton Millhauser, *Just Before Darwin: Robert Chambers and Vestiges* (Middletown: Wesleyan University Press, 1959); G. Roppen, *Evolution and the Poetic Belief* (Oxford University Press, 1956); and Lionel Stevenson, *Darwin among the Poets* (Chicago: University Press, 1959).
3. E. B. Mattes, *In Memoriam: The Way of a Soul* (New York: Exposition Press, 1951), pp. 65–6.

4. J. H. Buckley, *Tennyson: The Growth of a Poet* (Cambridge, Mass.: Harvard University Press, 1960), p. 276; Mattes, p. 69. Buckley's book will hereafter be cited as *Tennyson*.
5. Harold Nicolson, *Tennyson: Aspects of His Life, Character, and Poetry* (London: Constable 1923).
6. *The Works of Alfred, Lord Tennyson* (New York and London: Macmillan, 1894), p. 779—herafter cited as *WAT*.

11 God and Man

1. W. C. DeVane and Mabel P. DeVane (eds), *Selections from Tennyson* (New York: F. S. Crofts, 1940), p. 431.
2. R. H. Super, *The Time-Spirit of Matthew Arnold* (Ann Arbor: University of Michigan Press, 1970), p. 37.
3. A. M. Terhune and A. B. Terhune (eds), *The Letters of Edward FitzGerald*, vol. I (1830–1850) (Princeton University Press, 1980), p. 534; see also Wilson, III, pp. 352–6.
4. D. C. Somervell, *English Thought in the Nineteenth Century* (London: Methuen & Son, 1929), p. 163. C. H. O. Scaife, *The Poetry of Alfred Tennyson* (London: Cobden-Sanderson, 1930), p. 1.

PART TWO: PROPHET AND POET

12 Carlylean Caprice

1. Robert Bernard Martin, *Tennyson: The Unquiet Heart* (Oxford: Clarendon Press, 1980), p. 521.
2. Francis Espinasse, *Literary Recollections and Sketches* (New York: Dodd, Mead, 1893), p. 214.
3. *Maud* was dismissed with a single word, 'cobweb'; while 'Wellington', which Carlyle might have been expected to like, since it reflects many of the heroic qualities he admired, is called superfluous: 'Tennyson's verses are naught. Silence alone is respectable on such an occasion' (Wilson, V, 146; *CFS*, p. 210). Even Tennyson's first drama, *Queen Mary*, did not escape Carlyle's keen eye; it was Tennyson's 'so-called Shakespearean tragedy', with 'a dismal inclination to exclaim Scene after Scene, "Did you ever?"' It also was (as described to another correspondent) a 'stone-dead, ineffectual "Tragedy," ' which would do Tennyson 'neither ill na gude from this date' (*CFW*, p. 219).
4. Floyd Stovall (ed.), *Walt Whitman Prose Works* 1892, vol. 1, *Specimen Days* (New York: New York University Press, 1963), 255, 258—hereafter cited as Stovall. See also Whitman's note on p. 262 in which he mentions Carlyle's 'everlurking pessimism'.
5. Lawrence J. Starzyk, 'Arnold and Carlyle', *Criticism*, 12 (1970), 282.

6. See F. W. Roe, *Thomas Carlyle as a Critic of Literature* (New York: Columbia University Press, 1910); A. J. LaValley, *Carlyle and the Idea of the Modern* (New Haven: Yale University Press, 1968); Georg Tennyson, *Sartor Called Resartus* (Princeton University Press, 1965) and Ikeler.
7. See also Walter Houghton, *The Victorian Frame of Mind* (New Haven: Yale University Press, 1957), pp. 130–1. Houghton notes the same tendency in Carlyle, calling attention to his early praise of Shakespeare's plays as 'truer than reality itself', and then demonstrating his later unqualified admiration for 'a new literature of historical and biographical fact which he can feel is entirely true, which the whole man can believe'. Houghton attributes this change to Carlyle's loss of faith, his desire for a 'new religion', and he connects Carlyle's ideas about religion to literature: 'In that state of mind, hypersensitive to anything that can possibly be thought false, creative literature will be associated, however unconsciously, with Christian myth'.

13 Carlyle's Aesthetic Theory: The Aesthetic Whole

1. Roe, p. 53.
2. *A Carlyle Reader*, ed. G. B. Tennyson (New York: Modern Library College Edition, 1969), p. 55; see also John Rosenberg, *Carlyle and the Burden of History* (Cambridge, Mass.: Harvard University Press, 1985).
3. As Georg Tennyson has so acutely observed in his discussion of Carlyle's conception of poet and philosopher:

   It is in the means of presentation that the poet differs from the philosopher, not in what is presented; the philosopher, of course, uses systematic discourse, but the poet uses an imaginative creation. . . . Only the Germans, he felt, had wedded the unchanging essence of poetry to modern subject matter; only the Germans had found a means of bodying forth their insights into the Divine Idea of the World. *Sartor Called Resartus*, pp. 90, 92–3; hereafter cited as *SCR*.

14 Carlyle's Moral Aesthetic

1. For a valiant attempt to define some of Carlyle's favourite terms see C. R. Sanders, 'Carlyle, Poetry, and the Music of Humanity', *Western Humanities Review*, 16 (1962), pp. 53–66.
2. *William Allingham, A Diary*, ed. H. Allingham and D. Radford (London: Macmillan, 1907), p. 310.
3. All the quotations which follow are from *Works*, v, 78–114; I have used the accepted spelling of Shakespeare.

15 Carlyle and the Romantic Poets

1. *Byron: A Collection of Critical Essays*, ed. Paul West (New Jersey: Prentice-Hall, 1963), p. 155; Russell's work was published in 1945.
2. Jerome J. McGann, *Fiery Dust: Byron's Poetic Development* (Chicago: University of Chicago Press, 1968), p. 26.
3. Sanders has told much of the story in two different essays, 'The Carlyles and Byron' (*CFS*, pp. 61–93) and 'Carlyle and Leigh Hunt' (*CFS*, pp. 94–191), but he has not connected the various threads in a way that would appear to be natural in the light of chronology and the suddenness of Carlyle's shift in attitude towards doing a treatment of him.
4. Cosmo Monkhouse, *Life of Leigh Hunt* (London: Walter Scott, Ltd., 1893), p. 156; Barnette Miller in *Leigh Hunt's Relations with Byron, Shelley and Keats* (New York: Columbia University Press, 1910). One is tempted, too, to use the Hunt acquaintance to account for Carlyle's seemingly gratuitous references to Byron in his Review of the 'Corn-Law Rhymes' for the *Edinburgh Review* (1832). He had told Napier in the April 28 letter that the review 'has given some foolish trouble' and that it 'had better stay here yet a while' (*CL*, VI, p. 149). In the essay itself, Carlyle fairly early contrasts Byron and Burns:

   > they both, by mandate of nature, struggle and must struggle towards clear Manhood . . .; yet only the gifted Ploughman can partially prevail therein: the gifted Peer must toil and strive, and shoot-out in wild efforts, yet die at last in Boyhood, with the promise of his Manhood still but announcing itself in the distance. (*Works*, XXVIII, p. 140)

   Later in the essay he blames the 'worthy Rhymer' for imitating Byron's 'fierce vociferous mouthings, whether "passionate," or not passionate and only theatrical?' (*Works*, XXVIII, p. 153). Still later he refers to 'many a sickly and sulky Byron, or Byronlet, glooming over the woes of existence'; and, finally, towards the conclusion, Carlyle talks of these rhymes being interesting to 'one class of readers': 'To the highest, that is to say, the richest class' (*Works*, XXVIII, pp. 158, 163).
5. *Coleridge and the Pantheist Tradition* (Clarendon Press, 1969), pp. 9, 333. See also Ian Campbell, 'Conversations with Carlyle: the Monckton Milnes Diaries', *Prose Studies*, 8 (May, September, 1985), esp. Part 2, p. 23.
6. All following quotations are from *Works*, XI, p. 52ff. In connection with Carlyle's reference to Coleridge's being 'deficient in laughter' see the remarks by C.F.S. on 'the high value' Carlyle placed on humour (*CL*, I, p. xxviii).

16 Carlyle and Art: Symbol, Emblem and Image

1. *SCR*, p. 245.
2. Georg Tennyson, 'The Sacramental Vision' in *Nature and the Victorian*

Imagination, ed. G. Tennyson and U. Knoepflmacher (Berkeley: University of California Press, 1977), p. 370.
3. G. Tillotson, *A View of Victorian Literature* (Oxford: Clarendon Press, 1978), p. 82.

17 Wonder, Metaphor and Fact

1. Harrold has the following footnote on 'star-doomed' in his edition of *Sartor*: 'The title of St. Augustine's famous work, *De Civitate Dei*. Cf. also Richter's *Flower, Fruit, etc.*, p. 255: "The broad heaven, with the streets of the City of God all lit with the lamps which are suns," etc. (B) "Star-domed" is *star-doomed* by misprint, in the Centenary Edition'. One is tempted to say that star-doomed is as good a reading as star-domed in Carlyle's sense of things.
2. LaValley, p. 88.

18 The Ulyssean Strain: The Projection of Self

1. Raymond Williams, *Culture and Society: 1780–1950* (New York: Columbia University Press, 1958), p. 77; George Saintsbury. *A History of Nineteenth Century Literature* (New York: The Macmillan Company, 1920), p. 237.
2. David J. DeLaura, 'Ishmael and Prophet: *Heroes and Hero-Worship* and the Self-Expressive Basis of Carlyle's Art', *Texas Studies in Literature and Language*, 11 (1969), pp. 705–37.
3. Edward Dowden, *Transcripts and Studies*, 2nd edn (London: Kegan Paul, Trench, Trubner, 1896), pp. 185–6, 187; Edward Alexander, 'Thomas Carlyle and D. H. Lawrence: A Parallel', *University of Toronto Quarterly*, 37 (1968), p. 257; R. D. McMaster, 'Criticism of Civilization in the Structure of *Sartor Resartus*', *University of Toronto Quarterly*, 37 (1968), p. 276; John P. Farrell, *Revolution as Tragedy* (Ithaca: Cornell University Press, 1980), p. 288.
4. *Two Reminiscences of Thomas Carlyle*, ed. John Clubbe (Durham: N.C.: Duke University Press, 1974), p. 74—hereafter cited as *TR*.

19 Prophetic Utterances

1. Carlisle Moore, 'Thomas Carlyle', in *English Romantic Poets and Essayists*, revised edn (New York: Modern Language Association, 1966), p. 356; E. Bernbaum, *Guide through the Romantic Movement* (New York: Thomas Nelson and Sons, 1933), pp. 421ff.; Donald Stone, *The Romantic Impulse in Victorian Fiction* (Cambridge: Harvard University Press, 1980), p. 24.
2. Jonathan Loesberg, 'Self-Consciousness and Meditation in Victorian Autobiography', *University of Toronto Quarterly*, 50, (1980/81), pp. 200, 201.

3. David Masson, 'an unsigned review, *North British Review*', in Jules Paul Seigel (ed.), *Thomas Carlyle: The Critical Heritage* (New York: Barnes & Noble, 1971), p. 337.
4. Joel Porte, *Representative Man: Ralph Waldo Emerson in His Time* (New York: Oxford University Press, 1979), pp. 114–15; the text of the letter is from *CL*, which differs slightly from Porte.

20 Tennyson's Idylic Vision

1. Paull F. Baum, *Tennyson Sixty Years After* (Chapel Hill: University of North Carolina Press, 1948), pp. 145–6.
2. William E. Fredeman, ' "The Sphere of Common Duties": The Domestic Solution in Tennyson's Poetry', *Bulletin of the John Rylands Library*, 54 (1972), p. 362.
3. A. Dwight Culler, *The Poetry of Tennyson* (New Haven: Yale University Press, 1977), p. 128.
4. Richard D. Altick, *Victorian People and Ideas* (New York: W. W. Norton & Company, 1973), p. 282; see also my essay '"The Central Wish": Human Passion and Cosmic Love in Tennyson's Idyls', *Victorian Poetry*, 16 (1978), pp. 1–15; and Chapter 6 above, 'The Carlylean Dilemma: The Riddle of Destiny'.
5. Lionel Stevenson, 'Tennyson, Browning, and a Romantic Fallacy', *University of Toronto Quarterly*, 13 (1944), p. 182.
6. Charles Tennyson, *Alfred Tennyson* (London: Macmillan, 1968), p. 178—hereafter cited as *AT*.
7. Gerhard Joseph, *Tennysonian Love: The Strange Diagonal* (Minneapolis: University of Minnesota Press, 1969), p. 44.
8. J. H. Buckley, *The Triumph of Time* (Cambridge, Mass.: Harvard University Press, 1966), p. 146.
9. 'Arnold, Tennyson, and the English Idyl: Ancient Criticism and Modern Poetry', *Texas Studies in Literature and Language*, 16 (1974), pp. 135–46; Philip Drew, '"Aylmer's Field": A Problem for Critics', *The Listener* (2 April 1964), p. 553.
10. Christopher Ricks, *Tennyson*, Masters of World Literature Series, ed. Louis Kronenberger (New York: Macmillan, 1972), p. 290; Curtis Dahl, 'A Double Frame for Tennyson's Demeter?' *Victorian Studies*, 1 (1958), pp. 356–62.

21 'Aylmer's Field'

1. James R. Kincald, *Tennyson's Major Poems: The Comic and Ironic Patterns* (New Haven: Yale University Press, 1975), p. 14.

22 'Enoch Arden'

1. Douglas C. Fricke, 'A Study of Myth and Archetype in "Enoch Arden" ', *Tennyson Research Bulletin*, 2 (1974), p. 106; see also Winston Collins, 'Enoch Arden, Tennyson's Heroic Fisherman', *Victorian Poetry*, 14 (1976), pp. 47–53.

23 *Maud*

1. John Kilham, *Tennyson and 'The Princess': Reflections of an Age* (London: The Athlone Press, 1958), p. 191—hereafter cited as Killham, *The Princess*.
2. John Killham, 'Tennyson's *Maud*—The Function of the Imagery', in John Killham (ed.), *Critical Essays on the Poetry of Tennyson*, New York: Barnes and Noble, 1960), p. 228.
3. William E. Buckler (ed.), *The Major Victorian Poets* (New York: Houghton Mifflin, 1973), p. 643—hereafter cited as *MVP*.

24 *The Princess*

1. Edgar F. Shannon, Jr., *Tennyson and the Reviewers* (Cambridge, Mass.: Harvard University Press, 1952), pp. 135, 136.
2. Gerhard Joseph, for instance, has used the phrase 'of the valley' to designate what he thinks Tennyson meant by the term in connection with love. 'Princess Ida', Joseph writes, 'learns that human love is "of the valley," antithetical to the height of Princess Ida's mountain pride and the marine depth of the Kraken's abysmal sea'. In conjunction with Tennyson's choice of the idylic mode, then, I take the phrase to stand for Tennyson's choice of a mode that both encompassed the subject matter he felt was important to deal with and most effectively, not necessarily most directly, communicated those ideas and attitudes he wanted to communicate about that subject matter. It became the poetic vehicle that best suited his need, the one that reflected on the one hand the intensely personal, even mystical side, and, on the other hand, the prophetic voice. I suppose one can look at this as a kind of aesthetic 'compromise', but there is more involved; there is the question of Tennyson's ultimate meaning in the context of his age and his impact on future readers. Certainly, it serves to contradict the notion of Tennyson the 'mystic', the seer who sold his poetic soul for popularity. It also serves to answer those critics who would deny Tennyson's 'Victorianism', as the poet who best reflects his age. It demonstrates most vividly and forcefully Buckley's conclusion that Tennyson's 'development depends not on a sacrifice of the personal vision, but on the constant interaction between public knowledge and private feeling'. His choice of the idylic mode serves, further, to reinforce Buckley's central thesis:

   > [Tennyson] was the voice and sometimes indeed the conscience of Victorian culture; and his work will endure, even apart from its aesthetic worth, as a mirror of his civilisation. Yet the distinction that his critics have repeatedly drawn between the bard of public sentiments and the earlier poet of private sensibilities is ultimately untenable. For there was no real break in Tennyson's career; from the beginning he felt some responsibility to the society he lived in, and until the end he remained obedient to the one clear call of his own imagination. (Buckley, *Tennyson*, p. 255)

The idylic mode, most clearly, presents this balance between the poet's sense of responsibility to his society and his obedience to his own imagination, his 'soul'. In the idyls, written, it must be remembered, throughout his career, may be found Tennyson's transmutation into literary or artistic terms the values to which he adhered in life and to which he hoped his country and the world would adhere. To learn what these values were, and to see exactly how the poet developed and communicated them through the ideas, themes and attitudes found in the idyls, seems incumbent upon anyone who would understand both the poet and his age.

3. See Killham, *The Princess*, p. 261. Killham too writes of Ida's 'setback' in attempting to reconcile faith in a creator with the acceptance of evolution.

25 The Idylic Vision of *Idylls of the King*

1. See pp. 92–3 above.
2. See especially Pitt, Culler, and Donald S. Hair, *Domestic and Heroic in Tennyson's Poetry* (Toronto: University of Toronto Press, 1981), esp. pp. 47–102.
3. Caryl Emerson, 'The Tolstoy Connection in Bakhtin', *PMLA*, 100 (1985), 68.
4. George O. Marshall, Jr., *A Tennyson Handbook* (New York: Twayne Publishers, 1963), p. 136.
5. W. E. Gladstone, 'W. E. Gladstone on the *Idylls of the King* [1859] and Earlier Works', in John D. Jump (ed.), *Tennyson: The Critical Heritage* (London: Routledge & Kegan Paul, 1967), p. 259.

Epilogue

1. K. Z. Cieskowski, 'Grey Beard and Glittering Eye', *Times Literary Supplement* (9 October 1981), p. 1162.
2. Anthony J. Harding, 'Sterling, Carlyle, and German Higher Criticism: A Reassessment', *Victorian Studies*, 26 (1983), 269–85, esp. 279.
3. I have quoted directly from *Praeterita*, while Cate summarises the message from it (*Works*, XXXV, 545–8). *The Correspondence of Thomas Carlyle and John Ruskin*, ed. George Alan Cate (Palo Alto: Stanford University Press, 1982), p. 51.

Select Bibliography

Allingham, William, *A Diary, 1824–1889*, ed. H. Allingham and D. Radford (London: Macmillan, 1907).

Baum, Paull F., *Tennyson Sixty Years After* (Chapel Hill: University of North Carolina Press, 1948).

Baumgarten, Murray, *Carlyle and His Era* (Santa Cruz: Dean E. McHenry Library, 1975).

Becker, Carl L., *The Heavenly City of the Eighteenth-Century Philosophers* (New Haven: Yale University Press, 1932).

Buckler, William, E., *The Victorian Imagination* (New York: New York University Press, 1980).

Campbell, Ian, *Thomas Carlyle* (London: Hamish Hamilton, 1974).

Carlyle, Alexander (ed.), *Letters of Thomas Carlyle to John Stuart Mill, John Sterling, and Robert Browning* (London: T. Fisher Unwin, 1923).

Carlyle, Thomas, and Jane Welsh Carlyle, *The Collected Letters of Thomas and Jane Welsh Carlyle*, ed. Charles Richard Sanders, K. J. Fielding, *et al*. (Durham, N.C.: Duke University Press, 1970ff.).

Carlyle, Thomas, *Last Words* (London: Longman, Green, 1892).

——, *Lectures on the History of Literature*, ed. J. R. Greene (London: Ellis & Elvey, 1892).

——, *Reminiscences*, ed. C. E. Norton, 2 vols (London and New York: Macmillan, 1887), introduction by Ian Campbell, 1 vol (London: J. M Dent, 1972).

——, *Two Note Books*, ed. C. E. Norton (New York: The Grolier Club, 1898).

——, *Two Reminiscences*, ed. John Clubbe (Durham, N.C.: Duke University Press, 1974).

——, *Works*, Centenary Edition, ed. H. D. Traill, 30 vols (London: Chapman and Hall, 1896–9).

Cate, G. A., *The Correspondence of Thomas Carlyle and John Ruskin* (Palo Alto: Stanford University Press, 1982).

Cazamian, Louis, *Carlyle*, trans. E. K. Brown (New York: Archon Books, 1966); originally publ. 1932).

Clubbe, John (ed.), *Carlyle and His Contemporaries* (Durham, N.C.: Duke University Press, 1976).

Culler, A. Dwight, *The Poetry of Tennyson* (New Haven: Yale University Press, 1977).

——, *The Victorian Mirror of History* (New Haven: Yale University Press, 1986).

Cunningham, John, *The Church History of Scotland*, 2 vols (Edinburgh: A. & C. Black, 1859).

Davie, George Elder, *The Democratic Intellect: Scotland and Her Universities in the Nineteenth Century* (Edinburgh: Edinburgh University Press, 1962).

Dawson, Carl, *Victorian Noon: English Literature in 1850* (Baltimore: Johns

Hopkins University Press, 1979).
DeLaura, David J., 'Ishmael and Prophet: *Heroes and Hero-Worship* and the Self-Expressive Basis of Carlyle's Art', *Texas Studies in Literature and Language*, 11 (1969) pp. 705–37.
Drescher, Horst W. (ed.), *Thomas Carlyle 1981* (Frankfurt am Main: Peter Lang, 1983).
Duffy, Sir Charles Gavan, *Conversations and Correspondence with Carlyle* (London: Sampson Low, Marston, 1892).
Espinasse, Francis, *Literary Recollections and Sketches* (New York: Dodd, Mead, 1893).
Farrell, John P., *Revolution as Tragedy* (Ithaca: Cornell University Press, 1980).
Fielding, K. J., and Rodger L. Tarr (eds), *Carlyle Past and Present* (London: Vision Press, 1976).
Fredeman, William E., '"The Sphere of Common Duties": The Domestic Solution in Tennyson's Poetry', *Bulletin of the John Rylands Library*, 54 (1972), pp. 357–83.
Froude, J. A., *Thomas Carlyle: A History of the First Forty Years of His Life, 1795–1835; A History of His Life in London, 1834–1881* (London: Longmans Green, 1882; 1884).
Goldberg, Michael, *Carlyle and Dickens* (Athens: University of Georgia Press, 1972).
Hair, Donald S., *Domestic and Heroic in Tennyson's Poetry* (Toronto: University of Toronto Press, 1981).
Harding, Anthony J., 'Sterling, Carlyle, and German Higher Criticism: A Reassessment', *Victorian Studies*, 26 (1983), pp. 169–285.
Harrold, C. F., *Carlyle and German Thought: 1819–1834* (New Haven: Yale University Press, 1934).
Hume, David, *The Natural History of Religion*, ed. A. Wayne Colver (Oxford: Clarendon, 1976).
Joseph, Gerhard, *Tennysonian Love: The Strange Diagonal* (Minneapolis: University of Minnesota Press, 1969).
Kaplan, Fred, *Thomas Carlyle: A Biography* (Ithaca: Cornell University Press, 1983).
Killham, John, *Tennyson and 'The Princess': Reflections of an Age* (London: Athlone Press, 1958).
——, (ed.), *Critical Essays on the Poetry of Tennyson* (New York: Barnes and Noble, 1960).
Kincaid, James R., *Tennyson's Major Poems: The Comic and Ironic Patterns* (New Haven: Yale University Press, 1975).
LaValley, Albert J., *Carlyle and the Idea of the Modern* (New Haven: Yale University Press, 1968).
Martin, R. B., *Tennyson: The Unquiet Heart* (Oxford: Clarendon, 1980).
Mattes, E.B., *In Memoriam: The Way of a Soul* (New York: Exposition Press, 1951).
Maund, Constance, *Hume's Theory of Knowledge* (London: Macmillan, 1937).
Miller, R. K., *Carlyle's Life of John Sterling: A Study in Victorian Biography* (Ann Arbor: UMI Research Press, 1987).
Moore, Carlisle, '*Sartor Resartus* and the Problem of Carlyle's "Conversion"', *PMLA*, 70 (1955), pp. 662–81.

Newton, Sir Isaac, *Opticks*, reprinted from the 4th edn with a Foreword by Albert Einstein and an Introduction by E. T. Whittaker (London: G. Bell, 1931).
Nicolson, Harold, *Tennyson: Aspects of His Life, Character, and Poetry* (London: Constable, 1923).
Pitt, Valerie, *Tennyson Laureate* (London: Barrie and Rockliff, 1962).
Porte, Joel, *Representative Man: Ralph Waldo Emerson in His Time* (New York: Oxford University Press, 1979).
Rendall, Jane, *The Origins of the Scottish Enlightenment* (New York: St. Martin's, 1978).
Ricks, Christopher, *Tennyson* (New York: Macmillan, 1972).
Roe, F. W., *Thomas Carlyle as a Critic of Literature* (New York: Columbia University Press, 1910).
Rosenberg, John D., *Carlyle and the Burden of History* (Cambridge, Mass.: Harvard University Press, 1985).
Sanders, C. R., *Carlyle's Friendships and Other Studies* (Durham, N.C.: Duke University Press, 1977).
Shannon, Edgar, F., Jr., *Tennyson and the Reviewers* (Cambridge, Mass.: Harvard University Press, 1952).
Sinfield, Alan, *Alfred Tennyson* (Oxford: Basil Blackwell, 1986).
Slater, Joseph (ed.), *The Correspondence of Emerson and Carlyle* (New York: Columbia University Press, 1964).
Snow, A. J., *Matter and Gravity in Newton's Physical Philosophy* (London: Oxford University Press, 1926).
Tarr, Rodger L., and Fleming McClelland (eds), *Thomas and Jane Welsh Carlyle: The Collected Poems* (Greenwood, Florida: Penkevill, 1986).
Tennyson, Alfred Lord, *The Poems of Tennyson*, ed. Christopher Ricks (London: Longmans, 1969).
——, *Works* (London: Macmillan, 1894).
——, *Letters*, ed. Cecil Y. Lang and Edgar F. Shannon, Jr., vol. I, 1821–1850 (Cambridge, Mass.: Harvard University Press, 1981).
Tennyson, Sir Charles, *Alfred Tennyson* (London: Macmillan, 1968).
Tennyson, Hallam Lord (ed.), *Alfred Lord Tennyson: Memoir*, 2 vols (London: Macmillan, 1897).
——, *Tennyson and His Friends* (London: Macmillan, 1911).
Tennyson, G. B. (ed.), *A Carlyle Reader* (New York: Modern Library College Edition, 1969).
——, *Sartor Called Resartus* (Princeton: Princeton University Press, 1965).
Tillotson, G. *A View of Victorian Literature* (Oxford: Clarendon, 1978).
Timko, Michael, '"The Central Wish": Human Passion and Cosmic Love in Tennyson's Idyls', *Victorian Poetry*, 16 (1978), pp. 1–5.
Torrance, Thomas F., *Christian Theology and Scientific Culture* (New York: Oxford University Press, 1981).
Vijn, J. P., *Carlyle and Jean Paul: Their Spiritual Optics* (Amsterdam/Philadelphia: John Benjamins, 1982).
Williams, Raymond, *Culture and Society: 1780–1950* (New York: Columbia University Press, 1958).
Wilson, D. A. *Carlyle*, 6 vols (London: Kegan Paul, Trench; New York: E. P. Dutton, 1923–34).

Index